Buddhist
Landscapes

Buddhist Landscapes
Art and Archaeology of the Khorat Plateau, 7th to 11th Centuries

Stephen A. Murphy

© 2024 Stephen A. Murphy

Published by NUS Press with the Southeast Asian Art Academic Programme, SOAS, University of London under the Art and Archaeology of Southeast Asia: Hindu-Buddhist Traditions Series.

NUS Press
National University of Singapore
AS3-01-02
3 Arts Link
Singapore 117569

Fax: (65) 6774-0652
E-mail: nusbooks@nus.edu.sg
Website: http://nuspress.nus.edu.sg

All rights reserved. This book, or parts thereof, may not be reproduced in any form or by any means, electronic or mechanical, including photocopying, recording or any information storage and retrieval system now known or to be invented, without written permission from the Publisher.

ISBN 978-981-325-213-4 (casebound)
eISBN 978-981-325-217-2

National Library Board, Singapore Cataloguing in Publication Data

Name(s): Murphy, Stephen A.
Title: Buddhist landscapes : art and archaeology of the Khorat Plateau, 7th to 11th centuries / Stephen Murphy.
Other Title(s): Art and archaeology of Southeast Asia : Hindu-Buddhist traditions
Description: Singapore : Published by NUS Press with the Southeast Asian Art Academic Programme, SOAS, University of London, [2024] | Includes bibliography and index.
Identifier(s): ISBN 978-981-325-213-4 (casebound) | 978-981-325-217-2 (ePDF)
Subject(s): LCSH: Khorat Plateau (Thailand)--History. | Buddhism--Thailand--Khorat Plateau--History. | Buddhist art--Thailand--Khorat Plateau. | Buddhist architecture--Thailand--Khorat Plateau.
Classification: DDC 959.3--dc23

Cover image: Detail of The Buddha's return to Kapilavastu on a *sīmā* from Muang Fa Daed. 8th–9th centuries. Sandstone. National Museum Khon Kaen, Thailand.

Frontispiece: Detail of Buddha Mucalinda on a fragmentary *sīmā* from Muang Fa Daed. 8th–9th centuries. Sandstone. National Museum Khon Kaen, Thailand.

Concept and typographical design by: H55

Printed in Singapore

To my parents,
yes, it's finally done...

TABLE OF CONTENTS

Frontispiece   ii
List of Maps, Figures, and Tables   viii
Technical Notes   xix
Acknowledgements   xxi

CHAPTER 1
BUDDHIST ART AND ARCHAEOLOGY OF THE KHORAT PLATEAU
001

CHAPTER 2
THE CHI RIVER SYSTEM: THE MUANG FA DAED MANDALA
041

CHAPTER 3
BUDDHIST ART IN THE UPPER AND LOWER CHI RIVER SYSTEM
089

CHAPTER 4
THE MUN RIVER SYSTEM: ŚRI CANĀŚA AND BUDDHIST ART
IN THE LOWER KHORAT PLATEAU
123

CHAPTER 5
THE MIDDLE MEKONG: BUDDHIST ART FROM
VIENTIANE TO WAT PHU
165

CHAPTER 6
BUDDHIST LANDSCAPES OF THE KHORAT PLATEAU
201

Bibliography   209
Appendix: Tables 1–11   221
Index   231

MAPS, FIGURES, AND TABLES[1]

Map 1: The Khorat Plateau, its mountain ranges, and the locations of Buddhist sites in the Mun, Chi, and Mekong river systems. 3

Map 2: Modern-day provinces of Northeast Thailand (green), Central Laos (yellow), with bordering countries Cambodia (purple) and Vietnam (pink). 3

Map 3: The eight clusters on the Khorat Plateau. 9

Map 4: The distribution of moated sites, earthen mounds, and mountaintop sites on the Khorat Plateau. 21

Map 5: Sites in the Chi River system. 41

Map 6: Cluster 1. 43

Map 7: Cluster 2. 90

Map 8: Cluster 3. 102

Map 9: Cluster 4. 111

Map 10: Cluster 5: The Mun River system. 123

Map 11: Sites in the Middle Mekong group. 166

Map 12: Cluster 6. 167

Map 13: Cluster 7. 189

Map 14: Cluster 8. 192

Map 15: Hypothetical reconstruction of the extent of Wendan, Śrī Canāśa, Dao Ming, and Changzhou. 201

Figure 1.1: Satellite image showing the Khorat Plateau and its surrounding regions. Courtesy of Jacques Descloitres, MODIS Land Rapid Response Team, NASA/GSFC @ Thailand and Cambodia (nasa.gov). 2

Figure 1.2: The moated site of Ban Muang Fai, Buriram province, Thailand. Courtesy of Google Earth © 2022 Maxar Technologies. 20

Figure 1.3: Half-buried in situ *sīmā* dating to the 8th–9th centuries in a rice field on the outskirts of the village of Ban Na Ngam, Kalasin province, Thailand. 22

Figure 1.4: The four types of *sīmā*, from left to right: slab type,

---

1 All photographs by author unless designated otherwise. Photographs taken during fieldwork from 2007–2010 were done so with permission from the National Research Council of Thailand. All maps have been generated by the author unless indicated otherwise. Base map data for maps 1, 3–15 is sourced from OpenStreetMap (openstreetmap.org/copyright) and used under an Open Database License.

	pillar type, octagonal type, and unfashioned type.	27
Figure 1.5:	Axial *stūpa* design on a *sīmā* from Phu Phra Bat, Udon Thani province, Thailand. 8th–9th centuries. Sandstone. Height: 147 cm; width: 60 cm; depth: 30 cm.	30
Figure 1.6:	*Sīmā* with a *stūpa-kumbha* mounted on a stand from Wat Pho Si Mongkol Temple, Ban Tat Tong, Yasothon province, Thailand. 8th–9th centuries. Sandstone. Height: 180 cm; width: 80 cm; depth: 18 cm.	30
Figure 1.7:	*Sīmā* wrapped in a sacred banner and smothered in gold paint placed behind the *lak muang* (town pillar) of Kalasin town, Kalasin province, Thailand. 8th–9th centuries. Sandstone.	38
Figure 1.8:	*Sīmā* re-used as a town pillar in Wang Sapang, Loei province, Thailand. 8th–9th centuries. Sandstone. Height: 90 cm; width: 66 cm; depth: 23 cm.	38
Figure 1.9:	*Sīmā* placed under a signpost for the village of Ban Bua Simama, Khon Kaen province, Thailand. 8th–9th centuries. Sandstone. Height: 147 cm; 74 cm; width: 20 cm.	39
Figure 2.1:	The Prataduyaku Stūpa with *sīmā* placed around it at Muang Fa Daed, Kalasin province, Thailand.	46
Figure 2.2:	The *Temiya-jātaka* on a *sīmā* from Muang Fa Daed. Today kept at Wat Pho Chai Semaram Temple, Ban Sema, Kalasin province, Thailand. 8th–9th centuries. Sandstone. Height: 156 cm; width: 76 cm; depth: 26 cm.	48
Figure 2.3:	The *Kulāvaka-jātaka* on a fragmentary *sīmā* from Muang Fa Daed. 8th–9th centuries. Sandstone. Height: 84 cm; width: 90 cm; depth: 23 cm. National Museum Khon Kaen, Thailand. Inventory number K.K. 445/53. Courtesy of Thierry Ollivier.	50
Figure 2.4:	The *Sarabhaṅga-jātaka* on a *sīmā* from Muang Fa Daed. 8th–9th centuries. Sandstone. Height: 164 cm; width: 89 cm; depth: 14 cm. Today kept at Wat Pho Chai Semaram Temple, Ban Sema, Kalasin province, Thailand.	51
Figure 2.5:	The *Bhūridatta-jātaka* on a *sīmā* (possibly in situ) from Muang Fa Daed, Kalasin province, Thailand. 10th–11th centuries. Sandstone. Height: 130 cm; width: 83 cm; depth: 15 cm.	53
Figure 2.6:	The *Mahānāradakassapa-jātaka* on a fragmentary *sīmā* from Muang Fa Daed. 8th–9th centuries. Sandstone. Height: 120 cm; width: 60 cm; depth: 21 cm. National Museum Khon Kaen, Thailand.	

| | | Inventory number 17/242/2520. | 55 |

Figure 2.7: The *Vidhurapaṇḍita-jātaka* on a fragmentary *sīmā* from Muang Fa Daed. 8th–9th centuries. Sandstone. Height: 176 cm; width: 76 cm; depth: 25 cm. National Museum Khon Kaen, Thailand.   57

Figure 2.8: The *Mahāummagga-jātaka* on a *sīmā* from Muang Fa Daed. 8th–9th centuries. Sandstone. Height: 170 cm; width: 84 cm; depth: 24 cm. National Museum Khon Kaen, Thailand. Inventory number 17/19/2517.   58

Figure 2.9: The *Vessantara-jātaka* on a *sīmā* from Muang Fa Daed. 8th–9th centuries. Sandstone. Height: 144 cm. Today kept at Wat Sribunruang Temple, Kalasin town, Kalasin province. Thailand. Courtesy of River Books Bangkok.   60

Figure 2.10: *The Buddha Preaching to King Bimbisara or his Father* on a *sīmā* from Muang Fa Daed. 8th–9th centuries. Height: 156 cm; width: 74 cm; depth: 21 cm. National Museum Khon Kaen, Thailand. Inventory number 17/57/2522.   61

Figure 2.11: Indra offers fruit to the Buddha on a fragmentary *sīmā* from Muang Fa Daed. 8th–9th centuries. Sandstone. Height: 100 cm; width: 75 cm; depth: 23 cm. National Museum Khon Kaen, Thailand. Inventory number 17/58/2522.   62

Figure 2.12: Sotthiya offers *kusa* grass to the Buddha on a *sīmā* from Muang Fa Daed. 8th–9th centuries. Sandstone. Height: 167 cm; width: 83 cm; depth: 27 cm. National Museum Khon Kaen, Thailand. Inventory number K.K. 455/53. Courtesy of Thierry Ollivier.   63

Figure 2.13: The Buddha's return to Kapilavastu on a *sīmā* from Muang Fa Daed. 8th–9th centuries. Sandstone. Height: 200 cm; width: 80 cm; depth: 22 cm. National Museum Khon Kaen, Thailand. Inventory number 17/225/2516.   66

Figure 2.14: Unidentified Life of the Buddha scene on a fragmentary *sīmā* from Muang Fa Daed. 8th–9th centuries. Sandstone. Height: 110 cm; width: 60 cm. National Museum Bangkok, Thailand. Inventory number 01/435/2565. Courtesy of Nicolas Revire.   66

Figure 2.15: Buddha Mucalinda on a fragmentary *sīmā* from Muang Fa Daed. 8th–9th centuries. Sandstone. Height: 170 cm; width: 80 cm; depth: 27 cm.

Maps, Figures, and Tables

Figure 2.16: National Museum Khon Kaen, Thailand. Inventory number 17/56/2522/2. — 68

Figure 2.16: Tapered pillar type *sīmā* from Muang Fa Daed. 10th–11th centuries. Sandstone. Height: 298 cm; width: 50 cm; depth 50 cm. National Museum Khon Kaen, Thailand. — 70

Figure 2.17: Detail of a pillar type *sīmā* from Ban Nong Hang, Kalasin province, with an early 11th-century inscription and bodhisattva image. National Museum Khon Kaen, Thailand. — 73

Figure 2.18: Possible scene from The *Mahājanaka-jātaka* on a fragmentary *sīmā* from Ban Nong Hang, Kalasin province. 8th–9th centuries. Sandstone. Height: 64 cm; width: 60 cm; depth: 11 cm. National Museum Khon Kaen, Thailand. Inventory number 17/56/2517. — 77

Figures 2.19–2.21: Details of a pillar type *sīmā* from Ban Nong Hang, Kalasin province carved with three separate *jātaka* on its four faces. National Museum Khon Kaen, Thailand. Figure 2.19 is from the *Bhūridatta-jātaka*, and Figures 2.20 and 2.21 are from the *Vidhurapaṇḍita-jātaka*. — 78–79

Figure 2.22: Details of a pillar type *sīmā* from Ban Nong Hang, Kalasin province carved with three separate *jātaka* on its four faces. This figure is from yhe *Vessantara-jātaka*. National Museum Khon Kaen, Thailand. — 80

Figure 2.23: Aṅgulimāla threatens the Buddha on a fragmentary sandstone *sīmā* from Ban Nong Hang, Kalasin province. 8th–9th centuries. Sandstone. Height: 60 cm; width: 82 cm: depth: 9 cm. National Museum Khon Kaen, Thailand. Inventory number 17/25/2517. — 82

Figure 2.24: Image of a monk carved into the rockface at Wat Phu Kao Putthanimit Temple, Kalasin province, Thailand. 8th–9th centuries. — 84

Figure 2.25: Buddha image carved into the rockface in *mahāparinibbāna* posture at Wat Phu Bor Temple, Kalasin province. 8th–9th centuries. — 85

Figure 3.1: Unfinished Dvaravati-style Buddha located in an ancillary shire at Wat Ban Khon Sawan Temple, Ban Khon Sawan, Chaiyaphum province. 8th–9th centuries. Sandstone. — 91

Figure 3.2: The *Bhūridatta-jātaka* on a *sīmā* housed in a shed

	built by the FAD at Ban Kut Ngong, Chaiyaphum province, Thailand. 8th century. Sandstone. Height: 170 cm; width: 60 cm; depth: 22 cm.	92
Figure 3.3:	The *Bhūridatta-jātaka* on a *sīmā* located in a pavilion at Ban Khon Sawan Temple, Ban Khon Sawan, Chaiyaphum province, Thailand. 8th century. Sandstone. Height: 198 cm; width: 92 cm; depth: 15 cm.	92
Figure 3.4:	The *Mahāummagga-jātaka* on a *sīmā* housed in a shed built by the FAD at Ban Kut Ngong, Chaiyaphum province, Thailand. 8th–9th centuries. Sandstone. Height: 186 cm; width: 92 cm; depth: 22 cm.	94
Figure 3.5:	The *Mahānāradakassapa-jātaka* on a *sīmā* housed in a shed built by the FAD at Ban Kut Ngong, Chaiyaphum province, Thailand. 8th–9th centuries. Sandstone. Height: 175 cm; width: 82 cm; depth: 27 cm. Courtesy of River Books Bangkok.	94
Figure 3.6:	The *Vessantara-jātaka* on a *sīmā* housed in a shed built by the FAD at Ban Kut Ngong, Chaiyaphum province, Thailand. 8th–9th centuries. Sandstone. Height: 197 cm; width: 93 cm; depth: 23 cm.	96
Figure 3.7:	The *Vessantara-jātaka* on a *sīmā* located in a pavilion at Ban Khon Sawan Temple, Ban Khon Sawan, Chaiyaphum province, Thailand. 8th–9th centuries. Sandstone. Height: 198 cm; width: 82 cm; depth: 25 cm.	97
Figure 3.8:	*Stūpa-kumbha* motif with figure worshipping it on a sandstone *sīmā* located in a pavilion at Ban Khon Sawan Temple, Ban Khon Sawan, Chaiyaphum province, Thailand. 8th–9th centuries. Sandstone. Height: 233 cm; width: 90 cm; depth: 16 cm.	98
Figure 3.9:	*Dharmacakra stambha* from Wat Ban Pho Chai Temple, Ban Pho Chai, Khon Kaen province, Thailand. 8th–9th centuries. Sandstone.	101
Figure 3.10:	*Sīmā* with inscription from Wat Non Sila Temple, Ban Phai Hin, Khon Kaen province, Thailand. 8th century. Sandstone. Height: 185 cm; width: 89 cm; depth: 20 cm.	103
Figure 3.11:	*Sīmā* with inscription from Wat Non Sila Temple, Ban Phai Hin, Khon Kaen province, Thailand. 8th century. Sandstone. Height: 155 cm; width: 72 cm; depth: 30 cm.	103
Figure 3.12:	The *Mahājanaka-jātaka* from Wat Trairong Temple, Ban Non Chat, Khon Kaen province, Thailand. 8th–9th centuries. Sandstone. Height: 120 cm; width:	

Maps, Figures, and Tables xiii

	70 cm; depth: 20 cm.	104
Figure 3.13:	The episode of the Courting of Amarā from the *Mahāummagga-jātaka* on a *sīmā* from Kaset Sombun district, Chaiyaphum province, Thailand. 8th–9th centuries. Sandstone. Height: 117 cm; width: 61 cm; depth: 42 cm. Phimai National Museum, Thailand. Inventory number 39/12/2508.	106
Figure 3.14:	*Sīmā* depicting a bodhisattva or possibly Puṇṇaka, the *yakkha* General from the *Vidhurapaṇḍitajātaka* in a pavilion at Ban Phan Lam, Chaiyaphum province, Thailand. 8th–9th centuries. Sandstone. Height: 215 cm; width: 42 cm; depth: 37 cm.	107
Figure 3.15:	*Sīmā* with a *dharmacakra* motif from Wat Nong Sapung, Ban Bua Simama, Khon Kaen province, Thailand. 8th–9th centuries. Sandstone. Height: 140 cm; width: 53 cm; depth: 30 cm.	108
Figure 3.16:	*Sīmā* depicting a *dharmacakra* motif from Ban Phan Lam, Chaiyaphum province, Thailand. 8th–9th centuries. Sandstone. Height: 207 cm; width: 36 cm; depth: 51 cm.	108
Figure 3.17:	Detail of Buddha image carved into the rockface in *mahāparinibbāṇa* on the Phu Wiang Mountain range, Chaiyaphum province, Thailand. Late 8th– early 9th century.	109
Figure 3.18:	*Sīmā* depicting the Aminisa Jetiya episode from the Life of the Buddha at Wat Bueng Khum Ngoen Temple, Ban Khum Ngoen, Yasothon province, Thailand. 8th–9th centuries. Sandstone. Height: 115 cm; width: 65 cm; depth: 36 cm.	112
Figure 3.19:	*Sīmā* with a *stūpa-kumbha* motif at Wat Bueng Khum Ngoen Temple, Ban Khum Ngoen, Yasothon province, Thailand. 8th–9th centuries. Sandstone. Height: 112 cm; width: 56 cm; depth: 27 cm.	113
Figure 3.20:	*Sīmā* with a *stūpa-kumbha* motif at Wat Bueng Khum Ngoen Temple, Ban Khum Ngoen, Yasothon province, Thailand. 8th–9th centuries. Sandstone. Height: 114 cm; width: 58 cm; depth: 38 cm.	113
Figure 3.21:	*Sīmā* with a *stūpa-kumbha* motif at Wat Sri Thammaram Temple, Yasothon town, Yasothon province, Thailand. 8th–9th centuries. Sandstone. Height: 150 cm; width: 80 cm; depth: 25 cm.	115
Figure 3.22:	*Sīmā* with a *stūpa-kumbha* motif and *dharmacakra* finial at Wat Sri Thammaram Temple, Yasothon	

	town, Yasothon province, Thailand. 8th–9th centuries. Sandstone. Height: 140 cm; width: 90 cm; depth: 24 cm. Courtesy of River Books Bangkok.	115
Figure 3.23:	*Sīmā* with a *stūpa-kumbha* motif and *dharmacakra* finial at Wat Bueng Khum Ngoen Temple, Ban Khum Ngoen, Yasothon province, Thailand. 8th–9th centuries. Sandstone. Height: 133 cm; width: 77 cm; depth: 30 cm.	115
Figure 3.24:	*Sīmā* with a *stūpa*-Buddha motif at Wat Sri Thammaram Temple, Yasothon town, Yasothon province, Thailand. 8th–9th centuries. Sandstone. Height: 184 cm; width: 80 cm; depth: 34 cm.	118
Figure 4.1:	Detail of fired brick *stūpa* "Monument 9" at Muang Sema, Sung Noen district, Nakhon Ratchasima province, Thailand. 8th–9th centuries.	127
Figure 4.2:	Detail of the fired brick hemispherical threshold of the entrance to "Monument 4" at Muang Sema, Sung Noen district, Nakhon Ratchasima province, Thailand. 8th–9th centuries.	128
Figure 4.3:	*Mahāparinibbāṇa* Buddha image at Muang Sema, Sung Noen district, Nakhon Ratchasima province, Thailand. 8th–9th centuries. Sandstone. Approximately 11 metres in length.	129
Figure 4.4:	The Bo Ika inscription from Muang Sema, Sung Noen district, Nakhon Ratchasima province, Thailand, dating to 868 CE (K. 400). Sandstone. Height: 144 cm; width: 65 cm; depth: 27 cm. Phimai National Museum. Inventory number 39/89/2507.	130
Figure 4.5:	The head of a bodhisattva image found at Ban Tanot, Non Sung subdistrict, Nakhon Ratchasima province. 8th–9th centuries. Bronze. Height: 73 cm; width: 33 cm. National Museum Bangkok. Inventory number 01/684/2565.	132
Figure 4.6:	Seated Buddha image from Ban Muang Fai, Lam Plai Mat district, Buriram province, Thailand. 8th century. Sandstone. Height: 84 cm: width: 52 cm; depth: 25 cm. National Museum Bangkok. Inventory number 63/2510. Courtesy of Thierry Ollivier.	136
Figure 4.7:	Seated Buddha image (headless), exact provenance unknown. 8th century. Sandstone. Height: 66 cm; width: 52 cm. Phimai National Museum. Inventory number 39/1/2536.	137
Figure 4.8:	Standing Buddha image possibly in double	

	vitarkamudrā (right hand is missing) from Ban Muang Fai, Lam Plai Mat district, Buriram province, Thailand. 7th–8th centuries. Sandstone. Height: 115 cm; width: 34 cm; depth: 17 cm. National Museum Bangkok. Inventory number 323/2520. Courtesy of Thierry Ollivier.	139
Figure 4.9:	Standing Buddha image in double *vitarkamudrā* from Ban Muang Fai, Lam Plai Mat district, Buriram Province, Thailand. 7th–8th centuries. Bronze. Height: 109 cm. National Museum Bangkok. Inventory number 01/681/2565.	140
Figure 4.10:	Standing, four-armed bodhisattva from Ban Muang Fai, Lam Plai Mat district, Buriram province, Thailand. 8th–9th centuries. Bronze. Height: 137 cm. National Museum Bangkok. Inventory number 01/682/2565. Courtesy of River Books Bangkok.	141
Figure 4.11:	Standing bodhisattva Maitreya from Ban Muang Fai, Lam Plai Mat district, Buriram province, Thailand. 8th–9th centuries. Bronze. Height: 62 cm. National Museum Bangkok. Inventory number 01/683/2565.	142
Figure 4.12:	*Sīmā* with a four-armed bodhisattva, its face remodelled in modern concrete. Wat Phu Phra Angkhan temple, Phu Phra Angkhan, Chaloem Phra Kiat district, Buriram province, Thailand. 8th–9th centuries. Sandstone. Height: 174 cm; width: 91 cm; depth: 18 cm.	144
Figure 4.13:	*Sīmā* with *dharmacakra* surmounted by a truncated *stūpa-kumbha* motif. At Wat Pho Yoi Temple, Ban Prakham, Pakham district, Buriram province, Thailand. 8th–9th centuries. Sandstone. Height: 68 cm; width: 64 cm; depth: 12 cm.	146
Figure 4.14:	*Sīmā* with axial *stūpa* motif possibly in situ at Prasat Yai Ngao Temple, Ban Chop, Sangkha district, Surin province, Thailand. 8th–9th centuries. Sandstone.	147
Figure 4.15:	Four-armed Bodhisattva Avalokiteśvara. Reportedly found at Plai Bat II Temple, Lahan Sai district, Buriram province, Thailand. 8th century. Bronze with high tin content inlaid with silver and black glass or obsidian in eyes. Height: 142 cm; width: 58 cm; depth: 39 cm. Rogers Fund 1967. Acc. no: 67.234. Metropolitan Museum of Art, New York, USA. The Metropolitan Museum of Art/Art Resource/Scala, Florence.	151

Figure 4.16: Four-armed Bodhisattva Maitreya. Reportedly found at Plai Bat II Temple, Lahan Sai district, Buriram province, Thailand. 8th century. Copper alloy with inlays of silver and black stone. Height: 95 cm; width: 36 cm; depth 27 cm. Asia Society, New York: Mr and Mrs John D. Rockefeller 3rd Collection, 1979.63. Asia Society/Art Resource, NY/Scala, Florence. 152

Figure 4.17: Four-armed Bodhisattva Maitreya. Reportedly found at Plai Bat II Temple, Lahan Sai district, Buriram province, Thailand. 8th century. Bronze. Height: 123 cm; width: 51 cm; depth: 32 cm. AP 1965.01. Kimbell Art Museum, Fort Worth (TX), USA. Kimbell Art Museum, Fort Worth, Texas/Art Resource, NY/Scala, Florence. 153

Figure 4.18: In situ *sīmā* with *dharmacakra* motif and elaborate *kumbha* on stand with a monkey climbing up the right side. Peam Kre, Phnom Kulen, Cambodia. 8th–9th centuries. Sandstone. Height: 140 cm; width: 80 cm; depth 24 cm. 158

Figure 4.19: Detail of a *sīmā* with *dharmacakra* motif. Peam Kre, Phnom Kulen, Cambodia. 8th–9th centuries. Sandstone. 158

Figure 4.20: *Sīmā* with *dharmacakra* motif and elaborate *kumbha* on stand. Don Meas, Phnom Kulen, Cambodia. 8th–9th centuries. Sandstone. 160

Figure 4.21: Fragmentary *sīmā* with a *stūpa-kumbha* motif. Peam Kre, Phnom Kulen, Cambodia. 8th–9th centuries. Sandstone. Height: 96 cm; width: 60 cm; depth: 27 cm. 161

Figure 5.1: Buddha image from Ban Thalat, Vientiene province, today kept at Wat Ho Pra Keo Temple, Vientiane city, Laos. 7th–8th centuries. Sandstone. 169

Figure 5.2: Inscription from Ban Thalat, Vientiene province, today kept at Wat Ho Pra Keo Temple, Vientiane city, Laos. 7th century. Sandstone. 169

Figure 5.3: *Sīmā* with a *stūpa-kumbha* motif from Ban Muang Kao, Vientiane province, Laos. Today kept at That Luang, Vientiane. 8th–9th centuries. Sandstone. Height: 150 cm; width: 50 cm; depth: 20 cm. 170

Figure 5.4: A number of *sīmā* discovered at Ban Na Sone, Vientiane province, Laos have been gathered up and stored at a local shelter. 171

Figure 5.5: *Sīmā* from Ban Dong Phosy, Vientiane province

Maps, Figures, and Tables

xvii

	today kept at Wat Ho Pra Keo Temple, Vientiane city, Laos. 8th–9th centuries. Sandstone.	172
Figure 5.6:	Fragmentary *sīmā* from Ban Saphang Mo, Vientiane province with an unidentified narrative scene. Today kept at Wat Ho Pra Keo Temple, Vientiane city, Laos. 8th–9th centuries. Sandstone. Height: 70 cm; width: 50 cm; depth: 12 cm.	173
Figure 5.7:	Fragmentary *sīmā* from Ban Saphang Mo, Vientiane province showing the Courting of Amarā from the *Mahāummagga-jātaka*. Vientiane city, Laos. 8th–9th centuries.	174
Figure 5.8:	Buddha image carved into the rockface at Phu Phra Bat, Ban Phue district, Udon Thani province, Thailand.	176
Figure 5.9:	In situ *sīmā* placed around a rock shelter at Phu Phra Bat, Ban Phue district, Udon Thani province, Thailand. 8th–9th centuries.	177
Figure 5.10:	Rock shelter known as "Usa's Tower" at Phu Phra Bat, Ban Phue district, Udon Thani province, Thailand.	178
Figure 5.11:	Buddha images with modern gold leaf paint located under a rock shelter at Dan Sung, Vientiane province, Laos. 8th–9th centuries.	179
Figure 5.12:	Buddha images carved into the rockface at Vang Sang, Vientiane province, Laos. 9th–10th centuries.	181
Figure 5.13:	Detail of a *sīmā* depicting the *Sāma-jātaka* from Wat Non Sila Temple, Ban Nong Khleum, Ban Phue district, Udon Thani province, Thailand. 11th century. Sandstone. Height: 334 cm; width: 75 cm; depth: 48 cm.	184
Figure 5.14:	Detail of a *sīmā* depicting the *Suvannakakkata-jātaka* from Wat Non Sila Temple, Ban Nong Khleum, Ban Phue district, Udon Thani province, Thailand. 11th century. Sandstone. Height: 176 cm; width: 74 cm; depth: 35 cm.	184
Figure 5.15:	*Sīmā* with a *stūpa-kumbha* motif from Wat Phathsimaram Temple, Wang Sapung district, Loei province, Thailand. 8th–9th centuries. Sandstone. Height: 170 cm; width: 73 cm; depth: 30 cm.	187
Figure 5.16:	Detail of inscription K. 981 on a cylindrical *sīmā* from Wat Si That temple, Ban Don Kaeo, Ban Chiang Haeo subdistrict, Kumphawapi district, Udon Thani province. 7th–early 8th centuries. Sandstone. Length:	

114 cm; diameter: 55 cm. National Museum Khon Kaen. Inventory number 17/34/2517. 188

Table 1:	Sites in the Chi River system.	221
Table 2:	Sites in the Mun River System.	223
Table 3:	Sites in the Middle Mekong.	224
Table 4:	Cluster 1 sites.	226
Table 5:	Cluster 2 sites.	226
Table 6:	Cluster 3 sites.	227
Table 7:	Cluster 4 sites.	227
Table 8:	Cluster 5 sites.	228
Table 9:	Cluster 6 sites.	228
Table 10:	Cluster 7 sites.	229
Table 11:	Cluster 8 sites.	229

xix

TECHNICAL NOTES ON LANGUAGE

Both Sanskrit and Pāli appear in Thai and Lao usage over time. Pāli forms are used throughout this volume, with the exception of Sanskrit terms that have become commonplace and accepted forms of English language usage such as those included in the Oxford English Dictionary. For instance, this book uses the Sanskrit "bodhisattva" and "Maitreya" as opposed to the Pāli forms "bodhisatta" and "Metteyya". All Sanskrit and Pāli terms appear in transliteration with diacritics and/or in phonetic transcription. The only exceptions are common toponyms and other words commonly used in English. Regarding Buddhist funerary monuments, I acknowledge the diversity of terminology in Pāli, Thai, and Lao languages. For instance, the Pāli *cetiya* is used in Thai in both transliteration (*cetiya*) and phonetic transcription according to Thai pronunciation (*chedi*). *Chedi* is commonly used in academic literature on Thai and Lao culture. Additionally, the term *phra that* is often used in Northeast Thailand and Laos to designate Buddhist funerary monuments. This is a phonetic transcription of Khmer *braḥ* ('holy') + Pāli *dhātu* ('relic, reliquary'), commonly used in Tai languages. However, for consistency I have also chosen to use the Sanskrit term *stūpa* throughout, given that it is the best-known designation in English-language academic literature.

This book adheres to the Royal Thai General System of Transcription (RTGS) as published by the Royal Society of Thailand. The spelling of Thai proper names generally follows the rules of this system except when the preference of the author is known and it does not adhere to the RTGS. For example, Phasook Indrawooth is the author's own spelling and used here, and not Phasuk Inthrawut, as might be the case under Royal Institute rules. The spelling of Thai geographical names (villages, provinces, and districts) similarly follows the RTGS despite certain inconsistencies regarding its implementation and use by the Thai government. The exception to this is regarding well-known archaeological sites and monuments. In these cases, the book follows the prevailing conventions in the existing literature (i.e., Muang Fa Daed as opposed to Mueang Fa Daet). For geographical locations in Laos, the book also follows the prevailing conventions in existing literature.

To remain consistent with European language referencing conventions, Thai and Lao references in the bibliography and main body of text are given surname first. Full transliterations are given for references, and titles published in Thai are followed by an English translation.

Regarding country names, the name Thailand (or pre-modern Thailand) and the adjective Thai in this book refers to the area of the current Kingdom of Thailand, although Siam was its official name until 1939. The name Laos and adjective Lao refer to the area of the current Lao People's Democratic Republic founded in 1954. Similarly, the contemporary names of Cambodia and Vietnam are also used. Myanmar is preferred over Burma. The former is the official name of the country today, the latter that given to it during the colonial period by the British. However, it should be noted that all of these nation states are creations of the 19th and 20th centuries and have no historical presence in the first millennium CE.

Abbreviations and Acronyms

AA: *Arts Asiatiques*
BEFEO: *Bulletin de l'École française d'Extrême-Orient*
EFEO: École française d'Extrême-Orient
FAD: Fine Arts Department, Thailand
JSS: *Journal of the Siam Society*
K.: Inventory indicator for Khmer inscriptions
Wattanatum 2000: *Wattanatumphathtanakanthangprawatisateklaksanalae phumipanyachangwat Roi Et,* 2000.

ACKNOWLEDGEMENTS

This book grew out of my PhD, which I undertook between 2006–2010, subsequent fieldwork in 2011 and 2014, and further research that I have carried out in the intervening years. Consequently, most of the debts of gratitude that I owe were accrued during this period. And without the help, encouragement, support, and coaxing (gentle or otherwise!) from colleagues, friends, family, and innumerable others, this book would never have come to fruition. I would thus first and foremost like to thank everyone that has in some way assisted me in this journey.

It seems appropriate to start by thanking the people of Northeast Thailand and Central Laos. The welcome I received there was more often than not unconditional, and the assistance given to me was never with the expectancy of gaining something in return. In particular, I would like to thank the numerous *songtaow*, motorbike taxi, and tuk-tuk drivers who dropped me off at obscure archaeological sites; the monks who gave me access to their temples and storerooms; and the local villagers who oft times directed me to a main road so I could catch a bus back. These are fond memories of my time upon the Khorat Plateau that I hope will remain with me always.

In Thailand: at the Department of Archaeology, Silpakorn University, Bangkok, the late Professor Phasook Indrawooth for imparting to me some of her vast knowledge of all things Dvāravatī; to Associate Professor Surapol Natapintu for his help with research permission; at the Asian Institute of Technology, Bangkok, Dr Surat Lertlum for his initial assistance with arranging my fieldwork. Further thanks go to Khun Kroo Surapol from Ban Kruat, Buriram province for taking the time to show me around some key sites in Buriram province. Special thanks to the staff at the Khon Kaen National Museum, who made me feel welcome from day one and were a great help not only with my research regarding the *sīmā* at the museum but also in providing practical information on how to reach some of the more out-of-the-way sites. Additional thanks also go to the staffs at the Phimai National Museum and Ubon Ratchathani National Museum, who were also very helpful during my fieldwork as well as to Suppawan Nongnut at the National Museum Bangkok for her help in tracking down the accession numbers for many of the objects. For generously assisting with my fieldwork in 2014, I would like to thank both Lalita and Tanongsak Hanwong. In Laos, Dr Michel Lorrillard of the EFEO Vientiane generously shared the results of his fieldwork and provided me with information on how to reach many of the sites that I visited in Laos.

At SOAS University of London I would first and foremost like to thank my academic supervisor, Emeritus Professor Dr Elizabeth Moore who sadly passed away just as this book was going to print, for always generously giving her time. Her observations, suggestions, and support of my work throughout the years have been invaluable. To Professor Ashley Thompson, Hiram W. Woodward Chair in Southeast Asian Art for encouraging me to submit my manuscript to the SAAAP-NUS Press research publication series, Art and Archaeology of Southeast Asia: Hindu-Buddhist Traditions, and all of her subsequent support. I also wish to thank Dr Pamela Corey in her role as editorial board member of SAAAP-NUS Press research publication series for her comments and feedback. At NUS Press, I would like to thank Peter Schoppert and editor Lindsay Davis for steering this manuscript to its completion. I would also like to take this opportunity to register my thanks to the two anonymous peer reviewers for their insightful comments and critiques of the manuscript that have greatly helped in strengthening it.

In terms of language, many thanks to Dr Peter Skilling of the EFEO Bangkok and to Dr Hunter Watson (Mahidol University, Bangkok) for their advice regarding inscriptions on *sīmā*. To Pimchanok Pongkasetkan for the help and assistance with Thai language, both in terms of its usage and spelling throughout the book, as well as bringing to my attention countless Thai publications that were of great use to this study. For taking the time out from their busy schedules to read, comment, proofread, and advise on various chapters and final drafts of the manuscript, my thanks also go to Dr Nicolas Revire, Dr Pratapaditya Pal, and Dr Hunter Watson, all of whom supplied me with invaluable feedback.

On a personal level, thanks go first and foremost to my parents. Without their constant support from day one, this manuscript would never have seen the light of day. Perhaps the greatest debt of thanks, however, goes to my wife Mizuho, who spent many a month accompanying me on endless trips to remote villages in the middle of the hot season. Also for the many times we have been apart over the years due to research commitments. Her support and companionship over the years have kept me sane in what sometimes felt like an insane task.

In London, to my late aunt and uncle Maureen and Mick Sexton, who provided me with a roof over my head on my many return trips during my PhD and afterwards. To my cousin Angela Thompson and her husband Neil for being my much-needed support bubble during the long Covid lockdowns of 2020–2021, during which the final drafts of this manuscript were written.

Finally, I would like to thank the many institutions and authorities that have supported or part-funded either the research or the manuscript. Research permission for the PhD fieldwork was kindly granted by the National Research Council of Thailand (NRCT). Funding for the fieldwork was provided by the Empowering Network for International Thai Studies (ENITS), Institute of Thai Studies, Chulalongkorn University with support from the Thailand Research Fund (TRF); the University of London Central Research Fund; and the SOAS Fieldwork Grant. Fieldwork research in 2014 was undertaken while I was a Research Fellow at the Asian Civilisations Museum, Singapore; funding for indexing and images rights was kindly provided by the SAAAP Academic Support Fund.

This book was made possible through the publishing partnership between National University of Singapore Press (NUS) and the Southeast Asian Art Academic Programme (SAAAP) at SOAS University of London. SAAAP is generously funded by the Alphawood Foundation to whom I wish to register my sincere gratitude.

Stephen A. Murphy
London, 2024

Chapter 1

BUDDHIST ART AND ARCHAEOLOGY OF THE KHORAT PLATEAU

This book sets out to explore Buddhist art and archaeology on the Khorat Plateau – an area that encompasses Northeast Thailand and Central Laos – from the 7th to 11th centuries. To do so, it first investigates how widespread Buddhist material and visual culture was in this region during the 1st millennium CE. It then asks a number of questions of the surviving evidence. First, how did Buddhist art shape and in turn become shaped by the cultures, societies, and environments that it encountered? Second, how much can the surviving art and archaeology realistically tell us about Buddhist practices and beliefs during this period? Third, what is the *sīmā* tradition (stone boundary markers) and why did it prolificate so extensively in this region? And fourth, can the Khorat Plateau be seen as a region in its own right rather than as a peripheral interface between the Dvāravatī culture of the Chao Phraya basin to its west and the Zhenla and later Angkor civilisations to its south and southeast.

In an attempt to answer these questions, I undertook a study and review of the relevant literature in both European and Thai languages and carried out extensive fieldwork in the region for more than a decade. This led to the compiling of a comprehensive database of the material and visual remains of Buddhism on the Khorat Plateau. While it is not exhaustive, nor is the discussion in this book, I would argue that it is sufficiently robust to support the arguments and conclusions presented herein.

The key findings that will be examined in this book are that firstly, Buddhism spread along the major river systems and established itself primarily in the lowland, alluvial plains. In the course of this spread, a unique material and visual culture developed, which I refer to as "Khorat Plateau aesthetics" and "Khorat Plateau motifs". This started to occur in the 7th century with evidence becoming more abundant in the 8th and 9th centuries. This spread was facilitated by pre-existing settlement patterns – moated sites in particular – and the presence of well-travelled routes, particularly in terms of maritime, coastal, and inland waterways, which allowed this religion to work its way throughout Southeast Asia and beyond.

Fig. 1.1 Satellite image showing the Khorat Plateau and its surrounding regions. Courtesy of Jacques Descloitres, MODIS Land Rapid Response Team, NASA/GSFC @ Thailand and Cambodia (nasa.gov).

What then is the Khorat Plateau? It is a gently undulating landscape covering an area of about 155,000 square kilometres of what is now Northeast Thailand and Central Laos (Fig. 1.1, Maps 1 and 2). It has a distinctive geography, and the region's encounter with Buddhism brought a variety of new and innovative forms of art and architecture. These include sculpture in the round, richly symbolic religious motifs such as the *dharmacakra* (Wheel of the Law), and architectural remains such as *stūpa*. *Vihāra* (assembly halls) may have been present to a limited degree, but the evidence is inconclusive. It should also be noted that in the 1st millennium CE this term tends to refer to a Buddhist monastery in this context. It is only from the 14th century onwards that the term is more frequently used in the sense that it is today – to refer to assembly halls containing one or two images of worship (Chutiwongs 2009: 67). There is limited evidence, too, for the existence of the ordination hall during the 7th to 11th centuries (discussed below). Buddhism also introduced new forms of narrative art, as can be seen on the ornately carved relief scenes on *sīmā* or moulded in terracotta and stucco, decorating the facades of *stūpa*. The subject matter usually consists of scenes from the Life of the Buddha or *jātaka* tales (past lives of the Buddha). The Life of the Buddha scenes refer to the "Historical" Buddha, called the Sākyamuni Buddha (for his birth into the Śākya clan), or the Gotama Buddha (for his birth into the Gotama family), who reaches this point through the accumulation of merit over past lives as told in the *jātaka* tales. *Jātaka* tales are as Peter

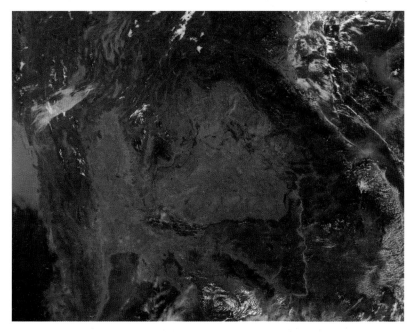

1.1

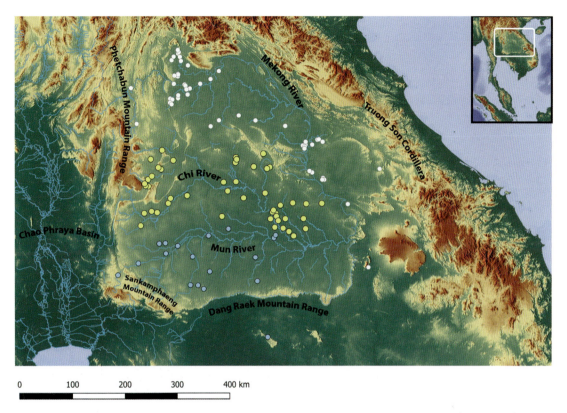

Map 1 The Khorat Plateau, its mountain ranges, and the locations of Buddhist sites in the Mun (blue circles), Chi (yellow circles), and Mekong (white circles) river systems.

Map 2 Modern-day provinces of Northeast Thailand (green), Central Laos (yellow), with bordering countries Cambodia (purple) and Vietnam (pink).

Skilling (2008a: 59) succinctly puts it "... a story of a past life of a Buddha – a life in which, as a bodhisattva, he underwent experiences or performed deeds that fortified him spiritually on his path towards full awakening." In discussing the evidence outlined above, this book aims to illustrate the extent and characteristics of Buddhist art and architecture during the 7th to 11th centuries on the Khorat Plateau.

Buddhism on the Khorat Plateau, as with anywhere else, spread by way of the *saṅgha*, the community of monks. Skilling (2012) cautions us to not think of the *saṅgha* as a centralised institution. Instead, he argues that:

> The *saṅgha* is a network of modules, self-governing and self-reproducing units (ten or even fewer qualified monks can ordain new members without recourse to external authority). Ideally, the modules are independent or at least autonomous, although at the same time they may be reinforced by networks of affiliation, including teaching lineages. This modular nature is the strength and also the weakness of the system. *Saṅghas* are free of interference insofar as they do not depend on any central authority, but at the same time they do not enjoy any centralised protection, and have to seek out secular support (2012: xiv).

It is this modularity that allows the religion to spread so freely and, as this book will show, is reflected by the archaeological and art historic evidence from the Khorat Plateau. The evidence shows that Buddhism followed the trajectories of the river systems and clusters into groups around several sites in particular. Skilling (2012: xv) argues that in order to understand more clearly the emergence of Buddhism in different regions, we must analyse "the interactions between *saṅgha* modules and their host environments – the social, economic, and political systems". Such interactions will be explored in this book through analysis of the available material and visual evidence.

THEORETICAL AND METHODOLOGICAL FRAMEWORKS FOR UNDERSTANDING BUDDHISM ON THE KHORAT PLATEAU: CONTEXTUALISING THE ART AND ARCHAEOLOGY THROUGH HISTORICAL ECOLOGY AND LANDSCAPE ARCHAEOLOGY

This book, and the research it is built on, is primarily an archaeological study. However, it also incorporates methods, theories, and approaches from art history and to a lesser extent the history of religions and Buddhist studies. From a regional perspective, it is a study in Southeast Asian archaeology and more specifically the archaeology of Thailand and Laos.

This archaeological approach to the study of Buddhism is in some ways inspired by the work of Gregory Schopen (1997) on early Indian Buddhism. Schopen has put forward a compelling argument that archaeological and epigraphic evidence – as opposed to Buddhist texts – provides the most direct access to the religion as it was practised at that time. He points out that:

> There was, and is, a larger body of archaeological and epigraphic material that is largely unedited...This material records or reflects at least a part of what Buddhists—both lay people and monks—actually practiced and believed. There was, and is, an equally large body of literary material that in most cases cannot actually be dated and that survives only in very recent manuscript traditions. It has been heavily edited, it is considered canonical or sacred, and was intended—at the very least—to inculcate an ideal (1997: 1).

Similar approaches to Schopen's have been taken in recent years in regard to contemporary Buddhist practice. For instance, Justin McDaniel's work (2015) on Thai Buddhism focuses on local forms of Buddhist knowledge and belief – specifically a magic monk and a lovelorn ghost. He convincingly shows that we can gain equally important insights into the nature of Buddhism from studying certain Thai Buddhist practices that provide a much more accurate picture of how the religion functions on a day-to-day basis. This again differs considerably from the perspective gained through the study of more traditional orthodox sources such as the manuscript tradition, which was historically the prism through which Western scholars studied and understood Buddhism.

All that being said, this book approaches the art historical and archaeological material of the Khorat Plateau fully aware of the limitations that this evidence poses. How much can objects and monuments alone actually tell us about Buddhist religious practice? They are silent in many ways until we make them speak through the various interpretative frameworks we apply to them. Falling back on the text thus becomes an obvious strategy. And of course, the Buddhists texts do indeed provide a wealth of information on how objects and monuments can be interpreted, and this book uses them in many instances to identify Buddhist narrative art and motifs, as well as in its analysis of *sīmā* stones – all the while with the caveats of Schopen in mind. However, we do need to be careful to not give primacy to the text. As this book will illustrate, and as Schopen has so persuasively shown us, archaeological evidence sometimes paints a different or somewhat alternate picture to the ideals stated in the textual sources.

Studies into the museology of religious displays can also be informative here. Even in a present-day context we can question how much material culture and textual sources can aid us in understanding religious belief. For instance, as Chris Arthur (2000: 2) has observed in his study of the St Mungo Museum of Religious Life and Art in Glasgow: "For if many, if not all, faiths have at their centre a key element which eludes expression, does this not drastically limit any attempt to exhibit religion from the outset? How should museums of, or concerned with, religion approach this tension between words, images, objects and an apparently incommunicable core?" This study thus cannot ever categorically reveal what Buddhists in the 7th- to 11th-century Khorat Plateau thought or believed and makes no claims whatsoever to do so. What it can do, however, is reveal how these beliefs and practices were made manifest in physical form – whether that be through Buddhist art, architecture, or the shaping of landscapes.

This book also attempts to reconcile what we see in archaeological and art historical records with what we see reflected in the texts, while also being fully cognisant of the parameters and limitations involved. In doing so, all types of evidence – archaeological, art historic, epigraphic, and textual – will be considered as I attempt to paint a fuller picture of Buddhism on the Khorat Plateau during the 7th to 11th centuries than what we have at present.

In approaching Buddhist material and visual culture, I view it through the lens of the physical and cognitive landscapes of the Khorat Plateau. To do this, I use both historical ecology and landscape archaeology as theoretical frameworks. In analysing the distribution patterns of this material, connections have been made and conclusions drawn that may not have been apparent from standard Western-centric art historical approaches. These have traditionally decontextualised the art and instead focus on issues of style, composition, and establishing chronologies. However, by contextualising Buddhist art back into the landscape, it allows us to understand that Buddhism was primarily a lowland phenomenon, which spread along the courses of the three main river systems on the Khorat Plateau – the Mun, the Chi, and Mekong (Maps 1, 5, 10, 11; Tables 1–3). Furthermore, by studying works of art in context, it is possible to propose the existence of ateliers/workshops, which is argued herein were central in developing distinct "Khorat Plateau aesthetics and motifs".

Landscape archaeologists conceptualise landscapes as cognitive constructs defined by how cultures or societies shape, create, and visualise them (Knapp and Ashmore 1999; Layton and Ucko 1999; Tilley 1994). In the context of Buddhist art and architecture, it means viewing this in terms of its relationship to the landscape and studying people's ability to manipulate and shape their environment through this material culture. Buddhist monasteries, architecture, artwork, and monks have all played active roles in physically and cognitively shaping landscapes.

Historical ecology develops this concept further. At its core, it is the study of human–environment interactions (Isendahl and Stump, 2015: 3). It bridges the divide between seeing humanity as the independent shaper of landscapes, on the one hand, and understanding nature as the dominant force in determining human society on the other. According to Balée (2006: 76), "Historical ecology is a research program concerned with the interactions through time between societies and environments and the consequences of these interactions for understanding the formation of contemporary and past cultures and landscapes." There is thus a dynamic interplay between humanity and the environment. Human beings manipulate their natural surroundings and endeavour to shape rather than be shaped by the landscape. In the context of Buddhism, this is reflected in the emergence of monumental architecture such as *stūpa*, the placement of *sīmā* within the landscape, and Buddha images carved into the rock faces of hills and mountainsides.

For Carole Crumley (2015: 2), another major proponent of this approach, "Historical ecology provides tools to construct an evidence-validated, open-ended narrative of the evolution and transformation of specific landscapes, based on records of human activity and changing environments." Historical ecology has also been shown to be most effective at bridging various spatial and temporal scales (Isendahl and Stump 2015: 6). And as Crumley (2015: 7) reminds us, landscapes are not fixed or timeless. They bear the traces of use and human–environment interactions over long and short timescales.

In this book, historical ecology is applied to analyse the spread of Buddhist art on the Khorat Plateau. This provides a framework that bridges various geographical and temporal scales. It is primarily located along the three major river systems on the Khorat Plateau. Its trajectory can be traced and understood by an analysis of the archaeological and artistic evidence located along these riverine routes. The Mun River system is located in the southern part of Northeast Thailand; the Chi River system cuts a diagonal path across the region, flowing in a southeasterly direction before joining the Mun at its confluence near Ubon Ratchathani; and the Middle Mekong is a section of this river that starts in the vicinity of Vientiane province and ends around Champassak in Southern Laos near the border with modern-day Cambodia (Maps 1, 2, 5, 10, 11; Tables 1–3).

The next geographical scale consists of moving from specific river systems to clusters within them. There are eight separate clusters: four in the Chi River, three in the Middle Mekong, and one in the Mun River system (Map 3; Tables 4–11). The clusters are determined based on factors such as geographical proximity, iconographic and stylistic similarities, typological similarities, chronological correlation, and the relationship to moated sites. The next spatial scale moves to specific sites within these clusters and finally to the objects located at the sites themselves. This final spatial scale allows for fine-grain analysis of the material evidence – objects such as *sīmā* or architectural features such as *stūpa* – to be done within clearly defined contexts such as moated sites. These contexts can then be understood within their wider landscapes (clusters) and relationships to ecological features such as rivers and mountain ranges. The temporal scale within which this takes place is the 400-year period between the 7th and 11th centuries. The book homes in on the 8th and 9th centuries in particular, as it is within this time frame that the majority of the evidence discussed emerges.

This multi-scalar and multi-temporal approach entails a number of methodologies. The first and foremost is mapping and survey work, two essential components of landscape archaeology. Sites and their material remains are recorded and plotted using Quantum Geographic Information System (QGIS). This software allows for large amounts of data to be analysed and arranged spatially, which in turn facilitates distribution analysis, as reflected in the maps present in this book. Distribution analysis considers factors such as the geographical proximity of sites to one another, their relationship to natural features such as rivers or topographic features such as hills and mountain ranges, the types of objects/artefacts/architecture found at sites, and again their proximity or relationship to one another and other sites. This is done by taking into consideration typological, stylistic, and iconographic characteristics.

Distribution analysis thus entails a detailed analysis of each site. This is done through the study of archaeological reports, site plans, site visits, and analysis of site morphology, the latter usually with the aid of Google Earth satellite imagery. This allows for sites to be classified into certain types (moated sites, earthen mounds, etc., see below) and these divisions are fed back into the mapping and distribution analysis. From site analysis, we move to a contextual analysis of the objects. This entails determining whether they are found in situ, and if so where and in relation to what other material, architectural remains, or archaeological features. If the material is not in situ, attempts have been made to ascertain their original findspots and, if known, where they are kept today in relation to this. This is again done with reference to site reports, site visits, as well as interviews or testimony from local people. Finally, we move to the visual analysis – stylistic, typological, and iconographic – of the objects themselves. The stylistic analysis aids in dating and the identification of distinctive characteristics of the objects and those that they share with other artworks. This, taken in conjunction with the contextual and distribution analysis, can help in identifying possible schools or centres. Finally, the iconographic analysis works to uncover the meaning embedded in these

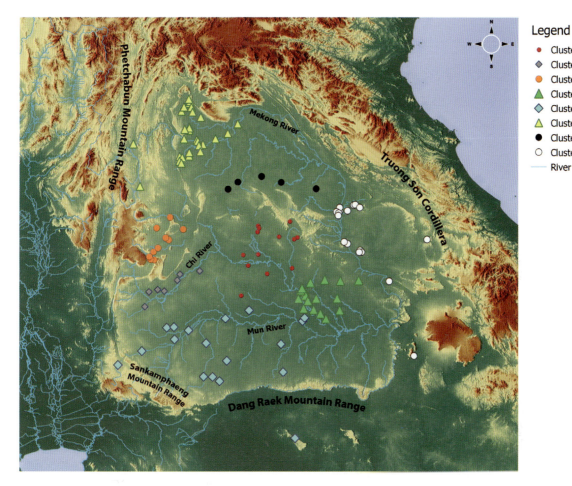

Map 3 The eight clusters on the Khorat Plateau.

objects. For this I have consulted both primary Buddhist sources (in translation) and secondary literature (discussed in detail below). Iconographic analysis coupled with the other methodological steps discussed above can lead to new insights into the nature and extent of Buddhist art on the Khorat Plateau, as will hopefully become apparent during the course of this book.

Chapters 2 to 5 are thus devoted to studying Buddhist art and archaeology, its spatial organisation and occupation patterns in these three river systems and eight clusters. The book will illustrate that the art flourished and developed more successfully in some areas than others, and that it is possible to identify certain centres in the region where this art took hold. For instance, in Chapters 2 and 3, I posit the idea that the site of Muang Fa Daed had direct political and administrative control over Cluster 1 and most likely over Clusters 2, 3, and 4 as well. These conditions would have enabled the spread of Buddhist art in a number of ways. In Chapter 4, I look at the Mun River system and propose that another site, Muang Sema, also exerted direct political control over the sites in its vicinity and perhaps over all or most of those along the Mun River. Furthermore, the epigraphic evidence in this river system points to an entity known as Śri Canāśa, which I argue was most likely centred around the site of Muang Sema. This site was also closely connected to Central Thailand, controlling the pass to and from the Khorat Plateau. At both of these political centres, there is strong evidence for the existence of Buddhist monasteries. The evidence from the Mekong discussed in Chapter 5 indicates that Buddhist art thrived in Cluster 6, an area located around Vientiane and sites in Udon Thani, Loei, and Nong Khai provinces (Map 2). The evidence from Clusters 7 and 8 is not as comprehensive, though it does indicate that Buddhism was present to a certain degree.

The river systems of the Khorat Plateau thus played a key role not only in the spread of Buddhist art, but also in the shaping of the societies of this region. The importance of waterways in the development of many Southeast Asian societies has been noted by scholars such as Veronica Walker Vadillo (2019). She highlights the key role of riverine culture within Angkorian society and urges that more consideration be given to this in studies on the subject. Regarding the Khorat Plateau, little in-depth research has been done in this area unfortunately, and this book is one attempt to address this dearth. At present there is no archaeological evidence for the type of boats that existed, though we can assume that dugouts were being used as well as more sophisticated craft made from planks. These vessels could either be paddled or rowed, which Walker Vadillo points out represent two distinct methods of propulsion and technological design (2019: 3). The seasons were also a factor, as travelling upstream during periods of heavy monsoon rainfall would have been difficult. Likewise, traversing narrow courses or rapids while travelling downstream under these conditions would have been ill-advised.

Historical evidence from the 19th century can shed some light on this matter. Étienne Aymonier's accounts of his travels throughout Northeast Thailand, Cambodia, and Laos from October 1883 to late April 1884 give some indication of how travel by river would have been carried out. It also gives information about the timescales involved. Travelling upstream required a combination of rowing and tacking along the banks with a boat hook and long poles, while rapids were traversed by hauling the boats with ropes (Aymonier 1895–1897: 1–29). While travelling in Cambodia, it took him two days to travel between Battambang and Monkolborei, a distance of approximately 48 kilometres (Aymonier 1876: 54). He thus managed to cover an average of 24 kilometres a day. A few years later in

1884, two of his assistants travelled over from Ubon Ratchathani to Khemerat on the banks of the Mekong in six days. This is approximately 100 kilometres as the crow flies (Aymonier 1895–1897: 183–90). They thus averaged around 14 kilometres per day.

As will be discussed in Chapters 2 to 5, most of the sites within the clusters studied are no more than 50 kilometres apart. Many are within 10 to 20 kilometres of each other and connected directly by river. This indicates that there was no great difficulty to journey between them with travel taking between one to two days only.

TAKING A CLOSER LOOK AT THE KHORAT PLATEAU

The Khorat Plateau encompasses the regions of Northeast Thailand and the lowland areas of Vientiane province in Central Laos and Bolikhamsai, Khammouane, Savannakhet, Salavan, and Champassak provinces of Southern Laos (Map 2). This definition is somewhat broader than most in the existing literature on the region, which usually considers the Khorat Plateau to consist of only the area of modern-day Northeast Thailand. The definition proposed in this book is arrived at by considering factors such as similarities in natural topography and geography, as well as that of material and visual remains. The present-day international border between Thailand and Laos centring on the Mekong River distorts the geographical homogeneity of the region. Furthermore, 7th- to 11th-century societies were not subjected to this political division.

Thongchai Winichakul (2004) explores how the British and French colonial powers, with their modern technology of mapping, introduced to the Thai geopolitical realm the idea of fixed boundaries on a map. The Thais had always viewed their borders as fluid spheres of influence based around local towns or settlements (*muang*). That territories could overlap, which was often the case on both sides of the Mekong region, was not seen in any way as conflicting or contradictory. In actuality, up until the 19th century, the Mekong River was a vital route of trade, transport, and communication, as opposed to the modern boundary between nation states that it has become.

The area of the Khorat Plateau that today forms part of the modern nation state of Thailand is commonly known as Isan. It consists of 20 provinces (Map 2). The majority of the population is ethnically Lao and there are also large ethnically Khmer populations in the southern part, particularly along or in the vicinity of the Dang Raek Mountain range in Buriram, Surin, and Si Sa Ket provinces. While the Khmer-speaking populations have been present from around the mid to late 1st millennium CE onwards, the presence of Lao and Thai ethnic groups mainly grew from the 17th century onwards. Northeast Thailand had been under the sway of the Lao kingdoms from around the 13th century. However, during the reign of King Rama I (1782–1809), Siamese influence expanded considerably, with areas previously under the kingdoms of Vientiane and Champassak now coming under direct administrative control of Bangkok. From this point onwards forced population transfers began, resulting in large numbers of Lao people being moved from the more populous left bank of the Mekong to its right. This intensified considerably after the Lao rebellion of 1826–1828. Today the region maintains a strong sense of regional identity, albeit within the overarching framework of the Thai nation state.

The Khorat Plateau lies at an average height of 90 to 200 metres above sea level. Its lowest point, located around the area of modern-day Ubon Ratchathani, is at no more than 60 metres above sea level (Pendleton 1962: 43). The Plateau is bordered by the Phetchabun and Dang Raek Mountain ranges to the west and south respectively, the Sankamphaeng range in the southwest, and to the north and east by both the course of the Mekong River and the Truong Son Cordillera (Map 1; Fig. 1.1).

The Khorat Plateau is comparatively ill-suited for rice cultivation (Kawaguchi and Kyuma 1977: 26–33). Soils are poor in quality and prone to salinity. Furthermore, rainfall throughout the region is irregular and can cause a combination of drought and flooding at various times throughout the year (Kermel-Torres 2004: 162). The Petchabun, Dang Raek, and Sankamphaeng mountain ranges, together with the Truong Son in the northeast, catch a large degree of rainfall. As a result, the southwest monsoon is less intense on the Khorat Plateau than in Central Thailand. The difference between the dry and wet seasons is therefore also greater. All of the above factors mean that the Khorat Plateau's rice yield today is significantly less than that of Central Thailand, and this was most likely the case in the 1st millennium CE as well. The Plateau consists of two plains: the southern Khorat plain, which is drained by the Mun and Chi rivers, and the northern Sakhon Nakhon plain/basin, which is drained by the Loei, Songkhram, and Mekong rivers. The two plains are separated by the Phu Phan Mountains.

The tendency for a high discharge of rainfall during monsoon season means that the low-lying floodplains of these major rivers would have been difficult areas in which to settle, at least until sufficient water management technologies were developed (Higham and Thosarat 1998: 18). Even today, areas of the Mun and Chi rivers are susceptible to severe flooding during the monsoon season. Floodplains are the area of land next to a river that stretches from the banks of its channel to the base of the enclosing valley walls. They flood during periods when there is a high discharge of water – such as that brought about by monsoon rains. The lower terraces and stream tributaries experienced much less severe flooding and thus provided more suitable locations for habitation. Terraces are step-like landforms that consist of flat or gently sloping surfaces. They are typically bounded on one side by a steeper ascending slope.

These observations are borne out by the archaeological record, with the majority of archaeological sites from prehistory onwards being located along the terraces of the Chi, Mun and Middle Mekong river systems or their tributaries. This settlement pattern has remained relatively unchanged until present day with the majority of villages, towns, and provincial centres still located on or close to major rivers. As Keizaburo Kawaguchi and Kazutake Kyuma (1977: 27) point out, in Southeast Asia one-third of the potentially arable land is alluvial lowlands, which necessitates that these areas be cultivated for rice crops. Furthermore, fieldwork and archaeological surveys over the past 50 years (FAD 1959, 1973, 1990) have by and large confirmed this with few moated sites being found in areas not closely located to river systems.

The Chi River system cuts its way through the very heart of the Khorat Plateau. It rises in the Phetchabun Mountain range and flows south towards Chaiyaphum province, after which it turns northeastwards towards the modern-day city of Khon Kaen. From here it takes on a southeasterly course, passing through the provinces of Maha Sarakham, Kalasin, Roi Et, and Yasothon respectively, before reaching its confluence with the Mun River 10 kilometres or so west of the city of Ubon Ratchathani. Its total length is approximately 450 kilometres.

The Chi River system has always been highly susceptible to severe flooding. The low terraces in particular are rich in alluvial and semi-alluvial deposits with poor drainage and low fertility. Today rice is the most suitable, and sometimes the only available, crop to be cultivated, particularly during the rainy season. Soil types on the middle and high terraces also produce low yields of rice (Lam Pao Project 1978: 8–9). Despite these factors, the Chi River system, cutting a roughly diagonal path across the middle of the Khorat Plateau, provides essential water resources and opportunities for agricultural cultivation, serving as a vital conduit for the human habitation of this region.

The Mun River system straddles the southern part of the Khorat Plateau. It flows eastwards on an approximately 700-kilometre journey from its source in Khao Yai National Park, close to Khao Khieo Mountain in the Sankamphaeng Range, through the modern-day provinces of Nakhon Ratchasima, Buriram, Surin, and Si Sa Ket, before joining the Mekong River at Khong Chiam in Ubon Ratchathani. There are numerous tributaries along its length, the largest of which is the Chi River, which joins the Mun in Kanthararom district, Si Sa Ket province.

The Mun River has to a large extent defined the settlement patterns and agricultural possibilities in this region from antiquity to the present day. Constant risk of flooding, coupled with the need to preserve and manage water resources, has resulted in settlements, both moated and unmoated, being located on three different zones – floodplain, lower terrace, and upper terrace areas. In Buriram, for instance, 11 per cent of sites are located on the floodplain, while 75 per cent are located on the low-middle terrace. In Nakhon Ratchasima province, 30 per cent of sites are located on the floodplain, while 55 per cent are located on the low-middle terraces (Moore 1988: 61–2, Fig. 4.8). Floodplains provide rich alluvial soil and thus are favourable areas for wet-rice cultivation. However, by their very nature, they are also challenging habitats to establish settlements due to the constant risk of flooding during the monsoon periods. The majority of settlements in the Mun River system are therefore located on the low-middle terraces, which provide protection from flooding while still being in reasonably close proximity to alluvial soils and their agricultural potential.

From its origins on the Tibetan Plateau, the Mekong River flows through China, Myanmar, Laos, Thailand, and Cambodia, before reaching its terminus in the delta of Vietnam. For millennia it has acted as a means of livelihood, trade, transport, and communication between the many cultures that straddle its course. The Mekong River hugs the northern and eastern edges of the Khorat Plateau and today this forms the modern border between the nation states of Thailand and Laos.

The term "Middle Mekong" is employed in this book to describe the section of this river and its tributaries starting at Vientiane province in Central Laos to Wat Phu in Champassak province of Southern Laos (Maps 2, 11; Table 3). This stretch of the Mekong encompasses the Thai provinces of Loei, Udon Thani, Nong Khai, and Bueng Kan and the lowland areas of Vientiane, Bolikhamsai, Khammouane, Savannakhet, Salavan, and Champassak provinces of Laos. The total length of this area of the Mekong River is approximately 700 kilometres.

The northwest part of the Khorat Plateau is characterised by the Phetchabun Mountain range. The northeast part is defined by the Sakhon Nakhon basin, which is bordered by the Mekong River to its north and east and the Phu Phan Mountain range to its south – this range reaches an elevation of 660 metres at its highest point. The basin is drained by the Songkhram River and its tributaries, the Lam Nam Yam River and the Huai Nam River, which all eventually flow into the Mekong River. The modern basin is characterised by paddy fields and swamps, while the Phu Phan Mountain range is still relatively densely forested (Kermel-Torres 2004: 164). The physical geography of the Sakhon Nakhon basin sub-region makes it much more unsuitable for substantial rice cultivation than the areas of the Mun and Chi River systems and is today characterised by the growing of cash crops. This fact is further emphasised by the much lower numbers of moated settlements and sites evidencing Buddhist art throughout this sub-region.

Vientiane province is bordered by the Mekong River to the south and the Nam Ngum River to the north. This latter river flows southward and meanders through the centre of the province before draining into the Mekong. Only a relatively small area of Vientiane province is lowland, the majority being mountainous uplands. It is within this lowland area, particularly along the Nam Ngum and Mekong rivers, that evidence for Buddhist art and archaeology is found. There is a high concentration of sites on the southern side of the Mekong around the area of modern-day Ban Phue district in Udon Thani province. Moving further south to Nakhon Phanom in Thailand and Khammouane and Savannakhet provinces of Laos, sites with Buddhist art cluster on both sides of the Mekong and its tributaries. Further south than this, the evidence thins out. There is one site in Salavan province and a limited amount of evidence from the Wat Phu complex in Champassak.

Overall, the Khorat Plateau represents a distinct geographical zone within the area of modern-day Northeast Thailand and Central/Southern Laos. Characterised by poor soils and unpredictable rainfall, ancient settlements had to locate themselves primarily along the lower terraces of the Mun, Chi and Mekong rivers or on their tributaries. It was in these locations of rich alluvial soil and manageable flood regimes that agriculture could be successfully undertaken. As a result, these river systems came to shape the direction and spread of the cultures that took hold within the region.

Dvaravatı and the Khorat Plateau

The Khorat Plateau is a distinct cultural and geographical region today. Despite this, many works on the art and archaeology of the Khorat Plateau regard it as either a derivative of the Dvāravatī culture based in Central Thailand or as an outer province of the Khmer Empire. Robert Brown (1996: 19–45) contends that the Khorat Plateau served as a link between the Khmers and Dvāravatī. In doing so, he unintentionally reduces the region to the role of passive go-between caught between two "great civilisations". Subhadradis Diskul (1956), on the other hand, looking from a Bangkok-centric viewpoint, wonders how Dvāravatī culture could have even reached the settlement of Muang Fa Daed.

The answer is that the Khorat Plateau is a region in its own right. It has a number of distinct cultural, religious, and artistic expressions, not least of which is the tradition of *sīmā* (discussed below). This viewpoint is supported by the prehistoric archaeological record, which depicts a region that developed its own traditions and characteristics while also displaying some interregional variation (White 1995). The Khorat

Plateau should thus be viewed as a region that incorporated elements of Dvāravatī culture from Central Thailand and Khmer culture from Cambodia. These then fused with local traditions, allowing it to form its own distinct identity.

Dvāravatī's political structure was based on a mandala-style system (Brown 1996: 10; Tambiah 1976; Wolters 1999). U Thong and subsequently Nakhon Pathom in the Lower Chao Phraya basin appear to have been the main power centres, followed by Si Thep in the Upper Chao Phraya basin. They would have had direct control over the surrounding areas of their cities and indirect control over areas further afield through vassal/tributary arrangements. These relationships could shift over time, creating a fluid political landscape. Similar political structures appear to have existed on the Khorat Plateau. Large sites like Muang Fa Daed and Muang Sema must have had considerable political reach and, as will be demonstrated in the following chapters, these centres play a significant role in the artistic trajectory of the *sīmā* tradition and Buddhist art in general. I am hesitant here to use the term "influence", particularly in light of the established art historical critiques of this term (Baxandall 1992; Wood 2016/17). The term connotes hierarchies and passive/active binaries that oversimplify the complex ways in which ideas, art styles, and iconographies circulate. Instead I rely on the concept of symbolic entrainment. This has been defined by archaeologist Colin Renfrew (1986: 8) as "the tendency for a developed symbolic system to be adopted when it comes into contact with a less-developed one with which it does not strikingly conflict".

While today the Khorat Plateau is made up predominantly of Lao, Thai, and Khmer speakers, the ethnicity and language(s) spoken by the people of both Central Thailand and the Khorat Plateau in the 1st millennium CE are the subject of much debate, disagreement, and misunderstanding. The most widely accepted theory holds that the majority of people in Central Thailand were ethnically Mon and thus spoke Mon. Today, the Mon are primarily concentrated in Mon State, Lower Myanmar. However, Gerard Diffloth (1984) contends that the Nyah Kur people, who are still present to a limited extent in Central Thailand today, are the direct linguistic descendants of the Dvāravatī-period Mon.

Inscriptions in Mon language have also led some scholars to believe that the Dvāravatī population was ethnically Mon. However, it is worth noting that inscriptions in Mon only indicate that it was one of the written languages in use (Watson 2020). It does not prove that it was the common vernacular spoken by the majority of the population, and any claims to the contrary are merely inferences drawn from an incomplete and fragmentary epigraphic record.

All that being said, the Mon were most likely one of the major ethnic groups in Central Thailand at the time. This is likely to be the case in the Khorat Plateau, though other Austro-Asiatic groups such as the Mon-Khmer and the Lawa people are also likely to have been present. However, these conclusions are based on a lack of evidence for other ethnic and linguistic groups, rather than a wealth of evidence for the Mon or Mon-Khmer. It is also extremely difficult and problematic to deduce ethnicity solely from art styles and material culture. Other ethnic groups may have existed but were unable to write or commission inscriptions and are thus invisible to us. For example, after reviewing the evidence for Mon inscriptions throughout Thailand, Hunter Watson (2020: 93) concludes that, "Old Mon may have been the vernacular of the ruling class or the ecclesiastic community, but that does not necessitate that all members of society were Mon or that other ethno-linguistic groups did not co-exist. Perhaps it would be preferable not to equate the population of Dvāravatī with any particular ethno-linguistic group."

The Dvāravatī polities of Central Thailand did not exert any form of direct control over the people of the Khorat Plateau. However, as Buddhism spread into this area, it brought the Dvāravatī art style and aspects of its culture with it. The archaeological record from the Khorat Plateau also demonstrates that the region adopted many of the material forms common to Central Thailand, particularly pottery styles (Ball 2019) and construction materials like finger-marked bricks.

The Khmer presence on the Khorat Plateau is still visible today in terms of both the ethnic Khmer language groups and monumental brick and stone temples. However, their impact on the material culture of the 1st millennium CE was overall far less pronounced than that of Dvāravatī. The earliest Khmer presence is found in Surin province in the form of a 6th-century inscription near Ta Muen, and in temples dating from the 7th century, such as Prasat Phumphon (Siribhadra and Moore 1992: 25). There is no clear evidence of Khmer political control in the region from the 8th to mid 9th centuries, and no temples were constructed during this period. It is not until the late 9th to early 10th centuries, under the reign of the Khmer king, Rājendravarman II (944–968 CE), that substantial control was exerted, and it was from this period onwards that the majority of Khmer temples on the Khorat Plateau were built. However, Khmer control still seemed to be primarily restricted to the Mun River system with Phimai, for example, becoming part of the Khmer kingdom sometime in the early 10th century (Woodward 1999: 76). By circa the 12th century, a royal road which ran directly between Phimai and Angkor had been established, thus strengthening the Khmer ties to the region (Hendrickson 2010). Areas such as the Chi River system and the Middle Mekong, on the other hand, still exhibited strong Dvāravatī artistic traits in the 10th and, to a lesser extent, 11th centuries.

As will be shown, the *sīmā* tradition flourished primarily in the Chi River system from the 7th to 9th centuries and shows little to no interaction with Khmer culture. By the 11th century and for most of the 12th, the entire Khorat Plateau, and all of Central Thailand for that matter, came under Khmer political control. Lopburi served as the seat of overall Khmer governance with Phimai also developing into an important regional centre. This period of Khmer domination is also reflected in the *sīmā* tradition, as from the 11th to 12th centuries Khmer-style art began to be incorporated into the motifs and narrative depictions.

Khmer art differs from that of Dvāravatī in a number of ways. In Khmer art, Hindu deities are typically depicted wearing a lower body cloth falling to below the knees, while bodhisattvas and female deities are depicted in a shorter lower-body cloth. Khmer images can also have an incised moustache, a detail that does not appear in Dvāravatī art. Lintel carving was another area in which the Khmers excelled, and it appears that this art form was readily adopted on the 11th-century *sīmā* carvings of Ban Nong Khluem and Ban Phailom (Figs. 5.13 and 5.14) (Kingmanee 1998b; Woodward 1997: 78).

Dvāravatī art, on the other hand, appears to have had an impact on the Khmer. For instance, a standing Buddha image from Kampong Speu province, Cambodia, today housed at the Musée Guimet (MG18891) dates to the late 7th century and has the distinctive Dvāravatī U-shaped robe, thick hair curls and is most likely in double *vitarkamudrā* (the teaching *mudrā*, one hand raised, palm facing outwards with forefinger and thumb pressed together). However, the left hand is missing, so it is impossible to tell for certain. Furthermore, seated Buddhas under the *nāga* appear to have spread from Central Thailand to the Khmer Empire via the Khorat Plateau (Fig. 2.15) (Gaston-Aubert 2010).

Despite competing stimuli from the Khmer and Dvāravatī, the Khorat Plateau developed its own aesthetics and religious culture, blending elements from its eastern and western neighbours. This is best exemplified by a variety of objects and stylistic modes. The *drapé-en-poche* (an art historical term for how the robe appears under the belt in two separate folds, forming a pocket above) is a stylistic variation that Diskul (1956) and H.G. Quaritch Wales (1969) first commented on. Both saw this as a borrowing from the Khmer, but as I will demonstrate in this book, it is better to understand it as a feature unique to the Khorat Plateau, as the form depicted in this region does not appear in Khmer art from any period (see Fig. 3.6). Another distinguishing feature of depictions of the *drapé-en-poche* from the Khorat Plateau is that the robe flares out to the right in a triangular shape. This type of robe configuration is never seen in Dvāravatī art of Central Thailand. When it does appear in Khmer art, it is never accompanied by the flared robe. This form of *drapé-en-poche* should thus be considered unique to the Khorat Plateau.

The depiction of bodhisattva with thick matted hair is another feature of the Khorat Plateau aesthetic. This can be seen in a number of *sīmā* as well as in sculptures from the Plai Bat II, "Prakhon Chai hoard" (discussed in Chapter 4, see Figs. 4.15–4.17). It is similar to Śiva's *jaṭā* (chignon) in Khmer art, but less rigidly stylised and is distinct enough to warrant its classification as a stylistic trait.

Buddha sculptures in *mahāparinibbāṇa* (the Buddha depicted entering nirvana, also known colloquially in modern Thai as a "sleeping Buddha") are a particular Khorat Plateau motif. These images appear to have been especially popular in this region from the 7th to 9th centuries and are typically found carved into hill and mountainsides. The Buddha in *mahāparinibbāṇa* is not commonly encountered in Central Thailand during this time period, though there is one known example from Tham Fa Tho Cave in Ratchaburi province and most likely associated with the ancient settlement of Khu Bua.

As the following chapters will demonstrate, motifs such as the *drapé-en-poche*, iconography such as the Buddha in *mahāparinibbāṇa*, and the exceptional quality of Khorat Plateau bronzes all exhibit Khorat Plateau aesthetics and motifs. *Sīmā*, in particular, are an important part of the region's material, religious, and artistic culture. However, the presence of Dvāravatī artistic traits on these objects must also be acknowledged, and an examination of the links between the Khorat Plateau, Central Thailand, and, to a lesser extent, Southern Thailand can be fruitful. What this book proposes therefore is a shift in perspective from viewing the Khorat Plateau as a peripheral zone to viewing it as a region in its own right. Using historical ecology as a framework, the region's Buddhist art is viewed, discussed, and interpreted within its own geographical and cultural context. In short, the Khorat Plateau is only a periphery if we choose to stand outside of it.

SITE ANALYSIS AND SETTLEMENT PATTERNS

The artistic, architectural, and archaeological remains discussed in this book can be found in four types of locations (Map 4). Moated sites are the most common type. The majority of the architectural remains, such as *stūpa* and possible ordination halls, are found in these settlements. Earthen mounds are less common, but when excavated, they can reveal evidence of *sīmā* or brick structures that are usually Buddhist in nature. While there are not many mountaintop and hillside sites, they do provide important evidence for the practice of Buddhism in more secluded locations. The final category, "undefined sites", also contributes to our

Fig. 1.2 The moated site of Ban Muang Fai, Buriram province, Thailand. Courtesy of Google Earth © 2022 Maxar Technologies.

understanding of the spread and extent of Buddhism; however, until further research or excavations are conducted at these types of locations, their exact nature will remain unknown.

Moated sites

Moated settlements are the most common type on the Khorat Plateau. They can be made up of single or multiple moats, with or without a rampart (Fig. 1.2). They can range in size from 40 to 170 hectares in total area (Supanjanya and Vanasin 1983). Some sites, such as Muang Sema, evolved and expanded over time, with additional moats added to increase the settlement's interior area (Moore 1988: 9; Murphy 2013: 311–4). They first appear around 500 BCE, coinciding with the conventionally accepted start of the Iron Age in the region (O'Reilly and Scott 2015). To date, nearly 300 sites dating from 500 BCE to 600 CE have been discovered, the vast majority of which are located in the Mun River system (O'Reilly and Scott 2015: 17). It should be noted, however, that the majority of these sites have not been verified by ground-truthing. My research has identified 45 potential 7th- to 11th-century moated sites on

1.2

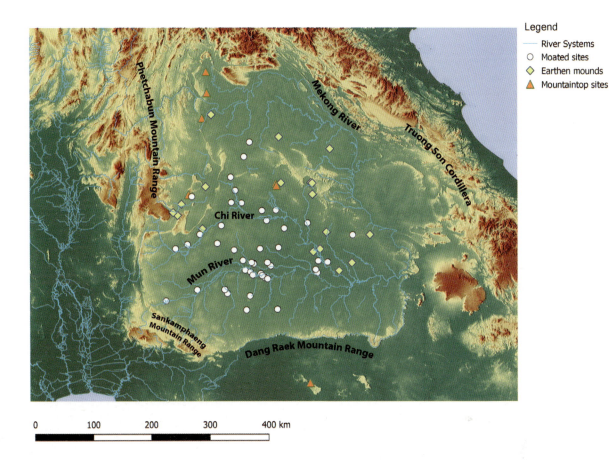

Map 4 The distribution of moated sites (circles), earthen mounds (diamonds), and mountaintop sites (triangles) on the Khorat Plateau.

the Khorat Plateau (Murphy 2010: 134–5, 138–40), some of which date back to the Iron Age.[2] Religious structures, such as *stūpa*, are clearly present at five of these locations. Future archaeological investigations at other sites could potentially reveal similar evidence.

A close examination of the distribution of moated sites during this time period reveals their reliance on the Mun and Chi river systems. All but three are located on these rivers or their tributaries. The paths of these tributaries and streams are typically channelled to feed the moats for flood control and irrigation. Their placement on or near these river systems would also have been crucial for trade, transportation, and communication

---

2   Many of these sites have been recorded by archaeological surveys of the region and dates have been attributed to them based on surface finds alone (see, for example, Fine Arts Department 1959, 1973, 1990). I have built on this published research with ground surveys and analysis of satellite imagery. Excavations would be needed, however, to accurately date occupation periods.

Fig.1.3 Half-buried in situ *sīmā* dating to the 8th–9th centuries in a rice field on the outskirts of the village of Ban Na Ngam, Kalasin province, Thailand.

in general. During the 7th to 11th centuries, the size, characteristics, and agricultural potential of moated sites on the Khorat Plateau would have been one factor in regards to the spread of Buddhism within the region. If monasteries wanted to keep large populations of monks, they needed a large enough lay community to support them. As Bronkhorst observes:

> Buddhism soon became a victim of its own success. The community of monks and nuns organized itself, and monasteries were created. Questions regarding the interaction between the buddhist community and society at large became inevitable. In order to build monasteries and places of worship, a steady stream of gifts from donors was necessary (2011: 99–100).

To support such monasteries, the lay community needed to produce a sufficient surplus of food and resources. As a result, large-scale monasteries would only thrive in areas with adequate agricultural resources or potential, hence the importance of identifying moated sites, as the spread and growth of Buddhism is governed by such settlement patterns.

Earthen Mounds

Earthen mounds are less common than moated sites during the 7th to 11th centuries across the Khorat Plateau. Earthen mounds are typically found within or near moated sites. It is also possible that earthen mounds discovered today in isolation were once part of a moated site and that the moats are no longer visible as a result of modern agricultural activity and

land use. Comparative evidence from the site of Dong Mae Nang Muang in Central Thailand's Nakhon Sawan province shows that earthen mounds are often Buddhist religious structures, most commonly small *stūpa* (Murphy and Pongkasetkan 2010).

Mountaintop and Hillside Sites

This site type is far less common than earthen mounds or moated sites, and I have only recorded seven to date (Map 4). They are typically found in heavily forested and isolated areas. These locations most likely served as sites of meditation for monks, particularly during traditional rainy season retreats. They could also have served as pilgrimage sites for the lay community. The site selection is less influenced by ecological factors than those in urban settlements. However, the monks are still affected by their environment in terms of the options available to them. If there are no suitable mountains or caves in the area, for example, a monk may opt for a forest instead. A monk may also choose a mountain or hilltop if there is little forest cover in the area due to swidden-type agricultural activity or large-scale rice farming. However, by its nature, this type of religious activity leaves little in the way of archaeological evidence, and the few surviving sites that we have today may only represent a small fraction of the total number that existed in the 7th to 11th centuries.

Undefined Sites

For lack of a better term, the fourth type of location where evidence for Buddhism has been discovered can be classified as "undefined sites". These sites lack clear boundaries or distinguishing features such as moats or earthen mounds that would allow them to be classified as a specific site type. *Sīmā* (discussed below) are still in situ in several places, such as Ban Ilay in Vientiane province, but the nature of the site itself cannot be determined without excavations. This is also the case at Ban Na Ngam in Kalasin province. Here, the *sīmā* are in situ in a rice field on the village outskirts and are currently lying in the ground, partially covered in soil (Fig. 1.3). While no structures or archaeological features are visible to define the site's boundaries, the *sīmā* are arranged in a circular pattern and spaced at regular intervals. The area enclosed by the *sīmā* would have been large enough to accommodate the performing of rituals such as ordinations or perhaps a religious structure of some sort. Excavations at both this site and that of Ban Ilai may reveal evidence for such a structure in the form of postholes or an earthen floor.

However, at the majority of undefined sites, Buddhist material evidence has been gathered up and stored in local temples or sheds in villages. Future research such as excavations, survey work, or remote sensing may help to determine the exact nature of certain sites.

OBJECT ANALYSIS: TYPES OF ARCHAEOLOGICAL AND ARTISTIC EVIDENCE FOR BUDDHISM ON THE KHORAT PLATEAU

Having discussed the geographical characteristics and types of sites, this section looks at types of Buddhist archaeological and artistic evidence. This consists primarily of architecture and artefacts such as stone and bronze Buddha images, *sīmā*, *dharmacakra* (Wheel of the Law), sculpture, votive tablets, and inscriptions. Taken altogether, they form a rich corpus of art and Buddhist symbolism.

Sīmā[3]

Sīmā, or Buddhist boundary markers as they are commonly referred to in English, provide some of the clearest and most abundant evidence for Buddhism in the region. They are very significant to this study because they provide some of the best testimony for tracing the trajectory and spread of Buddhist art in the region. These objects are used to demarcate Buddhist ritual space. This space could be an entire monastery, a specific building within it, or other areas such as forest dwellings. Today they are found in the majority of Southeast Asia's Buddhist countries, including Thailand, Laos, Myanmar, and Cambodia. However, archaeological evidence suggests that they first appeared in significant numbers on the Khorat Plateau around the 7th century CE. Early examples from Myanmar, dating from around the 6th to 9th centuries, have also been documented, albeit in far fewer numbers (Murphy 2014: 355–57).

Sīmā are typically arranged in groups of eight or sixteen. During the 7th to 11th centuries, some configurations could have comprised up to 24 *sīmā*. A manuscript from Bangkok's 19th-century Wat Suthat Dhepvararam temple shows *sīmā* arranged in groups of three, four, or seven to demarcate the sacred space (Paknam 1997: 60). There is therefore no fixed number. As long as a clear, unbroken boundary is formed, any amount is possible.

In Thai, *sīmā* are referred to as *sema* (เสมา) or more often than not, *bai sema* (ใบเสมา). "Bai" means "leaf", and this is reflective of the marker's shape, which from the Ayutthaya period onwards is predominantly leaf-like. The word *sīmā* in Myanmar refers to both a boundary and an ordination hall (pronounced *thein* in Burmese), as evidenced by the Kalyani Sīmā at Pegu and Thaton (Luce 1969: 252–3; Stadtner 2011: 154–5, 168–73).

The *Mahāvagga* of the *Vinaya Piṭaka* contains the canonical rationale for creating a *sīmā*, or sacred boundary (*Mahāvagga* II 5. 4–15. 2; Horner

---

3   For an in-depth study of *sīmā*, see Murphy (2010).

1951)[4]. According to this text, a *sīmā* must be created before certain rituals such as the *pāṭimokkha* and ordination ceremonies can take place. The *pāṭimokkha* ceremony, which consists of reciting the order's rules, is held twice a month, on the full and new moons, and once a year at the end of the rainy season.

The *sīmā* must be created by *nimitta* (boundary marks). However, as Pinna Indorf (1994: 19) notes, nowhere in this text does it specify what these *nimitta* are to be. It does provide a few options, stating that natural features like rocks, trees, and hillsides can be used, but rivers and lakes cannot (*Mahāvagga* II. 4–5, 12. 6–7; Nagasena and Crosby 2022). The use of sculpted stones as *nimitta* to create a boundary appears to be a Southeast Asian response to this need. Furthermore, archaeological evidence suggests that this tradition originated in the Khorat Plateau in the 7th to 9th centuries and to a lesser extent in Myanmar. It is possible that other forms of *nimitta* were created at the same time in other parts of Southeast Asia using perishable materials that no longer survive. For example, while sandstone is abundant on the Khorat Plateau, it is not in Central Thailand, which may explain their absence in this region. To date, no evidence for the *sīmā* tradition has been discovered in India or Khmer Buddhist practice prior to the post-Angkorian period. Meanwhile, as Buddhism spread into China in the early to mid 1st millennium CE, a raised platform was constructed to indicate the *sīmā* (Newhall 2022).

In modern-day Southeast Asian Theravāda Buddhism, the *sīmā* is subdivided into the *mahāsīmā* and the *khandasīmā* (Giteau 1969: 6–7; Kieffer-Pülz 1993: 242–58). A *mahāsīmā* is the boundary encompassing the entire monastery, whereas the *khandasīmā* demarcates a specific area within the monastery (or *mahāsīmā*) where a number of specific rituals take place. The *khandasīmā* is a section of the monastery defined by *sīmā* that usually includes a building that from around the 14th century onwards in Thailand is referred to by the term *ubosot* (Chutiwongs 2009: 67).[5] The term is based on the Pāli word, *"uposathāgāra"* – *"uposatha"* means ordination, *"agāra"* means building. It can also be referred to by its abbreviated form (*pos*, pronounced *bot* in Thai) while in Laos this building is referred to as a *"sim"*, presumably derived from *sīmā*. However, there is no epigraphic evidence to suggest that the term *uposathāgāra* was used on the Khorat Plateau from the 7th to 11th centuries. Furthermore, due to a lack of evidence, it is also unclear whether the divisions of *mahāsīmā* and *khandasīmā* existed during the 7th to 11th centuries. However, it appears that in some cases, *sīmā*

---

4   For an in-depth discussion of this text and its instructions regarding the creation of *sīmā*, see Nagasena and Crosby (2022).

5   However, this is not the case in modern Cambodia (or most of Middle Cambodia), where it is the *vihāra* which effectively doubles as an *ubosot*.

demarcated a structure that may have functioned as an ordination hall. There is also evidence for *sīmā* demarcating *stūpa* and rock shelters (see Chapters 2, 3, and 4). *Sīmā* in this period may thus have demarcated a variety of Buddhist space. It is only from the 14th century onwards that their usage becomes restricted to demarcating the *uposathāgāra/ubosot*. We must thus be careful not to project post-14th-century practice back onto earlier periods. For instance, the large quantity of *sīmā* discovered at sites such as Muang Fa Daed and Ban Khon Sawan suggests that they may have also demarcated the *mahāsīmā* in some cases.

Sīmā are classified into four main types: slab, pillar, octagonal, and unfashioned (Fig. 1.4).[6] Krairiksh (1974a: 38–40) proposed the first three classifications and Vallibhotama (1975: 90) added the fourth. The vast majority of *sīmā* are made of sandstone, though laterite is also used in some cases. It has been suggested that laterite *sīmā* represent an earlier form, possibly even a megalithic forerunner. The theory has been largely debunked, however (Murphy 2010: 365–74). The main flaw in this theory is that there is no evidence for megaliths on the Khorat Plateau. Despite this, the theory is still prevalent in the literature, owing largely to the assumption that incoming religions without fail co-opt indigenous practices (Wales 1969: 111; Phiromanukun 2009: 97–8; Hidalgo Tan Suwi Siang 2014: 72–4).

Outside of the Khorat Plateau, *sīmā* can be made from other materials such as schist and limestone, as in Nakhon Sawan (Murphy and Pongkasetkan 2010: 63), or fossilised wood as in Myanmar (Murphy 2014: 355–6). However, sandstone is the preferred material due to its abundance on the Khorat Plateau and ease of carving.

Slab *sīmā* are typically long and straight-bodied, with the sides occasionally tapering slightly outwards. The top of the stone ends in a leaf-like design, forming a curved triangle at the apex. Slab *sīmā* are approximately 175 centimetres tall, 70 centimetres wide, and 25 centimetres deep on average, but can reach heights of up to 3 metres in some cases. Pillar type *sīmā* are roughly squared-shaped with a pyramidal head and are usually devoid of artistic motifs other than a lotus band at their base. Their average size is 145 centimetres tall, 45 centimetres wide, and 45 centimetres deep. Octagonal *sīmā* are eight-sided and have a cone-shaped top. They are the rarest type of *sīmā* and are not found in the Mun River system. The Chi and, to a lesser extent, the Middle Mekong are home to the majority of them. Their overall average dimensions are 130 centimetres high, 55 centimetres in diameter, and 25 centimetres in width at the faces/sides. Finally, unfashioned *sīmā* are those with no artwork or carving on them. As a result, their form is crude. They can take

---

6   For a detailed typology of *sīmā*, see Murphy (2010: 344–65).

a variety of shapes but are typically slab or pillar in form. Caution should be used with this type, as what appears to be an unfashioned *sīmā* today is often the result of severe erosion. As a result, in many cases, these *sīmā* could have originated as a slab or pillar type. Certain *sīmā*, on the other hand, appear to be completely unfashioned.

The artwork displayed on *sīmā* can be divided into two main categories: narrative art and motifs. The narrative art consists of *jātaka* tales and scenes from the Life of the Buddha. The motifs include a wide range of images and symbols, almost all of which are Buddhist in nature. The *stūpa* is the most common Buddhist motif. There are also *kumbha* and *pūrṇaghaṭa* (vase of plenty) motifs, which are usually associated with *stūpa*. *Dharmacakra* are found in a few places, and lotus petals forming a band at the base of *sīmā* are also common.

As mentioned earlier, *sīmā* are significant because they provide some of the best evidence for tracing the trajectory and spread of Buddhist art in the region. Because of their large size, they are difficult to move, unlike bronze Buddha images and votive tablets, which were far more portable. To a large extent, they are still in situ or located close to their original findspots (Murphy 2010: 143–4). As previously stated, in order for ordinations to take place, a boundary must be created. This is done by the placement of *sīmā*. Therefore, we can deduce that the presence of *sīmā* at a site also indicates that there was once, in Skilling's (2012) terms, a

Fig. 1.4 The four types of *sīmā*, from left to right: slab type, pillar type, octagonal type, and unfashioned type.

1.4

self-governing *saṅgha* module at this location. It may also be the case that a *sīmā* represents locations of Buddhist monasteries. However, without clear archaeological evidence, it is most often impossible to establish whether this was in fact the case.

This has allowed me to map the distribution of *saṅgha* modules on the Khorat Plateau and enables a number of inferences to be drawn. First, it allows for the identification of clusters. Second, it sheds light on how the religion spread throughout the region. Third, by estimating the total number of *saṅgha* modules and associated communities, it is possible to gain some understanding of the extent of formal Buddhist practice (Murphy 2015).

A clear pattern emerges from analysing and plotting the distribution of *sīmā*. I surveyed 110 sites in total, 48 of which are located along the Chi River system, 49 in the Middle Mekong, and 14 along the Mun River system. In terms of percentage, the Chi has 45 per cent of *sīmā* locations, the Middle Mekong has 44 per cent, and the Mun has 11 per cent. This evidence strengthens the argument proposed in this book that the movement of Buddhism followed pre-existing routes along river systems.

Art on *sīmā* can be divided into two categories. The first is narrative art, which is the less common of the two. It usually depicts scenes from *jātaka* or the Life of the Buddha. The second category is that of Buddhist symbols and motifs. These are usually *stūpa* or *stūpa-kumbha* motifs (see below).

Visual Analysis: Narrative Art

The *jātaka*, an essential part of the Buddhist canon, recount the Buddha's legendary previous lives, with each successive rebirth representing a step toward Enlightenment. They number 547 in the Pāli tradition, with the last 10 known as the "Great Section" (*Mahānipāta*). The *jātaka*, however, are shared by all Buddhist traditions, be they Theravāda, Mahāyāna, or Vajrayāna, and represent a central part of Buddhist teaching (Skilling 2008a: 59).

The texts we have today can be divided into two categories: those of the Pāli canon and those of the Sanskrit schools. The most important relevant work in the Pāli tradition is the *Khuddaka-nikāya* [Miscellaneous Collection] of the Pāli *Tipiṭaka*, which contains 547 previous lives of the Buddha. It is unclear when this collection was written. However, by the early centuries of the 1st millennium CE, it was almost certainly a well-established piece of literature, with some scholars speculating that it was in existence by the 5th century (Krairiksh 1974b: 1; Skilling 2008a: 67).

A number of *jātaka* renditions were also produced by the Mahāyāna schools. The most famous of these is the *Jātakamālā* of Arya Sura [The Garland of Birth Stories], which consists of 34 stories in mixed Sanskrit prose and verse. It dates from the 4th century. Other examples include the *Mahāvastu* from the *Vinaya* [Collection of texts on "Discipline"] of the Lokottaravādin school, which contains many important *jātaka* written in Sanskrit specific to that school. Furthermore, the *Vinaya* of the Mūlasarvāstivādas contains *jātaka*, as does the Chinese *Fo Benxing Ji Jing*, which was translated from Sanskrit between 587–595 CE and contains *jātaka* from a variety of sources (Skilling 2008a: 65).

Attempting to link specific texts to the *jātaka* tales depicted on *sīmā* across the Khorat Plateau is a difficult task. For a start, there are no surviving texts from the Khorat Plateau during the time period in question, making it impossible to know with certainty which texts were in circulation. It is possible that many of the *jātaka* scenes found across the Khorat Plateau were transmitted as much by word of mouth and visual models such as palm leaf manuscript.

However, attempts to match specific schools and texts to the *jātaka* have been made, with mixed results. Art historian Piriya Krairiksh (1974a; 1974b) tried this in two different locations – the stucco panels at Chula Pathon Chedi in Nakhon Pathom and the *sīmā* at the Khon Kaen National Museum. However, Krairiksh appears to be unwittingly contradicting himself in the process. In one article (1974a), he claims that the *jātaka* on *sīmā* are from the Pāli tradition, stating, "The jātaka scenes can be identified with some certainty to have derived from a Pāli text, the *Jātaka-aṭṭhakathā*, since the illustrations closely follow this text" (Krairiksh 1974a: 45). In his other work from the same year (1974b), he argues that the *jātaka* tales depicted at Chula Pathon Chedi are derived from the Sanskrit *avadāna* of the Sarvāstivāda school, rather than the *Jātaka-aṭṭhakathā* (1974b: 1). However, Krairiksh must frequently refer to the Pāli *jātaka* in order to illustrate the *avadāna* tales, inadvertently highlighting the similarities between these texts and thus the difficulties involved in attempting to match specific texts to specific monuments or artefacts. Furthermore, as art historian Robert Brown (1997: 75–8) has highlighted, it is not always clear which *jātaka* is being depicted, making it even more difficult to match them to specific texts.

The basics of the narrative of the Life of the Buddha as we know them today do not come from a single definitive text but has been passed down in various forms. The Life of the Buddha, like the *jātaka*, was first preserved and passed down orally, with the earliest textual sources dating from the 2nd century CE. However, it is to the *Nidāna-Kathā*, an early Pāli work, that we must turn in order to find a complete life story of the Buddha (Jayawickrama 1990: xiv). The *Nidāna-Kathā*, which is part of the *Jātaka-aṭṭhakathā*, serves as an introduction to the work's *jātaka* texts. It does, however, have all the hallmarks of an independent work, as Pāli scholar Jayawickrama notes (1990: xi). It recounts the Life of the

Fig. 1.5 Axial *stūpa* design on a *sīmā* from Phu Phra Bat, Udon Thani province, Thailand. 8th–9th centuries. Sandstone. Height: 147 cm; width: 60 cm; depth: 30 cm.

Buddha from his birth to his acceptance of the monastery of Jetavana from King Bimbisara. N.A. Jayawickrama concludes from a careful examination of texts and sources that, while the text as we know it today was written down after Buddhist Sanskrit works such as the *Lalitavistara Sūtra* and the *Buddhacarita*, it is a chronologically earlier work that predates the texts of northern India (1990: xv). This would place the *Nidāna-Kathā* in the pre-2nd century CE.

It is difficult to say with certainty which texts inspired the various Life of the Buddha scenes depicted on *sīmā* throughout the Khorat Plateau. In many cases, scenes and episodes are described in the various sources in similar ways, making it impossible to give one text precedence over others. It should also be noted that in modern Thai Buddhism, the *Paṭhamasambodhi* is one of the preferred texts for reciting the Life of the Buddha. It is written in 29 sections and fills in details about the Buddha's life that are missing from some of the sources cited above (Swearer 1995: 41). However, because it was written much later than the period in question, it should be used with caution when identifying scenes on *sīmā*.

Visual Analysis: Stūpa Motifs

The *stūpa* is the most common Buddhist motif on the Khorat Plateau. However, *kumbha* and *pūrṇaghaṭa* motifs can also be found, usually in association with *stūpa*. *Stūpa-kumbha* motifs are typically found on votive tablets or *sīmā*, but they have also been discovered on gold repoussé sheets and as terracotta miniatures.

The axial *stūpa* is the most common motif depicted on *sīmā*. This motif consists of a straight ridge, usually no more than 10 centimetres wide, that bisects the *sīmā* vertically down the middle (Fig. 1.5). However, in some variants, the *stūpa* is wider and more triangular in shape. This motif appears only on slab *sīmā* and can be seen on both the front and back, or on one side only. It is frequently seen on the back of *sīmā* with narrative art depictions on the front. The axial *stūpa* can also sometimes form part of a narrative composition, rising out of the scene. In the Ayutthaya period, the motif is depicted more narrowly and represents the stylised spine of a leaf. This is an integral part of the leaf-shaped *sīmā* design that is still in use today.

It has also been suggested that this motif represents a sacred sword, similar to those figuring on *sīmā* found at the Kulen Mountains in what is now northern Cambodia (Wales 1980: 51). This association, however, is unconvincing. The majority of motifs are narrow and vertical in shape, with no evidence of a sword hilt, unlike the Phnom Kulen example. The presence of the *stūpa-kumbha* motif also suggests that this identification is incorrect. From the 7th century onwards, the axial *stūpa* appears on the earliest *sīmā* and is depicted until the 11th and 12th centuries. Its simplicity may be one factor in explaining why it spread throughout the Khorat Plateau – it met the need to indicate that *sīmā* were sacred Buddhist objects with the least amount of effort and artistic skill. The ease of execution of the axial *stūpa* would have made it a ready solution in areas and situations where the craftsmanship required to carve *sīmā* with narrative art was lacking.

The *stūpa-kumbha* is another prevalent motif on *sīmā*. A *kumbha* is an Indian water pot or jar that is associated with both Buddhism and Hinduism. It is also known as a *pūrṇaghaṭa* (full pot/vase of plenty) when it has overflowing foliate designs. While it is impossible to say for certain when and how the *kumbha/pūrṇaghaṭa* motif arrived on the Khorat Plateau, it is clear that this motif has had long and widespread usage in Buddhism with Indian examples dating back to the 1st century BCE. Its persistence over such a long period of time and its eventual spread into the Khorat Plateau demonstrate its durability and continuing symbolic significance.

The *kumbha* on *sīmā* from the Khorat Plateau can be seen as a simple water pot or as a more elaborate design, similar to the *pūrṇaghaṭa*, with foliate and vegetal motifs springing forth. The *kumbha* can either sit

Fig. 1.6 *Sīmā* with a *stūpa-kumbha* mounted on a stand from Wat Pho Si Mongkol Temple, Ban Tat Tong, Yasothon province, Thailand. 8th–9th centuries. Sandstone. Height: 180 cm; width: 80 cm; depth: 18 cm.

1.5   1.6

directly on the lotus band or on an ornate base. The *kumbha* is topped by a *stūpa*, hence the term *stūpa-kumbha*. As Thompson has observed, this reflects a gendered pairing. The *kumbha* represents the feminine, which receives and holds the *stūpa* or male aspect.[7] The *stūpa* motif can be devoid of decoration or ornately carved, and it is sometimes depicted with concentric rings, which are most likely meant to represent the *chattravali* (architectural term referring to *stūpa* rings) on actual *stūpa*. The *stūpa* can sometimes end in an elaborate finial, but more often its tip is left undecorated (Fig. 1.6).[8]

Throughout Central Thailand and the Khorat Plateau during the 7th to 11th centuries, the *stūpa-kumbha* motif was represented in a variety of forms and media. Excavations in Na Dun, Maha Sarakham province uncovered a bronze example that would have served as a reliquary (Sathaphon 1981). Another bronze reliquary was discovered at Si Thep, whose *stūpa-kumbha* motif is stylistically similar to that found at Na Dun (FAD 2007: 41). Another variant can be seen at U Thong, where a terracotta *stūpa-kumbha* was discovered and may have served as a reliquary or a finial for an actual *stūpa*. The motif can also be found on clay votive tablets, as seen at sites such as U Thong, Muang Fa Daed, and Khu Bua to name a few. The *stūpa-kumbha* motif is sometimes shown as part of a triad, as seen on a tablet from Khu Bua, with the Buddha in the centre, a *dharmacakra* motif to his left, and the *stūpa-kumbha* motif to his right (Baptiste and Zéphir 2009: 61–2). At other times, the Buddha is flanked by several *stūpa* motifs. The Buddha-*stūpa-dharmacakra* triad has been described as a uniquely Dvāravatī phenomenon with no precedents in India, and it is particularly common among votive tablets from Southern Thailand (Brown 1996: 85). *Stūpa-kumbha* flanking the Buddha in a triad configuration can also be found on stele, with two examples from Sri Mahosot in Prachinburi province amongst the finest (Murphy 2019: 304–5). However, it should be noted that neither of these triad types appears on *sīmā*. The motif has also been discovered on silver repoussé sheets from Kantharawichai, Maha Sarakahm province (Diskul 1973; Woodward 2005: 102–4).

The closest parallel to the *stūpa-kumbha* design found on *sīmā*, however, comes from Thamorat Cave, approximately 20 kilometres west of Si Thep in Petchabun province (FAD 2007: 125–7). The cave's walls are adorned with relief carvings of the Buddha and a bodhisattva, as well as a *stūpa-kumbha* motif depicted beside a seated Buddha image. Its style and iconography are strikingly similar to those found on the Khorat Plateau. Because of the numerous examples discovered, it is clear that the

---

7   "Recreating Angkorian Worlds: Out of Chaos" lecture given by Prof. Ashley Thompson, 15 March 2022, The Courtauld Institute of Art.

8   For a detailed typology of this motif, see Murphy (2010: 316–23).

stūpa-kumbha was an important and well-known motif both in Central Thailand and on the Khorat Plateau.

Architecture

Buddhist architectural remains from the 7th to 11th centuries on the Khorat Plateau are scarce. Brick *stūpa* foundations can still be found at a few locations, and the numerous earthen mounds found throughout the region may also reveal evidence of Buddhist architecture if excavated. There is also scant evidence of monastic buildings. However, because these structures were typically made of perishable materials such as wood, and bamboo and weave, it may be the case that they did exist but no longer survive. The only evidence we do have for these structures comes from the few instances where they were built in brick. The *stūpa* is arguably the most instantly recognisable form of Buddhist architecture. Most of the evidence for these structures of the 7th to 11th centuries comes from Central Thailand. There are, however, a few surviving examples from the Khorat Plateau, which can be seen at Muang Fa Daed, Muang Sema, and Na Dun (Fig. 2.1). During this time period, *stūpa* were made of fired bricks, which were sometimes finger-marked. The ground plan is typically made up of a square base surmounted by terraces, as seen at Chula Pathon Chedi in Nakhon Pathom (Dupont 2006: plan 6). The terraces are re-dented and adorned with a stucco façade. The *stūpa's* large central drum, also built of brick, rose out of the terraces. It is difficult to say exactly what shape this part of the monument took because they are usually in poor condition, do not exist at all, or have been completely replaced by renovations from later periods.

Surviving *stūpa* scattered across the Khorat Plateau are some of the only tangible forms of Buddhist architecture in the 7th to 11th centuries. To a certain extent, they would have shaped the urban planning of early settlements as they served as focal points within these societies for a variety of Buddhist rites, rituals, and activities.

If the *stūpa* is the most easily recognised form of Buddhist architecture, the ordination hall (*ubosot*) is possibly the most important. This position is derived from two specific rituals that must be performed within this monastic structure, namely, the ordination ceremony and the *pāṭimokkha*. However, there is little direct evidence for this structure in the Khorat Plateau during the 7th to 11th centuries. Only two or three examples are known to possibly exist. The archaeological record from Central Thailand is also unrevealing, with Si Thep being the only location where clear foundations of monastic buildings survive (FAD 2007). The lack of preservation is most likely due to the building materials used, as while *stūpa* were built of fired brick, ordination halls may have been built from perishable materials such as wood and woven bamboo strips, a tradition that continued until relatively recently (Matics 1992: 23–4). The other possibility is that ordination and *pāṭimokkha* ceremonies took place in the open. This would have been possible as long as the area was clearly demarcated by *sīmā*.

The other main monastic structure is the assembly hall (known from the 14th century onwards in surviving written records as a *vihāra*). It serves as an assembly or preaching hall for members of the laity and *saṅgha* to congregate. Muang Sema appears to be the only location with evidence for this architectural structure from the Khorat Plateau during the time period in question. We can speculate that if assembly halls did exist during this period, they too were made of perishable material, and thus no evidence survives today.

Buddha Images

Buddha images from the Khorat Plateau are found executed in the round, either carved in stone or cast in bronze. Otherwise they are found as relief carving. These images can be either seated or standing, with the former typically in *dhyānamudrā* (meditation *mudrā,* both hands on the lap, right on top of left, palms facing upwards) or *bhūmisparśamudrā* (representing the moment of Enlightenment under the Bodhi tree signified by the Buddha touching the earth with his right hand). They are frequently in double *vitarkamudrā* when standing. Relief carvings of the Buddha are typically found on *sīmā* or carved into rock faces or cave interiors. Buddha images in *mahāparinibbāṇa* etched into natural rockfaces on mountainsides become popular on the Khorat Plateau from the 7th to 11th centuries. They are, however, uncommon in Central Thailand.

To some extent, the Khorat Plateau has a sophisticated bronze casting tradition. This is best exemplified by medium- to large-scale images of the Buddha and bodhisattvas from the Mun River Valley region, some of which are larger than life-size. They include those from the sites of Ban Muang Fai and Ban Tanot, as well as the Prakhon Chai hoard supposedly discovered at Plai Bat II. Overall, it is possible to conclude that Buddhist images in bronze may have been just as common as those in stone. However, due to the nature of the medium, which corrodes over time, their rate of preservation would be much lower. They may have also been melted down and re-used at various times throughout antiquity. What is clear is that, at least in the Mun River system, there appears to have been at least one bronze atelier at work in some shape or form. The Prakhon Chai/Plai Bat II hoard and the image from Ban Tanot both suggest links to pre-Angkorian Cambodia, indicating the cultural and technological interaction that most likely existed between these two regions. This is discussed in detail in Chapter 4.

A number of small bronzes may also come from the Khorat Plateau.[9] One example, identified as the Buddha Vairocana, is now housed in the National Museum Bangkok (accession number SV.13). It was discovered in Kosumphisai, Maha Sarakham province, in 1927. This bronze is stylistically similar to those associated with Śrīvijaya (a maritime power based in South Sumatra and holding sway over the Straits of Malacca and the Thai–Malay Peninsula). The throne, with the oval back plates and ribboned umbrella, is reminiscent of those seen in Pala bronzes from Northern India, where Vajrayāna Buddhism had taken hold. Because they are highly portable, bronzes such as this most likely made their way to the Khorat Plateau via the maritime networks that connect Śrīvijaya and Dvāravatī sites in Central Thailand. It could have been carried into the region by practitioners/monks from here.

Votive Tablets

The practice of making votive tablets to be placed as offerings at sacred Buddhist sites or to be brought home as religious souvenirs from a pilgrimage date back to the 1st century BCE in India (Chirapravati 1999: 83). By the 7th century CE, there is clear evidence that this practice had spread to Thailand, first in the south, but soon after in the central and north-eastern regions as well. According to Skilling (2005: 677–85), these objects are among the most common artefacts discovered at Buddhist sites, sometimes numbering in the thousands. It should be noted that Skilling has raised concerns about the use of the term "votive". He argues that not all tablets were used in this manner. As an alternative, he suggests using "scalings" or moulded Buddhist tablets. To date, however, this new term has not been widely accepted by scholarship. This book retains the term "votive tablet", employing it in its broadest sense to describe this type of Buddhist material culture, while also acknowledging Skilling's caveat about its use.

Votives are typically made of terracotta and are rectangular or square in shape with an arched top. The Life of the Buddha and triads with the Buddha in the centre flanked by votive *stūpa,* or at times bodhisattvas, are popular themes (Chirapravati 1999: 83). They occasionally have inscriptions (see below) with the *Ye Dhammā* stanza (the dependent origination *dhāraṇī*) (Skilling 2008b; Revire 2014: 256–9) or other *dhāraṇī* (a Buddhist chant or mnemonic). They have been discovered on the Khorat Plateau at two specific sites: Na Dun in Maha Sarakham province and Muang Fa Daed in Kalasin province.

---

9   Sharrock and Bunker (2016: 238, Figs. 10.7a, 10.13a, 10.13b) discuss three bronzes that were reportedly found on the Khorat Plateau. However, these are part of the private collection of the late Douglas Latchford and are of dubious provenance and authenticity.

Inscriptions

The earliest inscriptions in Southeast Asia have traditionally been classified as being written in Pallava or post-Pallava script (Griffiths 2014: 54). Scholars in the early 20th century noticed similarities between Southeast Asian scripts and those used by the Pallava Dynasty in Southwest India around 300 CE. However, as Griffiths (2014) points out, the Pallava kings were not the only ones to use this script, and they had little direct connection with Southeast Asia. As a result, he proposes the more neutral term "Late Southern Brāhmī" to describe the script in this region. This script is in use from the 4th century until around 800 CE. Following this, the script evolves in different directions depending on the culture in which it finds itself (Griffiths 2014: 53–5). However, as previously stated, the terms Pallava and post-Pallava are still used in the literature, particularly in Thai. In these cases, Pallava roughly corresponds to what Griffith refers to as Late Southern Brāhmī. Post-Pallava refers to the regionalisation of this script, which occurred between the 8th and 10th centuries.[10]

When it comes to dating, there are two options. The most reliable method is if the inscription itself contains a date, which is either given numerically or in Sanskrit. If this is not the case, the inscription is dated based on palaeographic evidence, that is, by studying the script form and range of letters and other marks employed. This method of dating is based on comparisons with other inscriptions. As a result, this method of dating is far less accurate or reliable.

In terms of the languages used, Pāli inscriptions are limited to Central Thailand and primarily date from the 7th and 8th centuries. They do not appear on the Khorat Plateau, with the exception of Muang Sema. The majority of inscriptions in the region are instead in Old Mon (Revire 2014: 247–8). Old Mon inscriptions can also be found in Central Thailand, particularly at Tap Chumphon, though in smaller numbers than those in Pāli (Watson 2018: 119). Some inscriptions are bilingual, with the Pāli part containing the *Ye Dhammā* creed and the Old Mon part containing a message of some kind, usually referring to a donor or the attainment of merit (Watson 2018: 119).

Inscriptions in either Old Mon or Sanskrit can be found on Buddha images, particularly on their bases, and on *sīmā*. Christian Bauer (1991) was the first to study many of the Old Mon examples on the Khorat Plateau. Hunter Watson has recently re-examined and re-surveyed the region. To date, his research has yielded over 100 Mon inscriptions on a

---

10   My sincere thanks to Hunter Watson for guiding me through the literature and complexities of this issue.

variety of different artefact types ranging from *sīmā* to statues, and votive tablets. The length of an inscription is also variable. There are cases of entire *sīmā* covered in lines of script, to the other extreme of votive tablets containing only a word or two (Watson 2020: 87).

Watson categorises Old Mon inscriptions into three time periods. It should be noted, however, that only one Old Mon inscription from the Khorat Plateau bears a date. The remainder are dated based on palaeographic grounds (Watson 2020: 87). The first group, which dates from the 6th to 7th centuries, can only be found in Central Thailand. These are written in Pallava/Late Southern Brāhmī script (Watson 2020: 87). The second group, dating from the 8th to 10th centuries, are in post-Pallava script and consists primarily of inscriptions from the Khorat Plateau, though there are examples in Central Thailand as well, albeit to a lesser extent (Watson 2020: 87). The third group, which dates from the 11th to 12th centuries and is only found on the Khorat Plateau and at Lamphun in Northern Thailand, is written in Old Mon script (Watson 2018: 119; 2020: 87).

The inscriptions discovered on the Khorat Plateau and Central Thailand between the 7th to 11th centuries are almost entirely religious in nature. Their primary purpose is devotional. They largely comprise citations of canonical liturgical texts. The majority of the quotations are from texts shared by all forms of Buddhism, making it difficult to determine which school or sect they belong to.

Inscriptions on the Khorat Plateau are thus for the most part distinguished by their brevity. Many inscriptions record the donor's name along with dedications (Woodward 2005: 103–4). For example, the Hin Khon inscription (NM 31/K. 389) mentions royalty. It was founded by a prince who had become a monk (*rājabhikṣu*) and had not only dedicated four *sīmā* of high-quality stone to a royal monastery but also made significant donations (Woodward 2005: 104; Filliozat 1981: 84). This text gives us a tantalising glimpse of society at the time, and also emphasises the significance of using *sīmā* to fix and consecrate a boundary.

MODERN WORSHIP AND RE-USE

The re-use of ancient objects is a distinguishing feature of Thai Buddhism (and Buddhism in general). In this regard, some of the material discussed in this book provides several instructive examples. *Sīmā* dating to the 7th to 9th centuries have been re-used and are worshipped as sacred Buddhist objects in their own right at a number of sites and locations. Thai men and women often wear small-scale votive tablets as talismans, and Dvāravatī Buddha images can be found in temples and are still revered today.

Figure 1.7: *Sīmā* wrapped in a sacred banner and smothered in gold paint placed behind the *lak muang* (town pillar) of Kalasin town, Kalasin province, Thailand. 8th–9th centuries. Sandstone.

Figure 1.8: *Sīmā* re-used as a town pillar in Wang Sapang, Loei province, Thailand. 8th–9th centuries. Sandstone. Height: 90 cm; width: 66 cm; depth: 23 cm.

1.8

1.7

The re-use of *sīmā* is an intriguing phenomenon, as in some cases it begins to take on other religious functions. When this occurs, they develop "object afterlives". Deborah Cherry (2013: 3), for example, in her discussion of South Asian monuments says that afterlives are made up of a "multiplicity of co-existing versions, representations, imag(in)ings, and interactions taking place in widely distributed circuits of use, replication, and interpretation." Using *sīmā*, sometimes fragmentary ones, to create a new *sīmā* boundary is the most common form of re-use seen across the Khorat Plateau. This is most common when a temple constructs a new *ubosot*. Rather than carving new *sīmā*, they collect old *sīmā* and arrange them around the *ubosot* in groups of eight. As part of modern ceremony, gold leaf, paint, or candles are sometimes applied to these *sīmā*. *Sīmā* retain their original meaning and use in this context, albeit at a new temple. A *sīmā* may be carved with a modern inscription as part of this process, sometimes recording the year and month the new *sīmā* was created. Some inscriptions are older and contain astrological horoscopes or apotropaic spells. In these cases, the stone's age is likely to add to its sacredness. The meaning of *sīmā* begins to shift in these situations.

Sīmā are also commonly re-used in *vihāra* alongside Buddha images or in shrines of their own, where they are worshipped as sacred objects. The stone may be covered in gold leaf or candles may be placed on top of it as an offering. In front of the stone, there is usually an incense stand and a mat on which devotees can kneel and pray. The meaning of *sīmā* has shifted from an object used to define ritual space to one of religious devotion in this context. As a result, it has found a new afterlife.

Sīmā have at times been erected as the town pillar (*lak muang*/หลักเมือง) or in conjunction with it (Figs. 1.7 and 1.8). Every city or town in Thailand has a town pillar that marks the settlement's centre, and these shrines are revered as sacred places that house the local tutelary spirits. A *sīmā* has been used as a town pillar in Wang Sapung in Loei province, and in another example, a *sīmā* has been placed directly behind the town pillar in Kalasin town. The scene on the Kalasin *sīmā* (Fig. 1.7) appears to depict Sotthiya offering *kusa* grass to the Buddha. It is very similar in composition to another *sīmā* (Fig. 2.12) from Muang Fa Daed showing the same episode. It is highly likely that this *sīmā* originated at Muang Fa Daed which is only about 12 kilometres south of Kalasin town.

Two further *sīmā* have been placed at the city pillar shrine in Khon Kaen – one as the actual pillar and the other to be venerated from the outside.[11] The fact that *sīmā* were chosen in this way demonstrates their long-lasting sacred resonance and the fluidity of meaning they can have. This usage and emplacement reflects a similar principle to that of the *khandasīmā* and a certain overlapping between the political and religious spheres.

One final example is worth mentioning. A *sīmā* is used to mark the village boundary in Ban Bua Semama, Khon Kaen province, and is placed directly beneath a modern road sign (Fig. 1.9). This example demonstrates the variety of re-uses for *sīmā* in modern-day Thailand, as well as the ingenuity of the local villagers, who in a sense used the *sīmā* to demarcate the village's boundary.

The re-use of 7th- to 11th-century *sīmā*, Buddha images, and votive tablets demonstrates the latent sacred power that these objects still possess

Figure 1.9: *Sīmā* placed under a signpost for the village of Ban Bua Simama, Khon Kaen province, Thailand. 8th–9th centuries. Sandstone. Height: 147 cm; 74 cm; width: 20 cm.

1.9

---

11   My thanks to Hunter Watson for bringing the Khon Kaen example to my attention.

today. It reminds us that Buddhism is a living tradition in Thailand and Laos, and that the meanings of religious objects are not fixed but can shift to meet specific religious needs. It demonstrates that while textual and canonical definitions of *sīmā* limit them to demarcating ritual space, in actual religious practice they can assume much more varied purposes.

Chapter 2

THE CHI RIVER SYSTEM: THE MUANG FA DAED MANDALA

The distribution of sites along the Chi River system spans the entire length of its course from Chaiyaphum in the west to its confluence with the Mun River in Ubon Ratchathani province in the east. The largest concentration of sites is in the modern-day province of Yasothon. However, Kalasin, Khon Kaen, and Chaiyaphum provinces also have a significant number of sites (Maps 2, 5; Table 1). Evidence for Buddhist art

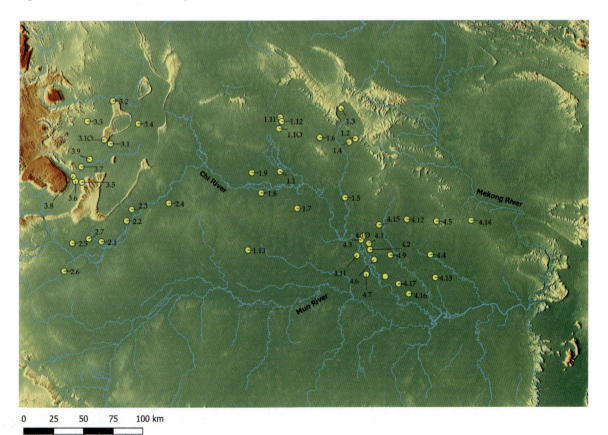

Map 5   Sites in the Chi River system. See Table 1 (pp. 221–222) for the corresponding site names.

and archaeology is extensive in this river system with *sīmā* alone found at 48 out of the 49 sites recorded. Distribution analysis indicates that the sites can be divided into four clusters. It appears that these clusters by and large form actual cultural and, in some instances, political units. Methodologically, this chapter moves from the spatial scale of the river system overall to that of Cluster 1 and its respective sites. Clusters 2, 3, and 4 are the subject of Chapter 3.

In this regard, this chapter pays particular attention to the site of Muang Fa Daed. Mapping and distribution analysis undertaken in this study illustrates it was strategically placed in the central section of this river system. It is located at the centre of a cluster of settlements and sites. Moving to the level of object analysis, this methodological step reveals that it has the most substantial evidence for Buddhist art and architecture anywhere on the Khorat Plateau. This comes primarily in the form of *sīmā* and brick monuments. The chapter thus first looks at the site, its characteristics and its wider context, including the possibility that it was the centre of a mandala, perhaps even the elusive Wendan mentioned in Chinese texts. It then carries out a fine-grain visual analysis of the art on the *sīmā* to tease out stylistic and iconographic aspects with the aim of gaining a better understanding of the Buddhist art being produced at the time. The chapter then moves on to examine the other sites within the cluster, their characteristics and relationship with Muang Fa Daed. Overall, the chapter provides a comprehensive and in-depth discussion of the Buddhist art and architecture of this cluster of sites within the Chi River system.

CLUSTER 1: THE MUANG FA DAED MANDALA

This cluster has the most extensive artistic and archaeological remains for Buddhism in the Chi River system (Map 6; Table 4). There are 13 sites in total located in and around the area of the modern-day provinces of Kalasin, Roi Et, and Maha Sarakham. The sites are situated in the vicinity of the Chi River and three of its tributaries – the Huai Kaeng River, the Lam Phan River, and the Lang Nam Yang River. The cluster includes sites such as Muang Fa Daed and Ban Nong Hang. *Sīmā* from both sites have a high number of narrative scenes.

Most of the land in the vicinity of the Chi River is flat and today covered in rice fields. The area to the north of Muang Fa Daed becomes hilly and two mountaintop sites – Phu Bor and Phu Kao Putthanimit – are located with this terrain and are discussed below. To the northeast, the cluster is bordered by the Phu Phan Mountain range, which is still relatively densely forested today (Kermel-Torres 2004: 164).

The moated site of Muang Fa Daed is one of the most significant in the Khorat Plateau. The settlement has been occupied from late prehistory up

The Chi River System: The Muang Fa Daed Mandala

until the present day. During the 7th to 9th centuries, it appears to have been the most powerful site within the Chi River system. As will be shown below, its reach and control most likely spread to the sites located in its hinterlands and somewhat further afield. Considering this, it seems plausible to speak of a Muang Fa Daed mandala. Several factors will be considered to explore this further. They include site size, agricultural yields, levels of urbanisation, and levels of symbolic entrainment. Urbanisation in this context is understood following the definition provided by archaeologist Michael Smith (2007: 4–5), who states that "…urban settlements are centers whose activities and institutions— whether economic, administrative, or religious—affect a larger hinterland… This functional definition allows the classification of a wider range of non-western settlements as urban than does the more common

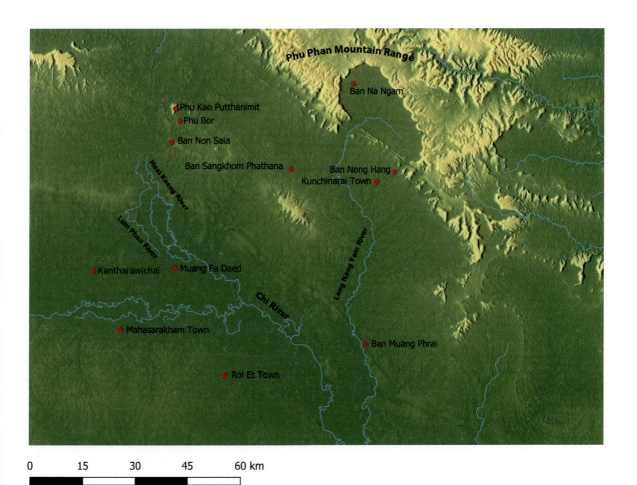

Map 6 Cluster 1.

demographic definition of urban settlements as large, dense, socially heterogeneous settlements."

Of the 13 sites in Cluster 1 considered as part of the Muang Fa Daed mandala (Map 6), 4 are moated sites, 2 are mountaintop sites, and 7 are sites identifiable by the presence of *sīmā*. The sites are on average 20 to 40 kilometres apart and the entire mandala has a diameter of approximately 100 kilometres. This in turn covers a total area of 10,000 square kilometres.

There is a proliferation of *sīmā* within the Muang Fa Daed mandala. They are notable for both the uniformity of their style and iconography and for the high quality of the artwork depicted on them. There are also more *sīmā* within this area than any other part of the Khorat Plateau. These factors can be explained by symbolic entrainment – the process by which symbolic systems become adopted by groups or cultures that have less-developed systems (Renfrew 1986: 8). It is argued that this process is taking place within this mandala and can help to explain the spread and profusion of both Buddhism and its art at this time.

Linguist Tatsuo Hoshino (2002: 25–72) has put forward the hypothesis that Muang Fa Daed may have been the outer capital of a polity known in Chinese records as Wendan (Map 15). He proposes that the inner capital corresponds to the modern-day site of Kantharawichai. He also notes that it had two vassals, Dao Ming and Can Ban (2002: 40). We will return to these later in the book when we discuss Cluster 6. Wendan is known to have sent tribute to China on four separate occasions: 717 CE, 753 CE (lead by a Wendan prince), 771 CE (including 11 trained elephants), and 798 CE, which represented the final known mission (Pelliot 1904: 211–5). These dates, spanning the 8th century, fall within the chronological period when Muang Fa Daed was at its height.

There is general agreement that Wendan was located somewhere on the Khorat Plateau, with Wat Phu being the preferred candidate as its capital (Jacques and Lafond 2007, 70–80; Woodward 2005: 98–9). Hiram Woodward (2010: 87–90), in discussing Hoshino's work, is in favour of locating Wendan in Northeast Thailand. He argues that Wendan is the "land Zhenla" mentioned in Chinese sources (2010: 87). These sources – more specifically the *New Tang Annals* (*Xin Tang Shu*) – divide the kingdom into a "Water Zhenla", which extended west as far as Dvāravatī, south to the Gulf of Thailand, and north as far as "Land Zhenla" (Wade 2014: 26–7). This description matches the general location of modern-day Cambodia (Map 15). Land Zhenla, which was said to be in a mountainous region, should therefore be located on the Khorat Plateau. Woodward, however, does not consider Muang Fa Dead as the possible capital of Wendan, as he follows the 10th-century dating of the site proposed by Krairiksh (2012: 345–8). However, as will be discussed in detail in this chapter, the artistic, historical, archaeological, and epigraphic evidence indicate that the *sīmā* tradition flourished at this site in the 8th and 9th centuries. It thus falls within the chronological span of Wendan.[12]

Furthermore, as archaeologist Phasook Indrawooth (2001) has shown, Muang Fa Daed has been continuously occupied since c. 300 BCE. It should also be noted that the absence of evidence for tribute missions to China from Wendan in the 9th century does not mean that it ceased to exist as Woodward presumes. It may instead mean that there are no surviving records of these missions, or that Wendan for some reason was either unwilling or unable to send further missions to China. Chronologically, Muang Fa Daed was at its height around the same time that Wendan was sending tribute to China.

I thus propose that Muang Fa Daed was the inner capital of Wendan. This is further supported by the fact that it is the largest site in Cluster 1 and occupies a central position. Its reach, as will be shown below, appears to have spread throughout the entire Chi River system. It may have subsequently extracted tribute from some of the other major moated sites in the region, as has also been highlighted by Hoshino (2002: 40–1). However, I argue that Kantharawichai was under Muang Fa Daed's control and not the other way around.

However, it should be noted that no inscriptions from Muang Fa Daed or the surrounding areas have ever been discovered that mention a polity called "Wendan" or anything even vaguely similar to this name. In fact, we have no inscriptional evidence to indicate what the site of Muang Fa Daed – or Kantharawichai for that matter – would have been called in antiquity. Until such time as evidence for this comes to light, the Wendan hypothesis will have to remain just that.

The Site of Muang Fa Daed

Muang Fa Daed is one of the largest moated sites in the Khorat Plateau. It is approximately 1,800 metres in length and 1,000 metres in width, with an area of around 171 hectares in total. It is situated on the Pao River, a tributary of the Chi. This location provides it with a reliable water supply and an advantageous position in terms of trade and transportation – it facilitated access to the Sakhon Nakhon basin to the north and the Chi River system to the south (Map 6).

The site became known to scholarship in the 1950s with the discovery of finely carved *sīmā* depicting *jātaka* and Life of the Buddha scenes

---

12   Woodward, in an earlier publication, notes that the *sīmā* tradition in general spans the 8th to 11th centuries and that those at Muang Fa Daed were from the 9th century (2005: 99, 101). It is not clear as to why he later favours the 10th-century date proposed by Krairiksh.

Figure 2.1: The Prataduyaku Stūpa with *sīmā* placed around it at Muang Fa Daed, Kalasin province, Thailand.

(Seidenfaden 1954: 643–7; Diskul: 1956: 362). I have documented over 170 *sīmā* at this site (Murphy 2010: 159), some of which are still located near their original findspots or in the village temple of Wat Pho Chai Semaram. The majority of the rest have been removed to Khon Kaen National Museum where they are on display. In recent years 70 more *sīmā* have been discovered during dredging of a pond at one of the local temples.

The first archaeological excavations were carried out in 1968 by the Thai Fine Arts Department. These uncovered 14 monuments, including foundations of a possible ordination hall with a number of in situ *sīmā* placed around it (Fig. 2.1). Excavations at the Prataduyaku Stūpa near the centre of the site revealed foundations dating to the 7th to 9th centuries and three in situ *sīmā* (FAD 1969–71). These *sīmā* were placed on three separate sides of the *stūpa*. This would suggest that they were used as boundary markers around *stūpa* as well as around ordination halls during this period.

In 1991 further excavations were undertaken by Phasook Indrawooth of Silpakorn University and the Fine Arts Department (Indrawooth et al. 1991; Indrawooth 2001). This excavation consisted of five test pits – three within the main enclosure, one outside the moat, and one near the rampart. It succeeded in establishing a clearer overall chronology for the site and divided the cultural sequence into five phases (Indrawooth 2001: 74–6). Occupation began in the late prehistoric period (phase 1) and stretched from around 300 BCE to 200 CE. The proto-historic phase begins around 200 CE and continues until the 7th century. Phase three (7th to 11th centuries) sees the appearance and growth of Buddhism, as reflected in the presence of *sīmā*, votive tablets, inscriptions, and religious architecture.

Phase four (12th to 13th centuries) shows clear evidence for Khmer cultural traits, particularly in the form of greenish-brown glazed Angkor-period stoneware (Indrawooth 2001: 76). Research has also pointed out similarities in the burial traditions between this site and that of Dong Mae Nang Muang, Nakhon Sawan province, located in the upper Chao Phraya basin. At both sites cremated human remains were placed in green-glazed Angkor-period stoneware (Pongkasetkan and Murphy 2012).

With the establishment of Buddhism at the site from around the 7th century onwards, changes took place in the urban planning and layout of the settlement. Seven of the monuments discovered during the 1968 excavations are *stūpa* located outside the moat, ringing the site (Indrawooth 2001: 104, Map 3) in a similar fashion to those at Muang Sema. It appears that this became an important practice during the Dvāravatī period and may have functioned to physically demarcate the boundary of the settlement.

This is an important cognitive shift in the way landscape was constructed and viewed. Prior to the arrival of Buddhism, there seems to

2.1

have been a clear separation between inside and outside the moat. However, with the flourishing of this religion, the divide was altered somewhat. Religious structures began to be also placed outside the moat. This calls into question the idea that the moats were primarily defensive, as it appears that from the 7th century onwards settlements could expand beyond these watercourses. However, it is still possible that the moats could have provided protection for the inhabitants, as those located outside of them could take refuge within if external threats arose.

Of the religious structures in the interior of Muang Fa Daed, two are possibly ordination or assembly halls. This would indicate that there were probably two monasteries within the settlement. One appears to be located near its centre and is aligned along an axis with the Prataduyaku Stūpa and three smaller *stūpa*. Today only the base of the Prataduyaku Stūpa dates to the Dvāravatī period – the superstructure is a later addition from the Ayutthaya period.

Evidence of what the vernacular architecture may have looked like can be gleaned from images on *sīmā*, as a number of examples depict wooden structures. They are simple buildings with gable roofs which sometimes terminate in upturned eaves. On one *sīmā* (Fig. 2.13) there is also a depiction of walls and gates indicating what they may have looked like at Muang Fa Daed. The gate is surmounted by a two-tiered tower, with guards flanking it on either side. However, apart from these glimpses on *sīmā*, there is no other evidence to substantiate what the wooden vernacular architecture may have looked like.

Figure 2.2: The *Temiya-jātaka* on a *sīmā* from Muang Fa Daed. Today kept at Wat Pho Chai Semaram Temple, Ban Sema, Kalasin province, Thailand. 8th–9th centuries. Sandstone. Height: 156 cm; width: 76 cm; depth: 26 cm.

Population estimates for the site suggest that it could potentially support up to 8,500 people (Murphy 2015: 94–5). This would be enough to support a sizeable monastic community. This figure could be as high as 1 per cent of the entire population, which would mean there could be about 85 monks based at this site at any given time (Murphy 2015:

94–5).[13] This figure seems entirely plausible, given the extent of the Buddhist remains at Muang Fa Daed. Buddhism had thus firmly established itself within this settlement. This is further evidenced by the high-quality artwork found throughout the site and best exemplified by *sīmā*. It points to the fact that Buddhism was receiving large-scale patronage from the settlement's inhabitants, whether that be from the elite ruling classes or the average lay worshipper.

The *Sīmā* Tradition at Muang Fa Daed

Having discussed Muang Fa Daed and its wider context, we now move to a fine-grain visual analysis of the *sīmā*. This allows for a closer interrogation of the Buddhist art from which a number of observations can be drawn. The *sīmā* tradition at Muang Fa Daed peaked in the 8th to 9th centuries and continues to a lesser extent in the 10th and 11th centuries (Murphy 2010: 339–42). The art mainly consists of *jātaka* tales, episodes from the Life of the Buddha, Buddha and bodhisattva scenes, and Buddhist motifs in general. Nine different *jātaka* have been identified on *sīmā*, all of which are slab type in form. Seven scenes from the Life of the Buddha have been identified and are discussed below.[14] They form the largest surviving corpus of evidence for Buddhist art on the Khorat Plateau and provide invaluable insights into the nature of the religion at this time. What follows is an art historical analysis – both stylistic and iconographic – on a selection of *sīmā*.[15]

The Temiya-jātaka

> "Our king has found his only son crippled and dumb, -an idiot quite; And I am sent to dig this hole and bury him far out of sight" (Cowell 1978: Vol. VI, 9).

The *Temiya-jātaka* is depicted on two *sīmā* from Muang Fa Daed, both of which show the same scene in almost identical compositions (Fig. 2.2; Murphy 2010: Fig. 5.10) (Kingmanee 1998a). This suggests that the stones were carved either by the same artist, produced by the same workshop, or at the very least, using the same template. In Figure 2.2,

---

13 These estimates are based on ethnographic and archaeological approaches using evidence from a range of sources such as population surveys of rural Thailand at the turn of the 20th century, archaeological excavations in the region, and calculations based on living space per person. Based on this, scholars have come up with a "ballpark" figure of 50 people per hectare. However, it must be stressed that these figures are only approximations (see Murphy 2015: 88–95).

14 The other two are the tale of the two merchants Tapussa and Bhallika and the First Sermon, see Murphy (2010: 277–8).

15 For a complete overview of all narrative art identified on *sīmā* from Muang Fa Daed, see Murphy (2010: 210–81).

2.3

The Chi River System: The Muang Fa Daed Mandala

Figure 2.3: The *Kulāvaka-jātaka* on a fragmentary *sīmā* from Muang Fa Daed. 8th–9th centuries. Sandstone. Height: 84 cm; width: 90 cm; depth: 23 cm. National Museum Khon Kaen, Thailand. Inventory number K.K. 445/53. Courtesy of Thierry Ollivier.

Figure 2.4: The *Sarabhaṅga-jātaka* on a *sīmā* from Muang Fa Daed. 8th–9th centuries. Sandstone. Height: 164 cm; width: 89 cm; depth: 14 cm. Today kept at Wat Pho Chai Semaram Temple, Ban Sema, Kalasin province, Thailand.

Temiya, identifiable by his hairstyle and nimbus, is standing to the right. The charioteer is kneeling to the left with the shovel clearly visible in his right hand. There is no sign of the chariot, however.

This *jātaka* extolls the act of renunciation, one of the 10 virtues attained by the Buddha that will lead to Buddhahood. The Buddha-to-be has been reborn as Prince Temiya. Wishing to avoid taking up his father's throne, he pretends to be dumb and crippled. However, he finally reveals that not only can he speak, but he also has full use of his body (Cowell 1978: Vol. VI, 1–18). This abrupt change of heart is brought about by the rather worrying fact that the king's charioteer is digging a grave to bury him in. Temiya lifts the chariot above his head and announces to the charioteer that he intends to spend the rest of his days as an ascetic.

The Kulāvaka-jātaka

The finely carved scene on this *sīmā* fragment (Fig. 2.3) has been identified as the *Kulāvaka-jātaka* (Phiromanukun 2009: 105). In it, the bodhisattva has four women in his household named Goodness, Thoughtful, Joy, and Highborn (Cowell 1978: Vol. VI, 76–83). The first three all performed acts of merit and as a result were reborn as the handmaidens of Indra. Highborn, however, carried out no such acts and was instead reborn as a lowly crane in a forest. The scene on the *sīmā* illustrates the results of this merit-making. Indra, seated in *lalitāsana* ("royal ease posture" whereby one leg is folded in half-lotus and the other leg hangs free, common in depictions of bodhisattvas) and holding his *vajra* (thunderbolt – the attribute of Indra) in his right hand, is located at the centre of the composition, most likely seated on Airavata, who may be indicated by the elephant to the left. However, the lower half of the *sīmā* is missing so we cannot be entirely certain. The three handmaidens are depicted to the right. We can presume that the bird in the palm of the foremost handmaiden represents Highborn reborn as a crane.

The Sarabhaṅga-jātaka

This *sīmā* (Fig. 2.4), today located at Wat Pho Chai Semaram, is one of the finest examples of Buddhist narrative carved in stone surviving from the Khorat Plateau. It is unusual in the fact that it appears to represent both a *jātaka* tale and a scene from the Life of the Buddha.

The Buddha is depicted in *vitarkamudrā* at the centre of the composition, legs crossed in *vīrāsana* (cross-legged posture – ankles are crossed, and the soles of the feet point downwards) on what appears to be a rectangular mat. He is flanked on either side by royal fans and flags. Behind him is a tree, perhaps the Bodhi. Below the Buddha, there are four seated figures surrounded by cloud motifs. Due to his headdress, the figure at the centre right appears to be a king. The figure to the centre left appears to be female and is perhaps a queen or princess. The figures to the far right and left appear to be attendants. Were the composition to stop at this point, a number of possible interpretations could be proposed. It could be the Buddha preaching to King Bimbisara or to his father King Suddhōdana, as is the case with another *sīmā* from Muang Fa Daed (Fig. 2.10, see below). However, below these four figures are three other carved figures, one of whom is nearly completely covered by a modern stepped altar platform. Two of the figures are armed with bows and arrows, while the figure in the centre is leaping upwards with what seems to be a weapon of some kind in his upraised right hand. This part of the *sīmā* has been

Figure 2.5: The *Bhūridatta-jātaka* on a *sīmā* (possibly in situ) from Muang Fa Daed, Kalasin province, Thailand. 10th–11th centuries. Sandstone. Height: 130 cm; width: 83 cm; depth: 15 cm.

identified by Phonpha and Suthilak (1974: 383) as a scene from the *Sarabhaṅga-jātaka*. In this *jātaka*, it is prophesied that the Buddha will be reborn as the best archer in the land. In order to prove this, the king arranges a contest whereby four renowned archers compete against the Buddha. The scene on the *sīmā* depicts this episode whereby the Buddha defends himself against the four archers by blocking their arrows with his own iron arrow (Cowell 1978: Vol. VI, 68).

On the lower section of this *sīmā*, the arrow in question appears to be depicted in the left hand of the central figure, while two of the archers are shown on either side. Stylistically, the lower section appears to be of the same handiwork as the rest of the composition and so does not represent a later addition. If the identification of the *Sarabhaṅga-jātaka* is correct, then it is unique in the *sīmā* tradition of the Khorat Plateau in that it shows both a Life of the Buddha scene and a *jātaka* in one composition. Perhaps the presence of the Buddha is meant to represent him telling the tale of this *jātaka* to those listening below?

The Bhūridatta-jātaka

This *jātaka* has been identified on a *sīmā* (Fig. 2.5) at the Prataduyaku Stūpa (Kingmanee 1997a: 104–9). In this incarnation the Buddha has been reborn as a *nāga*. It shows the episode quoted below where the brahmin Ālambāyana seizes him while he is meditating on an anthill.

> ... Ālambāyana, having first anointed his body with divine drugs ... uttered the divine spell, and going up to the Bodhisatta, seized him by the tail ... he stretched him out full length on the ground ... and then seizing his tail, pounded him as if he were beating cloth (Cowell 1978: Vol. VI, 97).

The brahmin wrestles the bodhisattva from his perch and into a basket. After that he brings him to a village and uses him to make money as a snake charmer. The artist has imparted a certain amount of dynamism and movement into his portrayal of this narrative. Ālambāyana is shown attempting to pull the *nāga* free from the anthill, the latter's tail is wrapped around the brahmin's neck and shoulders. Ālambāyana is leaning away to his right as he attempts to use gravity to aid in his struggle. The top half of the composition is flanked by two trees which enclose a stylised structure and/or cloud motif.

Based on the Khmer-style lower garment worn by Ālambāyana, this *sīmā* has been dated on stylistic grounds to the 10th to 11th centuries (Kingmanee 1997a: 104–9).

The Mahānāradakassapa-jātaka

This *jātaka* is present on two *sīmā* from Muang Fa Daed. In this tale the Buddha has been reincarnated in heaven. Meanwhile, King Aṅgati of the kingdom of Videha had heeded the advice of a Brahmin ascetic who convinced him that there were no karmic consequences to good or bad actions. The king thus stopped supporting good deeds or ruling justly. However, the king's daughter, Rujā, prays for assistance, and the Buddha, who has been reincarnated as Nārada Mahābrahmā, residing in heaven, hears her prayers. He descends to earth to convert the king from his heretical beliefs.

Figure 2.6: The *Mahānāradakassapa-jātaka* on a fragmentary *sīmā* from Muang Fa Daed. 8th–9th centuries. Sandstone. Height: 120 cm; width: 60 cm; depth: 21 cm. National Museum Khon Kaen, Thailand. Inventory number 17/242/2520.

Both *sīmā* depict this same scene in a very similar fashion (Fig. 2.6; Murphy 2010: Fig. 5.26). Figure 2.6 has been identified by the Khon Kaen National Museum, while the other has been identified by Paknam (1981: 114). As described in the quote below, the bodhisattva dresses himself in the guise of an ascetic and bears a yoke across his shoulder from which is suspended a begging bowl and a water pot.

> ... and having taken a golden begging bowl hung with a string of pearls, and having laid on his shoulders a golden carrying pole curved in three places, and taken up a coral water-pot by a string of pearls, he went with this garb through the heavens shining like the moon ... (Cowell 1978: Vol. VI, 122).

Both *sīmā* depict the yoke, bowl, and pot clearly and the bodhisattva is in *vitarkamudrā*, indicating he is teaching, which is consistent with the episode in question. The hair of the bodhisattva in Figure 2.6 is arranged in thick matted loops hanging from his *uṣṇīṣa* (cranial protuberance) while the earlobes are elongated in royal fashion. The other *sīmā* (Murphy 2010: Fig. 5.26) is executed in low relief with two figures kneeling on either side of him, most likely King Aṅgati on the left and his daughter, Rujā on the right, listening to the discourse of the bodhisattva. The classic Dvāravatī facial features of the bodhisattva in Figure 2.6, in particular, indicates that it dates to the 8th to 9th centuries. Furthermore, the matted hair of the chignon is extremely similar to that found on a number of bronze bodhisattva images from Prakhon Chai/Plai Bat II (see Fig. 4.16).

The *Mahānāradakassapa-jātaka* explains the causes and results of good and evil deeds and how there is a sensitive balance at play in the karma accumulated by individuals over their many successive rebirths. The depiction of the yoke balancing on the bodhisattva's shoulders is presumably meant to symbolise this.

The Vidhurapaṇḍita-jātaka

In this *jātaka* the bodhisattva was reborn as Vidhura, an advisor to King Dhanañjaya. One day the king was in discussion with three other kings – Indra, king of the gods; a *nāga* king; and a *garuda* king (a giant eagle-like bird usually depicted as part bird, part human) – about what were the greatest virtues. Unable to reach agreement between themselves, they asked Vidhura, who satisfied them all by telling them that each was equal, just like the four spokes of a wheel. They were all greatly impressed with his answer. Upon returning to the *nāga* realm, the *nāga* king informed his queen of what had occurred. She greatly desired to meet Vidhura and persuaded her husband to bring her Vidhura's heart. Unable to do this himself, he sought someone else to do it. Meanwhile, the *yakkha* (nature

The Chi River System: The Muang Fa Daed Mandala

Figure 2.7: The *Vidhurapaṇḍita-jātaka* on a fragmentary *sīmā* from Muang Fa Daed. 8th–9th centuries. Sandstone. Height: 176 cm; width: 76 cm; depth: 25 cm. National Museum Khon Kaen, Thailand.

2.8

spirit) general, Puṇṇaka had fallen in love with the king's daughter, Irandatī. Therefore, the king stipulated that if Puṇṇaka could achieve this, he would give his daughter's hand to him.

Two separate scenes of this *jātaka* are depicted on *sīmā* from Muang Fa Daed. Figure 2.7 shows the episode of the expounding of the law by the bodhisattva Vidhura to Puṇṇaka (Cowell 1978: Vol. VI, 149). In this episode, Vidhura dissuades Puṇṇaka from killing him by teaching him the dharma. Piriya Krairiksh (1974a: 53–5) has identified Vidhura located at the top left of the composition seated cross-legged in what appears to be *vīrāsana*, with his right hand in *vitarkamudrā*. Puṇṇaka, seated below him, is identifiable by his long, matted hair and horse, which is placed directly under him. Stylised cloud motifs above and below the protagonists indicates that this scene is taking place on a mountaintop.

The other *sīmā* (Murphy 2010: Fig. 5.33) may depict the moment when Puṇṇaka hears the song of the *nāga* princess while riding on horseback (Cowell 1978: Vol. VI, 131). It is badly eroded, but it appears that Puṇṇaka is shown on his horse at the bottom right of the composition, turning around with his right arm raised over his head. Placed above, directly in line with his gaze, is a female figure, possibly identifiable as the *nāga* princess Irandatī. However, the top of this *sīmā* is missing, so the princess's head and upper body are no longer visible.

The Mahāummagga-jātaka

In this *jātaka* the bodhisattva is reborn as a wise sage known as Mahosadha. King Vedeha had been foretold of his coming in a dream and asked his chief advisor Senaka whether he should summon him to his court. Senaka, fearful of losing his position of influence, suggests they observe him further to determine whether he is the one prophesised.

This *jātaka* appears on five *sīmā* at Muang Fa Daed. Two examples are discussed herein (Fig. 2.8).[16] The *sīmā* depicted in Figure 2.8 is unique in that it bears two scenes from the same *jātaka*, one on each side. Both scenes have been identified by Krairiksh (1974a: 48–50). The scene shown in Fig. 2.8 is described in the quote below, whereby Mahosadha forces the brahmin Kevaṭṭa into obeisance.

> "... today I have found this gem. Pray take it." The other [Kevaṭṭa] seeing the gem ablaze in his [Mahosadha's] hand, thought that he must be desiring to offer it and said "Give it me then," holding out his hand ... but the brahmin [Kevaṭṭa] could not support the weight of the gem in his fingers, and it slipt [sic] down and rolled to the Bodhisat's

Figure 2.8: The *Mahāummagga-jātaka* on a *sīmā* from Muang Fa Daed. 8th–9th centuries. Sandstone. Height: 170 cm; width: 84 cm; depth: 24 cm. National Museum Khon Kaen, Thailand. Inventory number 17/19/2517.

---

16 For the other three *sīmā*, see Murphy (2010: 244–9).

Figure 2.9: The *Vessantara-jātaka* on a *sīmā* from Muang Fa Daed. 8th–9th centuries. Sandstone. Height: 144 cm. Today kept at Wat Sribunruang Temple, Kalasin town, Kalasin province. Thailand. Courtesy of River Books Bangkok.

[sic] feet; the brahmin in his greed to get it, stooped down to the other's feet. Then the Great Being would not let him rise, but with one hand held his shoulder blades and with the other his loins... (Cowell 1978: Vol VI, 207).

The composition is framed by a stylised architectural feature, under which sit four figures, three of whom are attendants. Mahosadha is located on the far left of this group, identifiable by the parasol above his head. He is pushing down another figure with his hand and foot. This is the brahmin Kevaṭṭa whose forced obeisance is clearly depicted by the position of his

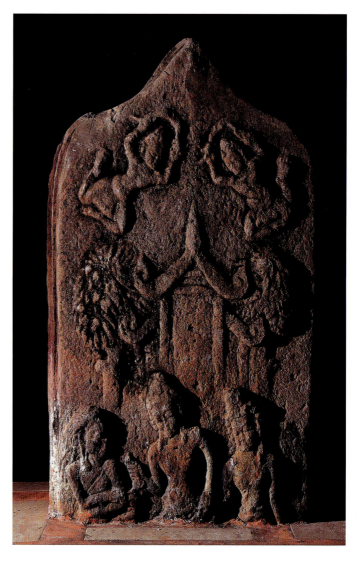

head and his hands, which are joined together in the traditional gesture of respect or worship.

The other side of this *sīmā* depicts the episode of the stolen child. The scene is too eroded today to photograph effectively. A photo reproduced in Krairiksh (1974a: Fig. 9) therefore provides the basis for the description and analysis given below.

In the episode of the stolen child (Cowell 1978: Vol. VI, 184–7) (Murphy 2010: Fig. 5.38), Mahosadha is seated at the centre of the composition gazing downwards at the two women to be judged, who kneel prostrate at his feet. In the background is an architectural detail of

Figure 2.10: The Buddha Preaching to King Bimbisara or his Father on a *sīmā* from Muang Fa Daed. 8th–9th centuries. Height: 156 cm; width: 74 cm; depth: 21 cm. National Museum Khon Kaen, Thailand. Inventory number 17/57/2522.

Figure 2.11: Indra offers fruit to the Buddha on a fragmentary *sīmā* from Muang Fa Daed. 8th–9th centuries Sandstone. Height: 100 cm; width: 75 cm; depth: 23 cm. National Museum Khon Kaen, Thailand. Inventory number 17/58/2522.

some kind, similar to that shown in Figure 2.8, perhaps meant to represent the roof of the palace. The woman to Mahosadha's right, holding the child, is a female goblin in disguise, while the figure to the left is the infant's true mother. The identity of the child's mother is proven by her reluctance to hurt the child in the ensuing tug-of-war.

Along with the *sīmā* from Ban Nong Hang (Figs. 2.19–2.22) discussed below, this represents the only other known example of the use of sequential, as opposed to mono-episodic, narrative on *sīmā*. The placement of these two scenes on either side of the same *sīmā* has precedent elsewhere. As Krairiksh (1974a: 49–50) has pointed out, they also appear side by side on terracotta plaques at the 11th-century Thagya Paya Stūpa at Thaton in Lower Myanmar. It is worth noting that while

2.11

Figure 2.12: Sotthiya offers *kusa* grass to the Buddha on a *sīmā* from Muang Fa Daed. 8th–9th centuries. Sandstone. Height: 167 cm; width: 83 cm; depth: 27 cm. National Museum Khon Kaen, Thailand. Inventory number K.K. 455/53. Courtesy of Thierry Ollivier.

the *sīmā* from Muang Fa Daed and the plaques from Thaton are stylistically rather different, in terms of content, they are identical. This most likely indicates that both areas were drawing on the same textual or oral sources and traditions, as opposed to any direct political or ethnic (Mon) connection between them (Murphy 2014).

Another *sīmā* (Murphy 2010: Fig. 5.42) shows the scene of the Courting of Amarā (Cowell 1978: Vol. VI, 184–7) and has been identified by Krairiksh (1974a: Fig. 15). Mahosadha is shown to the left while Amarā, one hand placed on her head to support the wood and the other at her hip, is located on the right. Mahosadha is depicted wearing a *drapé-en-poche* which flares out to the left in triangular fashion, a characteristic of the Khorat Plateau aesthetic. Stylistically this *sīmā* dates to the 8th to 9th centuries.

The Vessantara-jātaka

This *jātaka* is the penultimate rebirth, and in this life the bodhisattva perfects the virtue of generosity. He does this by gradually renouncing everything he owns. Born as Prince Vessantara, he first gives away the royal white elephant. This infuriates his father, the king, who banishes him and his family. In their exile Vessantara gives away their worldly goods and then his children to a wicked brahmin. Finally, Vessantara gives away his wife to Indra, disguised as a brahmin. The god did this to test Vessantara.

This *jātaka* is depicted on two *sīmā* from Muang Fa Daed. One (Murphy 2010: Fig. 5.46) depicts a scene preceding Vessantara's banishment from the palace (Krairiksh 1974a: 56). In this composition, Vessantara is seated on a throne in *lalitāsana* below a parasol, while his wife sits to his right, slightly below him in front of an architectural motif most likely meant to represent the palace. Vessantara's children are shown at the bottom of the scene, sleeping together on a mat. The throne and stylised architectural feature confirm that they are still within the palace.

The other *sīmā*, (Fig. 2.9) now kept at Wat Sribunruang Temple but originally from Muang Fa Daed, has been identified by Krairiksh (1974a: 57) as depicting the episode in which Vessantara gives away his wife Maddī to Indra, disguised as a brahmin (Cowell 1978: Vol. VI, 293). Vessantara is shown in the centre of the scene with Indra to his left and Maddī to his right. The donation of Maddī is symbolically depicted by the pouring of water onto the right hand of the recipient, who in this case is Indra. As is common on *sīmā* from Muang Fa Daed, the composition is framed by a stylised architectural motif – in this case, a pavilion with a two-tiered roof.

The Khaṇḍahāla-jātaka

In this *jātaka*, the bodhisattva is reborn as Prince Candakumara. The king has come under the sway of Khandahalā, a corrupt court brahmin. Khandahalā convinces the king that if he wishes to reach heaven, he must surrender all he holds dear, from his possessions to his queen and his sons. The king thus prepared for the ritual sacrifice outside the city. Prince Candakumara was brought to the sacrificial pit. However, at that moment, the queen prayed to Indra, who struck down the royal parasols with his lightning bolt, and the ritual was averted. The crowd rounded on Khandahalā and killed him. The king was exiled and Candakumara took the throne in his place.

The *Khaṇḍahāla-jātaka*, as depicted on one *sīmā* at Muang Fa Daed (Murphy 2010: Fig. 5.17), represents the climax of the tale where Indra descends from heaven to save the bodhisattva (Cowell 1978: Vol. VI, 68–80). This scene, identified by Krairiksh (1974a: 53), shows Indra clearly visible in the top centre of the composition surrounded by cloud motifs. He holds his *vajra* aloft in his right hand, preparing to strike, and is shown with his characteristic crown. His flowing lower garment, which trails out between his legs, is suggestive of the Khmer art of the 10th to 11th centuries. There seems to be an architectural motif depicted to Indra's right, perhaps a stylised palace of some kind. However, it cannot be clearly made out due to erosion. Unfortunately, the base of this *sīmā* is also badly eroded, making it impossible to establish what was depicted at the bottom section of the scene.

The Buddha Preaching to King Bimbisara or His Father, King Suddhōdana

This scene from the Life of the Buddha, depicted on a *sīmā* today housed at the Khon Kaen Museum, could represent either the Buddha preaching to King Bimbisara or King Suddhōdana (Fig. 2.10). The *sīmā* depicts the Buddha, seated in *vīrāsana* on what appears to be a cushion, which in turn possibly lies on top of a rug. There is an elaborate throne depicted directly behind the Buddha, which terminates in a tree of some kind. If this scene represents the Buddha preaching to King Bimbisara, then the tree might represent the bamboo grove of Veluvana, which the king donated to the Buddha (Jayawickrama 1990: 114; *Mahāvagga* I: xxii 13). The Buddha is depicted in *vitarkamudrā*, symbolising teaching, while his head is surrounded by a flaming nimbus, which also occurs on a number of other *sīmā* from Muang Fa Daed (see Figs. 2.11 and 2.12). Three figures are placed to the left of the Buddha, the largest of whom is in the centre and by virtue of his crown, can be identified as either King Bimbisara or King Suddhōdana. The two flanking figures can be assumed to represent his attendants.

Indra Offers Fruit to the Buddha

This *sīmā* (Fig. 2.11) has been identified by the Khon Kaen Museum as Indra offering the myrobalan fruit to the Buddha. This episode occurred

Figure 2.13: The Buddha's return to Kapilavastu on a *sīmā* from Muang Fa Daed. 8th-9th centuries. Sandstone. Height: 200 cm; width: 80 cm; depth: 22 cm. National Museum Khon Kaen, Thailand. Inventory number 17/225/2516.

seven weeks after the Buddha had attained Enlightenment. For that entire time, he had meditated and not eaten. Indra appears to offer him the medicinal myrobalan fruit to fortify him (Jayawickrama 1990: 107).

The Buddha is depicted to the left of the composition, his right hand in *vitarkamudrā* and left hand open, ready to receive the gift. His head is surrounded by a flaming nimbus similar to those found on Figures 2.10 and 2.12. The identification of the figure beside the Buddha is not certain, however. While the figure does hold a piece of fruit in his right hand, he is not depicted with any of Indra's usual attributes, such as a crown or *vajra*. Therefore, though it is a plausible identification, it cannot be said for certain that this scene is in fact Indra offering the myrobalan to the Buddha.

2.13

2.14

Sotthiya Offers Kusa Grass to the Buddha

This *sīmā* (Fig. 2.12) has been identified as the moment before the Buddha sits down under the Bodhi tree to meditate. Upon arriving at Gaya, the Buddha meets the grass cutter Sotthiya and asks him for some grass to sit on as a cushion while he meditates. The grasscutter humbly agrees and hands the Buddha as much grass as he requires (Jayawickrama 1990: 93–4). This is very similar in composition to Figure. 1.7, the *sīmā* today kept at the Kalasin town pillar shrine.

The Buddha is depicted to the right of the composition, his right hand in *vitarkamudrā* and his left hand open, palm downwards, ready to receive the grass from Sotthiya. The depiction and position of the Buddha's hands are almost identical to that of Figure 2.11, as is the flaming nimbus around the Buddha's head. As with the example of Indra offering fruit to the Buddha, the identification of this scene as Sotthiya offering grass to the Buddha hinges on the identification of the figure to the left. It is possible that this figure is Sotthiya, as it appears that he is holding cut grass in his left hand. However, it also looks similar to the fly whisks depicted in certain Dvāravatī scenes (Thamrungrueng 2009: 82). If this identification is correct, however, then the tree depicted in the background may represent the Bodhi tree under which the Buddha attained Enlightenment.

The Buddha's Return to Kapilavastu

This scene has been identified on three *sīmā* from Muang Fa Daed, one of which is discussed below.[17] It relates to the Buddha's return to Kapilavastu, the town of his birth. This is a dramatic event in the Buddha's life story as this is the first time he returns home after having left the palace in pursuit of Enlightenment. He returns to find his family at once proud of his accomplishments and made bereft by his abandonment. After first meeting with his father, the Buddha proceeds to meet with his wife and son. Yaśodharā, the Buddha's estranged wife, has coaxed her son Rāhula into asking his father for his inheritance. However, instead of receiving great material wealth as Yaśodharā had hoped, the Buddha instead bequeathed his son with the Four Truths and the Eight-fold noble path (Jayawickrama 1990: 123; *Lalitavistara* XII).

The art on this *sīmā* is some of the finest ever to be discovered from the Khorat Plateau (Fig. 2.13). It was first identified by Subhadradis Diskul (1956) and illustrates not only the well-structured compositional skills of the artists of Muang Fa Daed, but also their deft ability in depicting the main characters in this scene. Located in the top centre of the arrangement, the Buddha sits in *bhadrāsana* (legs pendant) while his

Figure 2.14: Unidentified Life of the Buddha scene on a fragmentary *sīmā* from Muang Fa Daed. 8th–9th centuries. Sandstone. Height: 110 cm; width: 60 cm. National Museum Bangkok, Thailand. Inventory number 01/435/2565. Courtesy of Nicolas Revire.

---

17   For the other two *sīmā*, see Murphy (2010: 269–73).

Figure 2.15: Buddha Mucalinda on a fragmentary *sīmā* from Muang Fa Daed. 8th–9th centuries. Sandstone. Height: 170 cm; width: 80 cm; depth: 27 cm. National Museum Khon Kaen, Thailand. Inventory number 17/56/2522/2.

wife and son are shown kneeling at his feet. The emotions of the Buddha's estranged wife are masterfully depicted by the sense of movement conveyed by her posture. She is leaning towards the Buddha, who in turn tilts his head to the side in order to address her. The Buddha seems to be almost stepping on her hair while she in turn is almost clasping his feet with her right hand, an arrangement which closely follows the description of this scene given in the *Nidana-katha*. The emotionally charged nature of the scene is further emphasised by the depiction of the Buddha's young son, who stretches out his small arms in an attempt to touch his father. Finally, the whole composition is neatly framed by the depiction of an architectural structure placed above the head of the Buddha. This structure is most likely a wooden pavilion of some kind. The overall sensitivity and balance of the composition illustrates the mastery reached by the artist in conveying Buddhist themes and narratives in this medium.

Unidentified Life of the Buddha Scene

There is one *sīmā* that depicts the Buddha in double *vitarkamudrā*, but the scene itself remains unidentified (Fig. 2.14). His face has the distinctive full lips, oval-shaped eyes, and thick hair curls, and his head is surrounded by a nimbus. The robe has the characteristic u-shape, clinging almost diaphanously to the rather androgynous body. To the left is a smaller figure in *vitarkamudrā*. It appears that this figure is a bodhisattva – both its nimbus and conical headdress point toward a divine nature. Furthermore, *vitarkamudrā* in the Dvāravatī period is primarily reserved for the Buddha or bodhisattvas. Could this scene represent the fully enlightened Buddha to the right and the Buddha in one of his previous reincarnations as a bodhisattva to the left? If so, as with the *Sarabhaṅga-jātaka* above (Fig. 2.4), this would represent the conflation of narratives. The scene is rounded off by the presence of a *deva* (celestial being) type figure flying above, hands pressed together in reverence of the Buddha.

Buddha Mucalinda

There are two examples of the Buddha sheltered under the hood of the *nāga* king Mucalinda (Jayawickrama 1990: 106–7) at Muang Fa Daed, one of which is discussed here (Fig. 2.15).[18] It comes from an earthen mound 3 kilometres away (Kingmanee 2007: 61) and has a superbly executed Buddha Mucalinda image. The Buddha is shown seated in *vīrāsana* on the coils of the five-headed *nāga*, whose hood is placed over the Buddha to protect him from the rainfall. The Bodhi tree appears from behind the five heads. The Buddha is shown in *vitarkamudrā*, which is unusual as Buddha Mucalinda images usually show him in *dhyānamudrā*,

---

18   For the other, see Murphy (2010: 274–5).

Figure 2.16: Tapered pillar type *sīmā* from Muang Fa Daed. 10th–11th centuries. Sandstone. Height: 298 cm; width: 50 cm; depth 50 cm. National Museum Khon Kaen, Thailand.

representing meditation. This *mudrā* may be explained by the presence of two kneeling figures at the bottom of the composition, intently looking up at the Buddha. The figure on the right is depicted with a crown and may represent the *nāga* king once he has reverted to human form. In this episode, after protecting the Buddha from the rain, Mucalinda then changed to human form and sat to hear the teaching of the Buddha. This would explain the *vitarkamudrā* gesture of the Buddha. If this is the case, then the artist has ingeniously conflated the narrative into one scene.

The preceding art historical analysis clearly reveals the popularity of the Life of the Buddha and *jātaka* tales at Muang Fa Daed. They represent one of the high points of artistic expression and carving on *sīmā*. Episodes such as the Buddha's return to Kapilavastu (Fig. 2.13) and the Buddha preaching to King Bimbisara (Fig. 2.10) truly represent masterpieces of the Khorat Plateau aesthetic. The proliferation of Life of the Buddha and *jātaka* tales is strongly suggestive of the presence of texts or oral traditions circulating at the site, which the *saṅgha* may have wished to express visually and for which *sīmā* provided a suitable medium. If this were the case, the artists would have had access to a variety of episodes and scenes from which to choose. The narratives may have been instructive to a certain extent and could have functioned as visual cues for the Buddhist faithful. However, Brown (1997) and Skilling (2008a) have cautioned against given primacy to the didactic function of *jātaka* and the Life of the Buddha. Skilling (2008a: 78–81) instead argues that it is secondary to the religious potency conveyed by these scenes. For instance, he states that in regard to architecture: "Representations of the life of the Buddha, of *jātakas*, of texts, invoke and install the power of the Buddha within the monument. The *jātakas* in particular invoke his perfections (*parāmitā*)" (2008a: 80). Brown (1997) has made similar arguments in regard to the placement of *jātaka* scenes at Borobudur, Java, Indonesia, the Ananda Temple in Bagan, Myanmar, and Wat Si Chum Temple in Sukhothai. In all of these instances, the *jātaka* were not placed in locations that could be easily viewed. In fact, at Wat Si Chum they are by and large inaccessible, while at the Ananda Temple many are placed at such a height on the monument as to be out of sight to all but those with the sharpest of eyesight. He thus concludes that the *jātaka* scenes function to invoke the presence of the Buddha. It seems reasonable to say that these narratives also imbued a similar potency in *sīmā*. They made him and his teachings manifest in the very stone itself.

Along with *jātaka* and Life of the Buddha scenes, there are several other images and motifs present at Muang Fa Daed. Two examples are discussed below.

Goddess Lakṣmī

There is one example of this goddess from Muang Fa Daed (Murphy 2010: Fig. 5.114). There is only one other known example of her on a *sīmā* from this period. It is from Don Meas on Phnom Kulen. The whereabouts of this *sīmā* is unknown today; however, there is a photograph in J. Boulbet and B. Dagens (1973: PL 131–132) and No Na Paknam (1981: 15).

Lakṣmī is the goddess of wealth, prosperity, and generosity. She is visible in the centre of the composition, flanked by two elephants and is depicted with a conical crown and nimbus. Water pots (possibly *kumbha*) are visible in the trunks of the elephants, which use them to pour lustral water over the goddess. The earliest depiction of this kind is from the *stūpa* at Bharhut, India circa 150 BCE. In Dvāravatī art, this scene also appears on a number of *abhiṣeka* tablets from Phetchaburi (Wongnoi 2009: 189) and Nakhon Pathom (Baptiste and Zéphir 2009: 55).

Arunsak Kingmanee (2002) has proposed that this scene represents the birth of the Buddha. To do so, he equates the figure of Lakṣmī with Queen Maya. The elephants presumably indicate her dream before she conceived. While it is true that in later Buddhist belief and Buddhism practised today in Thailand, this scene is associated with the birth of the Buddha, there is no clear evidence that it was viewed as such during the Dvāravatī period. While the goddess Lakṣmī is Hindu in origin, she can also appear in Buddhist contexts as this *sīmā* indicates.

Indra Mounted on Airavata

This *sīmā*, today in the British Museum comes from Muang Fa Daed.[19] This is one of three *sīmā* (acc. no. 1970,0310.1; the other two are 1975,0623.1 and 1975,0623.2) donated by the late Douglas Latchford, a disgraced collector, art dealer and smuggler who at the time of his death in 2020 was under investigation in the United States for antiquities smuggling of both Thai and Cambodian material. There is a very strong likelihood that these three *sīmā* were looted.[20]

The *sīmā* depicts Indra seated on his divine three-headed elephant Airavata, flanked by two of his handmaidens. In Buddhism, Indra is the king of Tāvatiṃsa heaven. He is shown sitting in *lalitāsana* with a nimbus encircling his head and crown, and a *vajra* in his right hand. He is surrounded by cloud motifs, perhaps emphasising his divine nature or a

---

19   https://www.britishmuseum.org/collection/object/A_1970-0310-1.

20   The Thai Fine Arts Department has documentary evidence in support of this. At the time of this book's publication, ongoing efforts by the Thai Fine Arts Department to repatriate this material has been unsuccessful. For the record, my view is that these three *sīmā* should be repatriated at the earliest possible opportunity.

celestial location. This *sīmā* is similar in composition and subject matter to the *Kulāvaka-jātaka* from Maung Fa Daed (Fig. 2.3). It too depicts Indra on his mount surrounded by his handmaidens. Perhaps one *sīmā* provided the inspiration for the other, or they could both have been executed by the same artist or school, thus explaining the similarities.

Other Motifs and Types

The numerous other *sīmā* from Muang Fa Daed are mostly slab type and

Figure 2.17: Detail of a pillar type *sīmā* from Ban Nong Hang, Kalasin province, with an early 11th-century inscription and bodhisattva image. National Museum Khon Kaen, Thailand.

have either axial *stūpa* designs or sometimes a *stūpa-kumbha*. Apart from this, there are also pillar type *sīmā* with one form, the "tapered pillar type" (Fig. 2.16) being found exclusively at this site and Ban Nong Hang (see below).

Stucco, Votives, and Inscriptions

Votive tablets, stucco decoration – which would have faced the brick monuments – and a few inscriptions have also been discovered at the site. The stucco mainly consists of Buddha and bodhisattva images, the majority of which is fragmentary and provides a hint of the artistic beauty of its original conception. Better preserved examples from the site of *stūpa* no. 40 at Khu Bua in Ratchaburi province and Khao Khang Nai Stūpa at Si Thep, Central Thailand give some indication as to how the stucco may have looked (Baptiste and Zéphir 2009: cat. 105–6).

The votive tablets are similar in fashion to those discovered at Na Dun in Maha Sarakham province and are similar in design to those found throughout the northeast of Thailand during the Dvāravatī period. They often depicted the Buddha flanked by *stūpa* and/or attendants. Other examples show multiple miniature *stūpa*.

There have been seven inscriptions recorded on *sīmā* from this cluster. Three of them have been read, the other four remain undeciphered. One from Muang Fa Daed has been dated to the 9th to 10th centuries and is in Old Mon. Another, from Ban Nong Hang, is in Old Mon and has been dated to the 10th century. Inscription (K. 510) also from Ban Nong Hang has been dated to the early 11th century (see Fig. 2.17 below). A further inscription from Ban Nong Hang is in Sanskrit but has not been read.

A Muang Fa Daed Atelier?

The sheer quantity and artistic skill reflected on the *sīmā* from Muang Fa Daed strongly point towards an active workshop at the site that may have acted as the source of inspiration for the rest of the sites in the Khorat Plateau, or in the Chi River system at the very least. This school was particularly fond of depicting scenes from the Life of the Buddha and *jātaka*.

This is reflected by five of the *sīmā* discussed above (Figs. 2.10–2.15). Based on the similarity in terms of style, composition, and subject matter, they strongly suggest the work of a single artist or workshop. Three of them depict the Buddha with a flaming nimbus, the other two depict the nimbus without flames. The flaming nimbus is found on a number of Buddha images in various media in the Dvāravatī period and has a date range stretching from the 7th to 10th centuries. For instance, it appears on votive tablets from Maha Sarakham dating to the 9th to 10th centuries (Baptiste and Zéphir 2009: 115), a bronze Buddha image from U Thong datable to the 7th century (Baptiste and Zéphir 2009: 251), and on relief Buddha images from cave sculpture in Phetchaburi dating to the 8th century (Khunsong 2009: 232). The presence of the flaming nimbus on *sīmā* from Muang Fa Daed provides a stylistic marker that indicates an 8th- to 9th-century date.

The hand positions of Figures 2.11 and 2.12 are identical. It appears that the left hand is open or could represent the Buddha clasping his robe. In these three *sīmā* and the *sīmā* with the unidentified scene, the attendant figures are shown in a similar manner and are almost identical in size in relation to the Buddha. Lastly, the face of the Buddha on all five *sīmā* is very similar, exhibiting the classic Dvāravatī-style hair curls, *uṣṇīṣa*, thick lips, and oval eyes. This too is indicative of the 8th to 9th centuries.

Often the figures are depicted in *vitarkamudrā*. The significance of this can perhaps be explained by the specific historical situation in the Khorat Plateau at the time. As monastic populations expanded, it is possible that images depicting the Buddha preaching to and/or converting kings, family members, and supernatural beings aided the *saṅgha* in their efforts in proselytising this new religion. Conversely, it is also possible that laypeople invited monastics to reside in their areas and financed the development of Buddhist centres and their satellites. This may go some way in explaining the proliferation of the theme of teaching on the narrative art of the *sīmā*.

Muang Fa Daed was the largest site in the Chi River system. The evidence from the surviving corpus of Buddhist architecture, art, and material culture in general points towards it being the location of an important religious centre, particularly in the 7th to 9th centuries. The remainder of this chapter discusses the sites in its vicinity which may have come under its artistic reach and political and economic control.

Ban Nong Hang, Kunchinarai, and Ban Na Ngam

Zooming back out from Muang Fa Daed to view Cluster 1 as a whole again, the distribution analysis brings three sites into focus. The modern district of Kuchinarai lies approximately 60 kilometres to the northeast of Muang Fa Daed. Here two sites, Ban Nong Hang and Kunchinarai town, have *sīmā*. Both are in close proximity to the Lang Nam Yang River. As the sites are only 6 kilometres apart, it is presumed that the material from both modern locations comes from one settlement. However, the exact nature of this site (or sites) is not clear at present, and analysis of the landscape using Google Earth imagery reveals no evidence for a moated site.

The site of Ban Na Ngam is located north of Ban Nong Hang in Khao Wong district. Five *sīmā* were discovered still in situ at this site lying face down in a paddy field (Fig. 1.3). They are the slab type variety with *stūpa-kumbha* motifs. Apart from this, no other evidence for Buddhism remains here. As the *sīmā* are still in situ, archaeological investigation of this site may prove fruitful.

Turning back to Ban Nong Hang, a total of 23 *sīmā* of the slab and pillar type have been found at this site. Thirty more are located at Kunchinarai town. Along with Muang Fa Daed, Ban Nong Hang exhibits some of the finest carved *sīmā* from the region, a number of which depict *jātaka* scenes and images of the Buddha. There is a high degree of uniformity in terms of style and iconography with those from Muang Fa Daed. Furthermore, tapered pillar type *sīmā* are only present at these two sites.

Tapered pillar type *sīmā* are the largest and most refined form (Krairiksh 1974a; Vallibhotama 1975). They have squared bases with elaborately carved floral motifs. The main body of the *sīmā* tapers inwards then outwards before tapering back inwards again to form a pyramidal top. They are the tallest of the pillar type *sīmā*, averaging 260 centimetres high, 55 centimetres wide, and 55 centimetres deep. Unlike all other examples of pillar type *sīmā*, they have narrative artwork depicted on the lower parts of their body, usually on all four sides. The style of the narrative art and the floral motifs exhibit Khmer traits and point towards a late 10th- to 11th-century date. This is confirmed by an inscription in Old Mon on one of the *sīmā* (Fig. 2.17) from Ban Nong Hang dated to circa 1000 CE (Krairiksh 1974a: 58).

There is thus a strong artistic connection between Muang Fa Daed and Ban Nong Hang. It is most likely that the *sīmā* at the latter site were executed by the artists of the Muang Fa Daed atelier, or at the very least, who were trained by this school. It is also possible to distinguish two distinct periods: *sīmā* dating to the 8th and 9th centuries and *sīmā* dating to the 11th century. A stylistic and iconographic analysis of a number of examples are discussed below to illustrate this.

The Mahājanaka-jātaka

This fragmentary *sīmā* dating to the 8th to 9th centuries (Fig. 2.18) has been identified by Krairiksh (1974a: 47–8) as depicting a scene from the *Mahājanaka-jātaka* – that of his encounter with his estranged wife, Queen Sīvalī, after he has renounced his kingship and become an ascetic (Cowell 1978: Vol. VI, 30–7). This *jātaka* centres around the bodhisattava Mahājanaka's quest to reclaim his father's kingdom of Videha, which has been taken over by a usurper. He sets out on a ship bound for Suvaṇṇabhūmi, the golden land of the east, to raise money for this venture by selling his cargo. After seven days at sea the ship sank and Mahājanaka jumped clear of the sea monsters waiting below to devour the crew. He treaded water for a whole week before being saved by a goddess who took him to dry land. He thus perfected the virtue of perseverance. He eventually regained his father's throne but in the end renounced it and became an ascetic.

Krairkiksh argues that the scene on Figure 2.18 represents Mahājanaka once he has become an ascetic. He identifies him as the figure depicted at the bottom centre of the composition in an ascetic's garb, holding an ascetic's staff. He argues that Queen Sīvalī is placed above him, shown leaning on her right shoulder, with her right hand raised to support herself. If this identification is correct, this posture may have been chosen to convey her grief and sorrow at the fact that Mahājanaka has resolved to remain an ascetic despite her pleas for him to return to the palace with her. Overall, the compositional arrangement is uncrowded and as far as can be made out from the fragment, there are no further motifs or features present in this scene. The viewer's attention is therefore solely focused on the interaction between the two figures.

Figure 2.18: Possible scene from *The Mahājanaka-jātaka* on a fragmentary *sīmā* from Ban Nong Hang, Kalasin province. 8th–9th centuries. Sandstone. Height: 64 cm; width: 60 cm; depth: 11 cm. National Museum Khon Kaen, Thailand. Inventory number 17/56/2517.

Figures 2.19–2.21: Details of a pillar type *sīmā* from Ban Nong Hang, Kalasin province carved with three separate *jātaka* on its four faces. National Museum Khon Kaen, Thailand. Figure 2.19 is from the *Bhūridatta-jātaka*, and Figures 2.20 and 2.21 are from the *Vidhurapaṇḍita-jātaka*.

This identification, while compelling, is far from certain. First, the identification of the lower figure as Mahājanaka rests solely on the assumption that the staff represents that of an ascetic. However, it has been pointed out by several authors that it represents a *khakkharaka* (a staff carried by Buddhist monks) (Lorrillard 2008, 123–4; Revire 2009: 120–3) whose use is not restricted to ascetics alone but common to monks of various sects. Furthermore, the *khakkharaka* is also depicted on another *sīmā* (Murphy 2010: Figure 5.74), and in this scene is held by the Buddha. Additionally, the figures on both *sīmā* have their hair cut short in the style of a monk, as opposed to the conical hairstyle of a bodhisattva. Nor do they have an *uṣṇīṣa*, which would at least indicate Buddhahood. The identification of the upper figure as a queen is also far from certain. It is more probable that this scene represents an unidentified episode involving a monk, as opposed to one from the *Mahājanaka-jātaka*.

The Sāma-jātaka

This *jātaka* tells the story of Sāma, who spent his days looking after his blind parents (Murphy 2010: 228–9). They were both ascetics and thus

2.19

the family lived in the forest. Sāma would fetch food and water every day for his parents. To assist him, he tamed deer to carry the large water containers on their backs. One day King Piliyakkha came to the forest to hunt for game. He witnessed Sāma leading the deer and wondered what type of great being could do such a thing. To find out, he decided to disable him by shooting him with an arrow. Sāma, while lying wounded, told the king all his actions were for the sole purpose of looking after his parents. The king was distraught and brought the dying Sāma back to his parents. Fortunately, a goddess intervened and not only healed Sāma but restored the sight of his parents. Sāma in this *jātaka* perfects the virtue of loving kindness.

I have identified the scene on one *sīmā* (Murphy 2010: Fig. 5.15) as depicting the episode in which King Piliyakkha mortally wounds Sāma (Cowell 1978: Vol. VI, 38–52). King Piliyakkha is shown standing to the left, bow in one hand and arrows in the other. Sāma stands to the right, water pot held high, two deer depicted directly behind him. This scene depicts the moment before the king lets fly his arrow.

2.20

2.21

Figure 2.22: Details of a pillar type *sīmā* from Ban Nong Hang, Kalasin province carved with three separate *jātaka* on its four faces. This figure is from the *Vessantara-jātaka*. National Museum Khon Kaen, Thailand.

The Bhūridatta, Vidhurapaṇḍita, *and* Vessantara-jātaka

This *sīmā*, dating to the 11th century, is carved on four sides with episodes from the *Bhūridatta*, *Vidhurapaṇḍita*, and *Vessantara-jātaka* respectively (Figs. 2.19–2.22). The face with the *Bhūridatta-jātaka* appears to depict the same episode as an example found at Muang Fa Daed (Fig. 2.7), where the brahmin Ālambāyana seizes the bodhisattva, who is meditating on an anthill. Alternatively, it could represent the episode where the brahmin makes the *nāga* dance. The scene shows Ālambāyana holding the *nāga* by its tail. However, in this depiction the violent sense of movement and struggle is absent, suggesting that this represents the snake dancing episode which follows directly after the *nāga*'s capture (Cowell 1978: Vol.

2.22

VI, 80–114). This is further emphasised by Ālambāyana's hand gesture, which seems to be instructing the *nāga*.

The *Vidhurapaṇḍita-jātaka* is depicted on two of its other faces (Figs. 2.20 and 2.21). Puṇṇaka is depicted on one face, shown with his matted hair standing alongside his horse. On the other, he is shown in the act of abducting Vidhura (Cowell 1978: Vol. VI, 146). Vidhura is shown with the ubiquitous Dvāravatī-style conical crown of a bodhisattva. There is a sense of dynamic movement in this scene as Puṇṇaka ushers Vidhura away.

The final face (Fig. 2.22) has a scene from the *Vessantara-jātaka*. It depicts the moment when Jālī and Kaṇhā, Vessantara's son and daughter, have been bound and are being led away by Jūjuka (Cowell 1978: Vol. VI, 283). The figure to the left is clearly male (Jālī) and the figure to the right female (Kaṇhā). Jālī's left hand is intertwined with Kaṇhā's left, and the creeper by which they are bound is visible, trailing away from Jālī's right hand. This compositional arrangement matches the description in the Pāli text almost verbatim. It states: "And Jūjuka went into the jungle, and bit off a creeper, and with it he bound the boy's right hand to the girl's left, and drove them away beating them ..." (Cowell 1978: Vol. VI, 283). This may indicate that the text or oral tradition that served as the basis for the execution of this scene has close similarities with the Sri Lankan Pāli rendition.

The *Vidhurapaṇḍita-jātaka* is present on one further *sīmā* from the site. One side, identified by Krairiksh (1974a: Figs. 17 and 18), shows Puṇṇaka depicted on his horse. He is turning backwards to hear the voice of Irandatī. The artist has depicted her on the next face of the *sīmā*. Following Puṇṇaka's gaze around the corner of the stone, we reach Irandatī, who is depicted dancing on a structure. Krairiksh (1974a: 54) explains that this is a Gupta device for depicting rocky terrain. This represents one of the few instances where two scenes from the same *jātaka* are placed alongside each other on separate faces.

This *sīmā* is also decorated on its two other faces (Fig. 2.17). One face has a banner motif of some kind while the other displays a bodhisattva whom Krairiksh (1974a: 58) identifies as Maitreya. However, it could also be Avalokiteśvara as both are frequently depicted with a lotus flower in their right hand. There is also an inscription (K. 510), which has been dated on palaeographic grounds to circa 1000 CE, located to the left of the image and possibly names the sculptor. However, it does not name the image itself (Krairiksh 1974a: 58). The bodhisattva is shown seated in *vīrāsana* on a polygonal throne with the lotus flower depicted in his right hand. His head and ears are bedecked with elaborate jewellery.

The episodes depicted on these two tapered pillar type *sīmā* form a uniform group in terms of content, iconography, and style, and are clearly the work of one particular school or artist. Both the inscription and the Khmer stylistic traits date these *sīmā* to the early 11th century.

Aṅgulimāla Threatens the Buddha

This *sīmā* (Fig. 2.23) dating to the 8th to 9th centuries has been identified by the Khon Kaen Museum as Aṅgulimāla threatening the Buddha. The story goes that Aṅgulimāla was an intelligent and keen student in Sāvatthī. He thus became the favourite of his teacher, which made the other students jealous. They set out to undermine this relationship and eventually succeeded in pitting him against his teacher. In an attempt to get rid of Aṅgulimāla, the teacher sent him on a mission to collect 1,000 human fingers in order to complete his studies. Aṅgulimāla thus became a bandit, killing any who crossed his path in his attempt to collect the required fingers.

In the episode on this *sīmā*, Aṅgulimāla, in attempting to obtain the finger of his 1000th victim, encounters the Buddha. He chases after the Buddha with his sword drawn ready to kill him. However, unable to catch

Figure 2.23: Aṅgulimāla threatens the Buddha on a fragmentary sandstone *sīmā* from Ban Nong Hang, Kalasin province. 8th–9th centuries. Sandstone. Height: 60 cm; width: 82 cm; depth: 9 cm. National Museum Khon Kaen, Thailand. Inventory number 17/25/2517.

or defeat the Buddha, he converts and becomes a monk instead (see the *Aṅgulimāla Sutta* in the *Majjhima Nikāya*). The moral of the story therefore is that anyone can change their life for the better if they follow the teachings of the Buddha.

The *sīmā* clearly shows the Buddha to the right of the composition. His head is missing but he is still identifiable by his robes and hand gesture. A figure to his left is attempting to attack him. This figure can tentatively be said to be Aṅgulimāla. However, his necklace of human fingers is absent, casting some doubt on this identification. Furthermore, there are numerous episodes during the Life of the Buddha where he is either attacked or accosted by ogres, so this could also be what is being depicted here. However, if this is Aṅgulimāla, then this depiction would be one of the earliest known examples of this scene anywhere in Southeast Asia.

The *sīmā* from Ban Nong Hang represent clear links with those from Muang Fa Daed, both in terms of the morphology of the *sīmā* and their content matter, namely, Buddhist narrative art. It is thus fair to assume that Ban Nong Hang fell within Muang Fa Daed's religious and artistic orbit.

Kantharawichai, Na Dun, and Roi Et

Three other sites in the vicinity of Muang Fa Daed also have evidence for Buddhist art. Kantharawichai is a large, moated site in Maha Sarakham province, 25 kilometres to the west of Muang Fa Daed. Sixty-six silver repoussé plaques were discovered here in 1972 (Diskul 1973; Brown 1996: 93–4). These plaques have a number of Buddhist motifs on them, including Buddha images, *cakra* and *kumbha*, and are today kept at Khon Kaen National Museum. Two plaques are of particular interest as they show a *cakra* placed on top of a column emerging from a *kumbha* pot bearing a striking resemblance to designs on *sīmā* discovered on Phnom Kulen (Figs. 4.18–4.20). Excavations at the site have also revealed a brick structure that is possibly an ordination hall (Diskul 1973: 302, Fig. 1). Six *sīmā* and the lower half of an over life-size sculpture have also been discovered at the site. Today a modern torso and head have been attached and it rests up against a tree, somewhat entangled by its roots. This makes close analysis of the sculpture difficult. However, it could perhaps be from the Dvāravatī period or possibly later.

As discussed above, Hoshino had proposed that this site represented the inner capital of Wendan. However, the archaeological and art historic evidence from this site does not come close to rivalling that of Muang Fa Daed. Based on this, it is thus difficult to accept Hoshino's hypothesis.

A number of votive tablets have been discovered at the site of Na Dun in southern Maha Sarakham province. Chirapravati (1997: 25–7) has identified three phases of stylistic development. The first group dates to the 9th century and bears all the hallmarks of the Dvāravatī style. Some

Figure 2.24: Image of a monk carved into the rockface at Wat Phu Kao Putthanimit Temple, Kalasin province, Thailand. 8th–9th centuries.

depict the Buddha in standing posture under the Bodhi tree, flanked by a *stūpa* on each side. These *stūpa* are similar in form to the *stūpa-kumbha* seen on *sīmā*. However, the finial is depicted in sun-like fashion (Skilling 2009: Figs. 31 and 32). Other votive tablets from this period show the Buddha either seated in meditation or with legs pendant (Skilling 2009: Figs. 33–37).

The second phase, dating to the 10th century, fuses elements of Khmer art with the Dvāravatī style. In the third period, dating to the 11th century, the votive tablets take on a distinctive iconography – they all show the Buddha seated in meditation with his hands in *dhyanamudrā*.

The site also has a small number of laterite *sīmā* with axial and *stūpa-kumbha* designs. Another 38 *sīmā* have been gathered up at a temple in Maha Sarakham town; however, their exact provenance is uncertain.

Roi Et, located 30 kilometres to the southeast of Muang Fa Daed, is also a moated site. Parts of the moat remain, despite it being in the centre of a busy modern town. Evidence for Buddhism can be found at Wat Nuea Temple. The brick foundations of a *stūpa* at the temple possibly date to the

Dvāravatī period (Wattanatum 2000: 43). Eleven *sīmā* are also still located there. Another 29 Dvāravatī-period *sīmā* are located at a number of other temples in the town, though their exact findspots are unknown.

Mountaintop Sites

Shifting focus to the landscape almost directly north of Muang Fa Daed, we encounter two mountaintop sites – Phu Bor and Wat Phu Kao Putthanimit. They both have Buddha images in *mahāparinibbāna* carved into the rock face. Here we begin to see some of the earliest evidence for a cognitive shaping of the landscape by Buddhist practitioners.

The site of Wat Phu Kao Putthanimit is located on a hilltop 45 kilometres north of Muang Fa Daed. It commands excellent views of the plains below. Evidence for the existence of a monastic community is attested by *sīmā* and an image carved into the rockface. The presence of *sīmā* indicates that there was probably some form of religious structure, but no evidence survives. The nearby image is in a reclining posture and on first viewing, one might assume it is a Buddha in *mahāparinibbāna* (Fig. 2.24). However, on closer inspection this does not appear to be the case. First off, the image is resting on its left hand. Normally the Buddha in *mahāparinibbāna* is shown resting on its right side. Secondly, the face of the image does not correspond to that of a Buddha – it has no *uṣṇīṣa* or snail-curl hair. Instead, it appears to be sporting the hairstyle of a Buddhist monk.

Figure 2.25: Buddha image carved into the rockface in *mahāparinibbāna* posture at Wat Phu Bor Temple, Kalasin province. 8th–9th centuries.

2.25

The site of Phu Bor is located 35 kilometres to the northeast of Muang Fa Daed and only 16 kilometres south of Phu Kao Putthanimit. This site has two images carved in relief into the rockface – one located on the bottom slope of the mountain and another about 80 metres higher up. Both represent the Buddha in *mahāparinibbāna*. The lower of the two (Fig. 2.25) has classic Dvāravatī features. The robe clings diaphanously to the rather androgynous body of the Buddha and the hair is depicted in tight curls with a cone-shaped *uṣṇīṣa* similar in form to that found on some Dvāravatī bronze images (see Fig. 4.9). The head, which rests on a pillow, is surrounded by a halo in a similar fashion to examples on *sīmā* from Muang Fa Daed (Figs. 2.14 and 2.15). A small worshipping figure (not visible in the image), possibly Ānanda, has been carved at his feet, presumably mourning his passing. There appears to be an inscription at the bottom right, but the image is today covered in gold paint and makes this hard to ascertain. The second image appears to be later in date. It still retains the Dvāravatī-style hair curls; however, its face is gentler, and the robes no longer cling to the body to the same extent. It may therefore date from the 12th to 14th centuries onwards and could thus be roughly contemporary with the *mahāparinibbāna* from Wat Preah Ang Thom Temple on Phnom Kulen (discussed in Chapter 4). This Buddha image also indicates that the site of Phu Bor was active to at least the 12th to 14th centuries. Whether this was continuous or not is impossible to say, but the carving of the later Buddha in *mahāparinibbāna* does signal that it held an enduring sacred appeal to the surrounding inhabitants.

The sites of Phu Kao Putthanimit and Phu Bor most likely functioned as both a location for forest retreats for monks and places of pilgrimage for the Buddhist faithful. For monks it would have provided a place for those who wished to live a more ascetic lifestyle altogether, as well as for monks to come during the rainy season retreats. This may also explain the choice of depicting the Buddha in *mahāparinibbāna*. The *mahāparinibbāna sutta* starts just before the rainy season retreat and the narrative continues beyond the three months of the retreat and records the passing away of the Buddha. It then details his cremation, the division of relics, and the building of the eight *stūpa* enshrining the relics of the Buddha. Either way, the fact that at Phu Bor and Phu Wiang in Cluster 3 (discussed in Chapter 3), the artists decided to specifically depict the Buddha in *mahāparinibbāna* indicates that there was some clear reason for this. Did some form of pilgrimage arise on the Khorat Plateau at this time that consisted of ascending a mountaintop to commemorate the *mahāparinibbāna* of the Buddha? Perhaps. Phu Wiang in Cluster 3 (Fig. 3.17), for instance, has epigraphic evidence to suggest such a function. However, we cannot say for certain what the exact nature of this pilgrimage was.

Given the proximity of both sites to Muang Fa Daed, it is likely that the initiative to create these sites came from monks located here. Both sites show how Buddhist art started to be gradually inscribed on the surrounding landscape and how elevated locations became integrated into the ritual practices of the populace.

SUMMARY

The evidence discussed in this chapter illustrates that the Muang Fa Daed mandala was strategically placed in the central section of this river system. The site of Muang Fa Daed, lying at the heart of a cluster of sites in the central Chi River system, has the most substantive material evidence for Buddhist art and architecture anywhere on the Khorat Plateau. This leads to the conclusion that there was a Buddhist monastery at this site. Muang Fa Daed also appears to have been powerful politically and may have exerted control over the surrounding sites too, perhaps even being the enigmatic Wendan mentioned in the Chinese sources.

The sheer volume of *sīmā* found at Muang Fa Daed, together with their harmony of style and the iconographic unity of much of the imagery – nine out of the ten *Mahānipāta-jātaka* are present – points towards the existence of a major workshop. Whether the *sīmā* tradition originated here or not is impossible to tell, but it is clear that by the 8th to 9th centuries, the art from this site inspired the *sīmā* tradition throughout the Chi River system. In the next chapter, we will look at Clusters 2 and 3, which provide further evidence to indicate this. The reach of Cluster 1 was also felt much further afield. For instance, I have identified strong stylistic similarities on *sīmā* from Muang Fa Daed with art from the Cham culture located in present-day Vietnam at the sites of Mỹ Sơn, Đồng Dương, Ưu Điềm, and Trà Liên in particular (Murphy 2019). This indicates that artists were moving back and forth between these two cultures. This adds further weight to the argument that Muang Fa Daed was an important religious, artistic, and political centre during the 7th to 9th centuries.

Chapter 3

BUDDHIST ART IN THE UPPER AND LOWER CHI RIVER SYSTEM

This chapter looks at the evidence for Buddhist art in two areas, the upper and lower sections of the Chi River system. While Buddhist art spread along the entire course of the Chi River system, there is a certain degree of regional variation in terms of both its concentration and the stylistic and iconographic features. The survey work and site distribution analysis that I undertook reveals that there are a significant number of sites located in the upper reaches of the Chi River system, particularly in the areas of modern-day Khon Kaen and Chaiyaphum provinces. The Buddhist art and material remains share certain similar characteristics with that found in Cluster 1, indicating clear links between these two areas. However, the highest concentration of sites in the Chi River system is within the area of modern-day Yasothon province (Map 2) in the system's lower reaches. This material also shares similarities with the art from Clusters 1 to 3, but also some differences in terms of the iconography. Once again, the evidence for Buddhist art comes primarily from *sīmā* as there are very few examples of surviving Buddha images or architectural remains. The narrative art on the *sīmā* is also more limited than Cluster 1 and instead *stūpa-kumbha* motifs predominate. A close visual analysis of the *sīmā* indicate a number of similarities, both stylistically and iconographically between Clusters 1, 2, and 3 and is indicative of the links between the sites in these respective areas. Cluster 4, however, tends to focus more on aniconic representations, as seen in the profusion of the *stūpa-kumbha* motif. By focusing on Clusters 2, 3, and 4, this chapter builds on the analysis in Chapter 2 to give a more complete picture of Buddhist art in the Chi River system in the 7th to 11th centuries.

CLUSTER 2: THE UPPER CHI RIVER

Cluster 2 consists of seven sites, two of which are moated (Map 7). They are located in the upper section of the Chi River system situated in the modern-day provinces of Chaiyaphum and Khon Kaen (Table 5). This section of the river meanders downstream in a northeasterly direction.

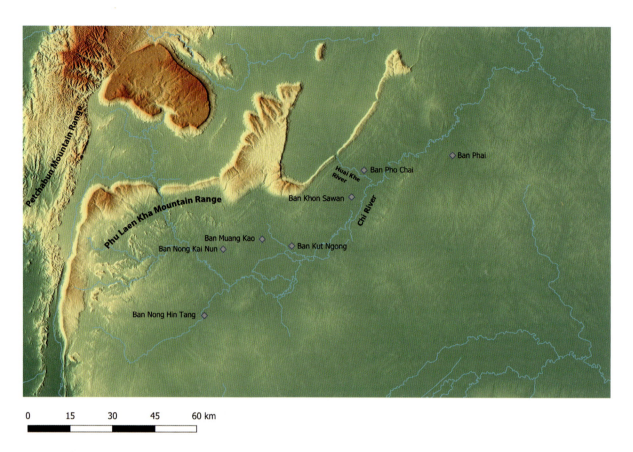

Map 7 Cluster 2.

The landscape is dominated by the Phu Laen Kha Mountain range located about 15 to 20 kilometres north of the river. This range consists of mountains and plateaus that reach between 200 and 720 metres above sea level. Of the seven sites in the cluster, five of them are located north of the Chi River in a corridor between it and this mountain range. They thus have good access to both the wooded upland environs and the floodplains of the river system. The other two sites are located just to the south of the Chi River. Two out of the seven sites – Ban Kut Ngong and Ban Khon Sawan – have *sīmā* with narrative art. Cluster 3 (discussed below) is located to the north, on the other side of the Phu Laen Kha Mountain range.

Stylistically, the narrative art from Ban Kut Ngong and Ban Khon Sawan shows close similarities with that on *sīmā* from Muang Fa Daed and Ban Nong Hang. Furthermore, the epigraphic evidence indicates a similar date range of the 8th to 9th centuries CE (Bauer 1991: 58–60). The *sīmā* from the other five sites are carved with axial *stūpa* motifs or are left largely undecorated, apart from the lotus band carved around their bases.

Site Analysis: Ban Kut Ngong and Ban Khon Sawan

Ban Kut Ngong is located 10 kilometres east of modern-day Chaiyaphum town and about 5 kilometres west of the banks of the Chi River on a tributary called the La Pa Thao. It is a moated site of about 1 kilometre in diameter. The La Pa Thao River forms part of the moat system, which would have aided in mitigating flooding and water management in general. The site is thus well placed on the Chi riverine network. Ten of the 27 *sīmā* that have been collected and are kept at Wat Kut Nong Temple have narrative art on them.

Figure 3.1: Unfinished Dvaravati-style Buddha located in an ancillary shire at Wat Ban Khon Sawan Temple, Ban Khon Sawan, Chaiyaphum province. 8th–9th centuries. Sandstone.

Figure 3.2: The *Bhūridatta-jātaka* on a *sīmā* housed in a shed built by the FAD at Ban Kut Ngong, Chaiyaphum province, Thailand. 8th century. Sandstone. Height: 170 cm; width: 60 cm; depth: 22 cm.

Figure 3.3: The *Bhūridatta-jātaka* on a *sīmā* located in a pavilion at Ban Khon Sawan Temple, Ban Khon Sawan, Chaiyaphum province, Thailand. 8th century. Sandstone. Height: 198 cm; width: 92 cm; depth: 15 cm.

Ban Khon Sawan lies 2 kilometres west of the Chi River and about 30 kilometres downstream from Ban Kut Ngong. It too is a moated site of about 1 kilometre in diameter. The feeder canal to the Chi River is still visible today and connects to the moat in its southeast corner.

There are 46 *sīmā* located at this site. In addition, there are three roughly carved Buddha images that appear to date to the Dvāravatī period. Today they are under worship in the local village temple. Two of them have lost their original heads, making it difficult to identify for certain which period they date from. The other, however, appears to be an unfinished Dvāravatī Buddha image (Fig. 3.1). Its feet have not been fully carved, nor have its hair curls, but all of the salient features are present.

Art Historical Analysis: Narrative Art from Cluster 2

Twelve out of the 46 *sīmā* at Ban Khon Sawan have narrative art. Taken together with the ten from Ban Kut Ngong, this represents the highest concentration of narrative art outside of Muang Fa Daed and Cluster 1 in general. A discussion of a selection of these *sīmā* is given below.

3.2   3.3

The Bhūridatta-jātaka

The *Bhūridatta-jātaka* has been identified on one *sīmā* apiece from Ban Kut Ngong (Fig. 3.2) and Ban Khon Sawan (Fig. 3.3). It is also present at Muang Fa Daed and Ban Nong Hang (Figs. 2.5 and 2.19). All four *sīmā* show the same scene – the brahmin Ālambāyana wrestling with the *nāga*. Its depictions at Ban Kut Ngong and Ban Khon Sawan are very similar in composition and style. In both cases Ālambāyana is depicted at the left centre with both hands clasping the tail of the *nāga*.

In the Ban Kut Ngong example, the *nāga*, with its body in three coils, is placed directly above Ālambāyana. The composition is rounded off by a cloud motif decoration above. The coils of the *nāga* wrap around both the right- and left-hand sides of the stone, as the artist has skilfully incorporated the shape of the *sīmā* into the composition.

In the Ban Khon Sawan example, the *nāga* is depicted to the top right of Ālambāyana, again in three coils. The closeness in composition and style of these two *sīmā*, coupled with the geographical proximity of the sites, strongly points towards the work of a single artist or school. This can be seen in both the similarity in the depiction of the *nāga*'s face and how the artist conveys a real sense of movement and energy in the posture of Ālambāyana, who in both incidences is leaning away to the right, his weight placed on his right knee as he strains to wrestle the *nāga* free from the anthill.

A Mon inscription (Jy. 9) on the back of the Ban Kut Ngong example has been dated on palaeographic grounds to the 8th century (Bauer 1991: 35), thus providing a date range for these two examples.

The Mahāummagga-jātaka

The episode of the Courting of Amarā from this *jātaka* is present on one *sīmā* from Ban Kut Ngong (Fig. 3.4) and one *sīmā* from Ban Khon Sawan (Murphy 2010: Fig. 5.39). It is also present on one *sīmā* from Muang Fa Daed (Murphy 2010: Fig. 5.42). All three *sīmā* show almost identical compositions – Mahosadha is placed to the left and Amarā is on the right, with one hand placed on her hip and the other on her head to support the wood she is carrying. The similarity in the compositions between the two sites, as also seen in the *Bhūridatta-jātaka* above, indicates that these *sīmā* are the work of one school/artist, or at the very least, that they are all working from the same template, which could have been a palm manuscript.

The Mahānāradakassapa-jātaka

This *jātaka* is present on one *sīmā* from Ban Kut Ngong (Fig. 3.5) and two *sīmā* from Muang Fa Daed (Fig. 2.6; Murphy 2010: Fig. 5.26). All

Figure 3.4: The *Mahāummagga-jātaka* on a *sīmā* housed in a shed built by the FAD at Ban Kut Ngong, Chaiyaphum province, Thailand. 8th–9th centuries. Sandstone. Height: 186 cm; width: 92 cm; depth: 22 cm.

Figure 3.5: The *Mahānāradakassapa-jātaka* on a *sīmā* housed in a shed built by the FAD at Ban Kut Ngong, Chaiyaphum province, Thailand. 8th–9th centuries. Sandstone. Height: 175 cm; width: 82 cm; depth: 27 cm. Courtesy of River Books Bangkok.

three depict the same episode in a very similar fashion. The bodhisattva on the *sīmā* from Ban Kut Ngong (Fig. 3.5) has classic Dvāravatī facial features, and the matted hairstyle of the chignon, characteristic of the Khorat Plateau aesthetic, is extremely similar to that found on bodhisattva images from the Prakhon Chai/Plai Bat II hoard (Figs. 4.15–4.17). The site of Ban Tanot, where an over life-size bronze bodhisattva was discovered, is approximately 60 kilometres due south of Ban Kut Ngong and could have provided the inspiration for this depiction (Fig. 4.5). Hunter Watson (2013: 182, 187, 191, 402–7) has identified a Mon inscription on this *sīmā*, located below the *kumbha* pot on the right. However, it has not been dated. The *sīmā* can, however, be dated to the 8th to 9th centuries based on the Dvāravatī style exhibited.

The Khaṇḍahāla-jātaka

This *jātaka* is depicted on one *sīmā* from Ban Kut Ngong (Murphy 2010: Fig. 5.18). There is also one *sīmā* from Muang Fa Daed with this *jātaka* (Krairiksh 1974a: 53; Murphy 2010: Fig. 5.17). Both *sīmā* depict

3.4   3.5

the same episode – that of Indra descending from heaven to save the bodhisattva, who reincarnated as the just Prince Candakumāra, is about to be ritually executed by his misguided father, King Vasavatti (Cowell 1978: Vol. VI, 68–80). In the *sīmā* from Ban Kut Ngong, Indra is located in the centre of the composition, ready to strike. King Vasavatti is visible at the bottom left of the *sīmā*, crouching down in fear with his right arm raised above his head in a vain attempt to protect himself from the impending divine wrath.

The Vessantara-jātaka

This *jātaka* is present at both Ban Kut Ngong (Fig. 3.6) and Ban Khon Sawan (Fig. 3.7), but the episodes they depict differ. It is also present at Muang Fa Daed (Murphy 2010: Fig. 5.46). The Ban Kut Ngong *sīmā* depicts the episode of the "Children and the Fruit" (Cowell 1978: Vol. VI, 266). In this scene, Vessantara and his family encounter fruit trees on either side of the road. His children wish to pick the trees' fruit, but they are not tall enough to do so. Vessantara therefore causes the branches to drop down so that they can reach the fruit. Vessantara, identifiable by his earrings and conical headdress, is depicted to the right, gesturing to his child standing beside him to pick the fruit from the tree to the left of the composition. The fruit is clearly visible above the child's outstretched arms and the trunk of the tree seems to be bending ever so slightly to the right. Also noteworthy on this *sīmā* is Vessantara's pronounced *drapé-en-poche*, which provides a clear illustration of this salient characteristic of the Khorat Plateau aesthetic of the 8th to 9th centuries.

The episode depicted at Ban Khon Sawan (Fig. 3.7) is that of Vessantara giving away his two children to the brahmin Jūjuka (Cowell 1978: Vol. VI, 280–90). The *sīmā* shows Vessantara in the centre, carrying a water pot in his right hand. One of his children is depicted to the right, trying to pull away from his father, perhaps in an attempt to escape from the brahmin Jūjuka. Jūjuka is depicted to the left, with his right hand outstretched, in anticipation of the imminent donation symbolised by the act of pouring water on the right hand of the recipient.

The Vidhurapaṇḍita-jātaka

This *jātaka* is present at both Ban Kut Ngong and Ban Khon Sawan (Murphy 2010: Figs. 5.28 and 5.29), as well at Muang Fa Daed and Ban Nong Hang in Cluster 1 (Figs. 2.7, 2.20, 2.21). In both cases they show Vidhura and Puṇṇaka seated beside each other. Puṇṇaka is identifiable by his long-matted hair. In the example from Ban Kut Ngong, the composition is encircled with cloud motifs indicating the mountaintop setting. In the example from Ban Khon Sawan, the clouds are absent, but the bodhisattva seems instead to be surrounded by a nimbus type motif.

Figure 3.6: The *Vessantara-jātaka* on a *sīmā* housed in a shed built by the FAD at Ban Kut Ngong, Chaiyaphum province, Thailand. 8th–9th centuries. Sandstone. Height: 197 cm; width: 93 cm; depth: 23 cm.

Figure 3.7: The *Vessantara-jātaka* on a *sīmā* located in a pavilion at Ban Khon Sawan Temple, Ban Khon Sawan, Chaiyaphum province, Thailand. 8th–9th centuries. Sandstone. Height: 198 cm; width: 82 cm; depth: 25 cm.

The *sīmā* from Ban Kut Ngong has a two-line Mon inscription (K. 1100) on its lower section, in between the two rows of lotus petals. Watson (2013: 83, 117, 182–7, 393–6) has read the inscription, which refers to merit-making.

The Temiya-jātaka

The *Temiya-jātaka* is present on one *sīmā* from Ban Khon Sawan (Murphy 2010: Fig. 5.11). There are also two examples from Muang Fa Daed (Fig. 2.2; Murphy 2010: Fig. 5.10). All three *sīmā* depict the same episode – Temiya and the charioteer (Cowell 1978: Vol. VI, 1–18) – and are extremely similar in composition and style. All three *sīmā* depict Temiya standing to the right with the charioteer kneeling to the left. The

3.6

shovel is clearly visible in the charioteer's right hand. The *sīmā* from Ban Khon Sawan, while sharing the same compositional arrangement as those from Muang Fa Daed, is executed in lower relief.

Buddha and Bodhisattva Images

As well as narrative art, a number of *sīmā* have either Buddha or bodhisattva images depicted on them. For instance, one *sīmā* from Ban Kut Ngong depicts the Buddha seated cross-legged in what appears to be *vīrāsana*, placed on a high, three-tiered throne beneath the Bodhi tree, which is shown rising from behind (Murphy 2010: Fig. 5.90). The Buddha is in *vitarkamudrā* and is depicted with a ball-shaped *uṣṇīṣa* and round nimbus.

3.7

Figure 3.8: *Stūpa-kumbha* motif with figure worshipping it on a sandstone *sīmā* located in a pavilion at Ban Khon Sawan Temple, Ban Khon Sawan, Chaiyaphum province, Thailand. 8th–9th centuries. Sandstone. Height: 233 cm; width: 90 cm; depth: 16 cm.

One *sīmā* from Ban Kut Ngong may have a bodhisattva figure depicted on it. This can be inferred as it is standing on lotus petals in *tribhaṅga* (three bends) posture and wears a conical crown surrounded by what appears to be a nimbus (Murphy 2010: Fig. 5.96). Unfortunately, there are no further iconographic clues available – such as a *stūpa* or Amitabha Buddha in the headdress or flower in the figure's upraised right hand – to identify exactly which bodhisattva this may be.

One *sīmā* from Ban Khon Sawan also depicts a bodhisattva image (Murphy 2010: Fig. 5.67). The *sīmā* has been whitewashed at some stage and the carving has eroded over time. However, the bodhisattva is still clearly visible on its top right. He is seated in *vīrāsana* with his hands in *dhyānamudrā* and is adorned with a conical headdress. There is perhaps a tree behind him; however, it is no longer possible to tell for sure. To the left, a seated figure gazes up at the bodhisattva. There are three other *sīmā* from this site which may depict bodhisattva figures. However, due to their eroded and fragmentary nature, it is impossible to tell for certain (Murphy 2010: Figs. 5.127–5.129).

There is one unique *sīmā* from Ban Khon Sawan that shows a *stūpa-kumbha* motif and a figure beside it who appears to be worshipping it (Fig. 3.8). The figure is placed to the right side of the *stūpa-kumbha* image, hands clasped together in prayer. There appear to be festoons either side of the *stūpa-kumbha,* perhaps either flags or banners. Could this representation be taken as evidence for *stūpa* worship on the Khorat Plateau? This question is dealt with in more detail later. The rest of the *sīmā* from Ban Khon Sawan and Ban Kut Ngong are largely undecorated and there are very few examples of axial *stūpa* or *stūpa-kumbha* motifs.

Summary: Combining Art Historical Analysis and Landscape Archaeology

By analysing the art historical evidence in tandem with the site distribution informed by landscape archaeological approaches, a number of observations can be made. First, Ban Kut Ngong and Ban Khon Sawan are the only two sites outside of Cluster 1 that have narrative art to any significant degree. The similarity both in terms of content (the *jātaka* depicted) and style/composition of the episodes indicate direct links with Muang Fa Daed. This may reflect the process of symbolic entrainment proposed by Colin Renfrew (1986) by which satellite sites adopt the dominant iconography and iconology of the cultural and political centre. Furthermore, Peter Skilling (2012) sees Buddhist art spreading by means of a network of self-governing modules. It is thus possible that the *sīmā* at these sites reflect this process. Could it be that the monks making up these modules received ordination from Muang Fa Daed and then sometime after this, set sail upriver to set up new monastic communities? This would be one possible explanation for the appearance of the workshops at both sites, albeit on a smaller scale to the one at Muang Fa Daed. They too produced a number of highly accomplished compositions (Figs. 3.2, 3.3, 3.5, and 3.6 in particular), though the quality of those from Ban Khon Sawan is somewhat lesser than Ban Kut Ngong. It is also worth noting that there are a number of roughed out and uncompleted *sīmā* present at Ban Kut Ngong. This is one more piece of evidence that points towards it functioning as a *sīmā* workshop.

Of the remaining sites in Cluster 2, Ban Pho Chai is also noteworthy. It lies about 10 kilometres upriver from Ban Khon Sawan. Thirty-nine *sīmā* were recorded at this site. They are located near an earthen mound and are mostly plain or decorated with axial *stūpa* designs. One in particular stands out. At over 260 centimetres in height and over 80 centimetres wide, it is one of the tallest examples from the Khorat Plateau. Furthermore, its base is elaborately carved with Khmer-style floral motifs and designs, indicating that aspects of this culture had begun to spread to this site, most likely in the 9th or 10th centuries. A *dharmacakra stambha* was also found here, but there is no trace of the wheel or socle (Fig. 3.9). Along with that discovered at Muang Sema, they represent the only known examples outside of Central Thailand.

Cluster 2 illustrates the extent to which the *sīmā* tradition and Buddhism in general spread along the Chi River system. Narrative art is found at two sites, while axial *stūpa* motifs proliferate at all others. There are strong artistic as well as typological similarities between Clusters 1 and 2. The sites from Cluster 2 are located in close proximity to the Chi River system, no more than a day or two's journey from each other, and this would have facilitated easy access back and forth between them, as well as travel further afield to Muang Fa Daed. Buddhism most likely spread out from this latter location in the form of independent, self-governing modules of *saṅgha* who made their way up the Chi River to spread the religion amongst the smaller settlements in this area.

CLUSTER 3: TRIBUTARIES OF THE UPPER CHI RIVER

This cluster is located on two tributaries of the Chi River – the Huai Soen River and the Nam Phom River. It is situated approximately 50 kilometres north of Cluster 2, in the modern-day districts of Chum Pae and Phu Wiang in Khon Kaen province and Kaset Sombun in Chaiyaphum province (Map 8). The cluster consists of ten sites in total (Table 6), the majority of which are located on the Nam Phom River, with the remainder in close proximity to the Huai Soen River. Nowadays both rivers drain into the Ubolratana Dam and its adjoining reservoir. The dam, located about 50 kilometres north of the modern-

Buddhist Art in the Upper and Lower Chi River System

Figure 3.9: *Dharmacakra stambha* from Wat Ban Pho Chai Temple, Ban Pho Chai, Khon Kaen province, Thailand. 8th–9th centuries. Sandstone.

day city of Khon Kaen, was constructed in 1964, and its adjoining reservoir covers an area of over 12,104 square kilometres. The Nam Phom River enters the reservoir from the south and the Huai Soen River enters it from the west. One further river, the Nam Phong, enters the reservoir from the north. Before the dam and reservoir were constructed, all three rivers joined in the area today submerged by the reservoir to become the Nam Phong River, which today exits to the east, after which it joins the Chi River near the modern-day city of Khon Kaen. The sites in this cluster are located near the confluence of these three rivers and this would have provided them with easy access to waterborne travel and communication routes.

Cluster 3 lies between the Petchabun Mountain range proper to its west, which can reach up to 1,000 metres above sea level, and the Phu Laen Kha Mountain range to its south. The Huai Soen and the Nam Phom rivers have their sources in the Petchabun range and flow eastwards down to the plains. The cluster is also bordered by the Phu Wiang

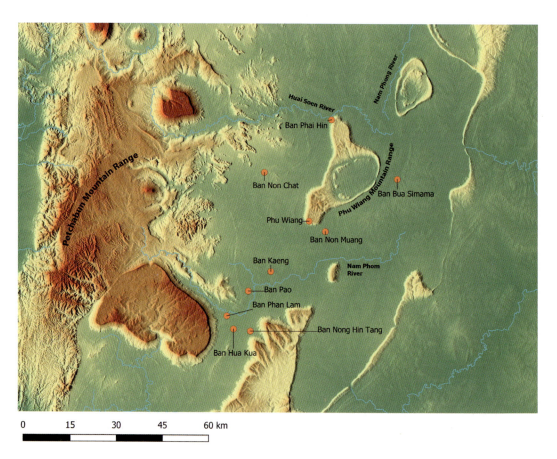

Map 8 Cluster 3.

Mountain range to its northeast. This hollow, circle-shaped mountain range has a basin at its centre. Its highest point in the westernmost mountain range is 844 metres above sea level and it is thickly covered with evergreen forest.

Inscriptional Evidence

Ten *sīmā* from this cluster have inscriptions. At Wat Non Sila Temple in Ban Phai Hin, two *sīmā* (Figs. 3.10 and 3.11) have Mon inscriptions that have been dated paleographically to the 8th century (Bauer 1991: 61–5; Champa and Mitem 1985: 83–9). The *sīmā* are slab shape in design with axial *stūpa*. The inscriptions have been incised over the *stūpa* motif, indicating that they were added afterwards. One further *sīmā* also has an inscription but it is now illegible. A *sīmā* at Ban Phan Lam also has a short Mon inscription (Watson 2013: 191, 197, 236, 407–9).

At Ban Kaeng, three *sīmā* have Mon inscriptions that have been dated paleographically to the 9th century. Three further *sīmā* at the Phimai

Figure 3.10: *Sīmā* with inscription from Wat Non Sila Temple, Ban Phai Hin, Khon Kaen province, Thailand. 8th century. Sandstone. Height: 185 cm; width: 89 cm; depth: 20 cm.

Figure 3.11: *Sīmā* with inscription from Wat Non Sila Temple, Ban Phai Hin, Khon Kaen province, Thailand. 8th century. Sandstone. Height: 155 cm; width: 72 cm; depth: 30 cm.

National Museum, but originally from Kaset Sombhun district, have inscriptions. According to the museum labels for these objects, they are in Sanskrit in post-Pallava script and have thus been dated on palaeographic grounds to the 10th to 11th centuries.

Art Historical Analysis: *Jātaka* and Buddha Images

A number of *sīmā* from this cluster have narrative art or Buddha images depicted on them. One is at Ban Non Chat and two more are kept at the Phimai National Museum. A *sīmā* at Ban Phan Lam possibly has one narrative scene, but its identification is uncertain. Ban Hua Kua has two *sīmā* with Buddha images depicted on them.

At Ban Non Chat, I have identified one scene from the *Mahājanaka-jātaka* – the episode of the shipwreck (Cowell 1978: Vol. VI, 22) (Fig. 3.12). As discussed previously, Mahājanaka set sail to Suvaṇṇabhūmi, but after seven days the ship sank. On this *sīmā,* a large fish is shown at the bottom right corner and to the left, two figures are clinging to the mast of a ship shown just to the left of the central *stūpa* motif. There is another figure placed above the large fish to the top right. It is possible that this latter figure represents Mahājanaka, as in this episode the protagonist climbs to the top of the mast as the ship begins to sink, while his shipmates, unable to do so, are eaten alive by sea creatures, symbolised in this case by the large fish.

Arunsak Kingmanee (1997b) proposes an alternative identification for this scene. He argues that it is the *Devedhamma-jātaka*. In this past life, three brothers enter a forest and are captured by an ogre. He proposes that the three figures represent the three brothers and that the creature at the bottom right is the ogre. This is very doubtful, however, as it clearly looks like a sea creature of some kind.

There is one further *sīmā* from Ban Non Chat that appears to have narrative art. It is extremely very badly eroded; however, the waist and belt of a figure are still just about visible (Murphy 2010: Fig. 5.64).

Of the two *sīmā* at Phimai National Museum, I have identified one as depicting the episode of the Courting of Amarā from the *Mahāummagga-jātaka* (Fig. 3.13). Its depiction is very similar in composition to those at Ban Khon Sawan, Ban Kut Ngong, and Muang Fa Daed. The scene on the other *sīmā* has been identified by No Na Paknam as being from the *Chaddanta-jātaka* (1981: 104). He gives no explanation for this, however. We can assume it is because the *sīmā* has two elephants, which Paknam has identified as the bodhisattva and one of his queen consorts. In this *jātaka* the bodhisattva is reincarnated as an elephant and has two queens. One of them takes offence at a perceived slight and subsequently plots her revenge (Cowell 1978: Vol. V, 20–31). The elephant on the right of the scene could possibly be the bodhisattva,

Buddhist Art in the Upper and Lower Chi River System

Figure 3.12: The *Mahājanaka-jātaka* from Wat Trairong Temple, Ban Non Chat, Khon Kaen province, Thailand. 8th–9th centuries. Sandstone. Height: 120 cm; width: 70 cm; depth: 20 cm.

with the elephant to the left, which is shown bowing down to the elephant on the right, as one of the queen consorts. However, there are numerous instances of elephants appearing as characters in *jātaka* tales, so this identification is far from certain.

One *sīmā* (Fig. 3.14) from Ban Phan Lam has a figure depicted on its lower half that may represent a bodhisattva. Alternatively, it could be Puṇṇaka, the *yakkha* General from the *Vidhurapaṇḍitajātaka*. The image is seated with one hand placed behind him and the other on his thigh. However, it is unclear if this is meant to represent him with his legs pendant (*bhadrāsana*) or in the *lalitāsana* posture common for

3.13

Buddhist Art in the Upper and Lower Chi River System

3.14

Figure 3.13: The episode of the Courting of Amarā from the *Mahāummagga-jātaka* on a *sīmā* from Kaset Sombun district, Chaiyaphum province, Thailand. 8th–9th centuries. Sandstone. Height: 117 cm; width: 61 cm; depth: 42 cm. Phimai National Museum, Thailand. Inventory number 39/12/2508.

Figure 3.14: *Sīmā* depicting a bodhisattva or possibly Puṇṇaka, the *yakkha* General from the *Vidhurapaṇḍitajātaka* in a pavilion at Ban Phan Lam, Chaiyaphum province, Thailand. 8th–9th centuries. Sandstone. Height: 215 cm; width: 42 cm; depth: 37 cm.

bodhisattvas. The figure does not appear to be wearing a Buddhist robe but instead is depicted with a short lower garment hanging from his waist.

Art Historical Analysis: *Dharmacakra* and *Stūpa* Motifs
Dharmacakra motifs are present on two *sīmā* from this cluster, one at Ban Phan Lam and one at Ban Bua Simama. The *sīmā* from Ban Bua Simama (Fig. 3.15) shows a *dharmacakra* in low relief, placed on top of what appears to be a stylised *stambha* and a socle, the latter depicted by three concentric rings. The wheel consists of eight diamond-like spokes reminiscent of flower petals radiating out from a circle in the centre.

3.15

3.16

The *dharmacakra* motif on the *sīmā* from Ban Phan Lam (Fig. 3.16) also appears to be mounted on a *stambha* and socle, or perhaps a *stūpa*. The spokes of the wheel are very similar to the example from Ban Bua Simama; however, there are 12 in total, packed closer together. Furthermore, there is a two-ringed circle in the middle, which is suggestive of the centre of a flower.

The only other example of a *dharmacakra* motif on a *sīmā* from the Khorat Plateau comes from the site of Ban Prakham in Buriram province in the Mun River system (Fig. 4.13). Further examples are also seen at Phnom Kulen in Cambodia. These are discussed in some detail in the next chapter (Figs. 4.13, 4.18–4.20).

The majority of remaining *sīmā* from this cluster are slab type in design and are either plain or depicted with an axial *stūpa* or *stūpa-kumbha* motif on either one or both sides.

Phu Wiang Mountaintop Site

Cluster 3 has one mountaintop site located in Chum Phae district at the southern end of what is today Phu Wiang National Park in the Phu Wiang Mountain range. It consists of a Buddha image in *mahāparinibbāna*, lying on its right side, approximately 3.70 metres long (Fig. 3.17). Its facial features bear all the salient characteristics of Dvāravatī art. Overall, this Buddha is depicted in a very similar fashion to the example from Phu Bor, suggesting a close connection between these two sites. There is a two-line inscription which, according to Kaeoklai (2001), is written in Pallava or

Figure 3.15: *Sīmā* with a *dharmacakra* motif from Wat Nong Sapung, Ban Bua Simama, Khon Kaen province, Thailand. 8th–9th centuries. Sandstone. Height: 140 cm; width: 53 cm; depth: 30 cm.

Figure 3.16: *Sīmā* depicting a *dharmacakra* motif from Ban Phan Lam, Chaiyaphum province, Thailand. 8th–9th centuries. Sandstone. Height: 207 cm; width: 36 cm; depth: 51 cm.

Figure 3.17: Detail of Buddha image carved into the rockface in *mahāparinibbāṇa* on the Phu Wiang Mountain range, Chaiyaphum province, Thailand. Late 8th–early 9th centuries.

post-Pallava script and dates paleographically to around the late 8th to early 9th century CE. It is located above the head of the Buddha. Kaeoklai (2001) has read and translated it into Thai. He proposes that it says "the people of the town have arrived to make merit". If this reading is correct, then the townspeople were presumably making offerings to the image. A further inscription from Chumpae (K. 985) mentions *puṇyakṣetra*, which George Cœdès suggested means a place of pilgrimage (cited in Woodward 2005: 109). Hiram Woodward (2005: 109) suggests that the location mentioned in the inscription is referring to the *mahāparinibbāṇa* Buddha image. If so, and it seems highly likely, then these two inscriptions give clear indication that this site functioned in part as a location for pilgrimage.

The site itself is approximately 400 metres above the surrounding plains and provides a commanding view of the landscape below. It is located a mere 7 kilometres or so northeast of Ban Non Muang and about 20 kilometres southeast of Ban Non Chat. Furthermore, the site of Ban Phai Hin lies at the other end of this mountain range while Ban Bua Simama is located 30 kilometres or so to the northeast. This Buddha image is ringed by these four sites and thus could have served any or all of these Buddhist communities. One of these sites is most likely the location referred to in the inscription above the Buddha image.

As suggested in the previous chapter, it appears that a tradition of making pilgrimage to *mahāparinibbāṇa* Buddha images arose during this time. The exact reasons and meanings for doing so are uncertain but it is clear that mountaintop locations such as this transformed features in the landscape into sacred sites. As Buddhism settled and flourished in this region, it reshaped the surrounding landscape, not just physically but potentially on a cognitive level too.

Summary

Cluster 3 represents evidence for the further spread of Buddhist art westwards along the tributaries of the Chi River system. While not possessing *sīmā* executed to the same artistic level as those in Cluster 1 and, to a lesser extent, Cluster 2, it does have other forms of important evidence. The evidence from inscriptions on *sīmā* and the *mahāparinibbāṇa* image illustrates that Buddhism was active in the area from the 8th to 9th centuries onwards. The two *dharmacakra* motifs from two separate sites indicate that this symbol was known and used in this area during this period. The tradition of carving *mahāparinibbāṇa* images into hill and mountainsides also speaks to a wider Buddhist tradition of pilgrimage that spread across the Khorat Plateau.

CLUSTER 4: THE LOWER CHI RIVER SYSTEM

Travelling downstream in a southeasterly direction from Muang Fa Daed brings one to Cluster 4 in the lower reaches of the Chi River system. This cluster is primarily located in the modern-day province of Yasothon, but also stretches into Roi Et, Ubon Ratchathani, and Amnat Chareon provinces (Map 9). The distribution analysis reveals that the majority of the 17 sites (Table 7) that make up this cluster are situated along a 30-kilometre stretch of the Chi River system, which starts around the modern-day town of Yasothon and continues southward. A number of other sites in this cluster are located along the Huai Phong River, a tributary that runs on a parallel course to the Chi River and joins the Mun River close to the modern-day city of Ubon Ratchathani. In addition to this, one site, Ban Pueai Huadong, is located on the Huai Se Bok River while another, Muang Samsip, is in close proximity to the Huai Chaevarnae River. In contrast to Clusters 1 to 3, the terrain here is flat with no mountain ranges or ridges in close proximity. The Chi River

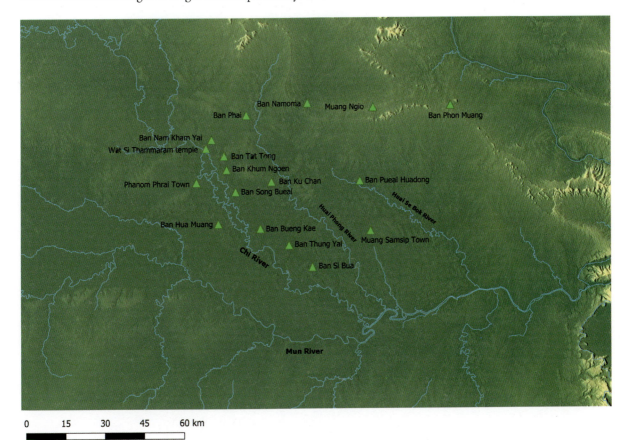

Map 9 Cluster 4.

Figure 3.18: *Sīmā* depicting the Aminisa Jetiya episode from the Life of the Buddha at Wat Bueng Khum Ngoen Temple, Ban Khum Ngoen, Yasothon province, Thailand. 8th–9th centuries. Sandstone. Height: 115 cm; width: 65 cm; depth: 36 cm.

meanders gently through this lowland landscape, frequently oxbowing through the swampy floodplain as it makes its way down to its confluence with the Mun River.

The art historical analysis reveals that this cluster is extremely homogenous in terms of the iconography and style of art depicted on *sīmā*. The most defining characteristic is the *stūpa-kumbha* motifs. While present in other areas of the Khorat Plateau, they are not found to the same extent or level of artistic execution as they are in Cluster 4. This leads to the conclusion that the *stūpa-kumbha* motif had particular relevance to the Buddhist communities of this area. Moreover, only one *sīmā* in the entire cluster depicts a narrative art scene.

Ban Tat Tong and Ban Khum Ngoen

Two sites in the cluster are closely associated with the *stūpa-kumbha* motif. One, Ban Tat Tong, is a moated site located approximately 10 kilometres southeast of the modern-day town of Yasothon. The other, Ban Khum Ngoen, is 5 kilometres to the southeast of Ban Tat Tong. Furthermore, there are 13 *sīmā* in the compound of Wat Si Thammaram Temple in Yasothon town, three of which are stylistically very close to those from Ban Tat Tong and Ban Khum Ngoen. Given Ban Tat Tong's proximity to Wat Si Thammaram Temple, they most likely came from this site.

Ban Tat Tong lies 6 kilometres due east of the Chi River. There are 26 *sīmā* at the site, the majority of which are decorated with *stūpa-kumbha* motifs. Add to this the 13 from Wat Si Thammaram Temple and that gives 39 in total – enough to represent a sizeable *saṅgha* module. The *sīmā* at Ban Tat Tong were found in the immediate vicinity of an earthen mound. Excavations indicate that it appears to have been inhabited from prehistoric times onwards. There are three phases of occupation. The first two periods show evidence of jar burials and were thus assigned to the prehistoric period. The final phase revealed stoneware and Lopburi ware.

Figure 3.19: *Sīmā* with a *stūpa-kumbha* motif at Wat Bueng Khum Ngoen Temple, Ban Khum Ngoen, Yasothon province, Thailand. 8th–9th centuries. Sandstone. Height: 112 cm; width: 56 cm; depth: 27 cm.

Figure 3.20: *Sīmā* with a *stūpa-kumbha* motif at Wat Bueng Khum Ngoen Temple, Ban Khum Ngoen, Yasothon province, Thailand. 8th–9th centuries. Sandstone. Height: 114 cm; width: 58 cm; depth: 38 cm.

Figure 3.21: *Sīmā* with a *stūpa-kumbha* motif at Wat Sri Thammaram Temple, Yasothon town, Yasothon province, Thailand. 8th–9th centuries. Sandstone. Height: 150 cm; width: 80 cm; depth: 25 cm.

Figure 3.22: *Sīmā* with a *stūpa-kumbha* motif and *dharmacakra* finial at Wat Sri Thammaram Temple, Yasothon town, Yasothon province, Thailand. 8th–9th centuries. Sandstone. Height: 140 cm; width: 90 cm; depth: 24 cm. Courtesy of River Books Bangkok.

Figure 3.23: *Sīmā* with a *stūpa-kumbha* motif and *dharmacakra* finial at Wat Bueng Khum Ngoen Temple, Ban Khum Ngoen, Yasothon province, Thailand. 8th–9th centuries. Sandstone. Height: 133 cm; width: 77 cm; depth: 30 cm.

We can thus infer that the site was occupied throughout the Dvāravatī and Lopburi periods (Dumrigon 2006: 33–45).

Ban Khum Ngoen is located about 7 kilometres east of the Chi River. There are 19 *sīmā* at the site today, most of which have been re-used to form a *sīmā* around the modern *ubosot* at Wat Bueng Khum Ngoen Temple. The majority of *sīmā* have *stūpa-kumbha* motifs. However, one has a scene from the Life of the Buddha (Fig 3.18). This *sīmā* depicts the Buddha standing with his arms folded. There is a tree and polygonal throne placed to his left. Kingmanee (2001: 73) has suggested that this scene represents the Aminisa Jetiya episode. This event took place in the second week after Enlightenment, when the Buddha stood and contemplated the Bodhi tree for seven days without blinking. Kingmanee points out that the *mudrā* in this particular *sīmā* is interesting, being found in a few instances only during this period. The *mudrā*, where both hands are placed crossed on the chest is usually interpreted as a gesture of respect. The presence of the tree and the posture of the Buddha, whose eyes do appear to be gazing at it, make Kingmanee's argument a compelling one and it is likely that this *sīmā* does represent the Aminisa Jetiya episode. If this were the case, it would represent the earliest example of this *mudrā* in Thailand, as it is more usually associated with Sri Lanka in this period.

Only one other *sīmā* depicts this *mudrā*. It is from Muang Fa Daed and today is kept in the Khon Kaen Museum which has identified the scene as Sujātā's gift. However, this is problematic as the gift in question, a bowl of milk-rice, is nowhere to be seen (Murphy 2010: Fig. 5.81).

A Lower Chi River Workshop

By considering the distribution analysis in tandem with what the art historical analysis is telling us, we can once again propose the location of a workshop. The uniformity of the *stūpa-kumbha* iconography from Ban Tat Tong and Ban Khum Ngoen is strongly suggestive that there was a school of artists at these sites. Being only 5 kilometres apart, it may be that all of the *sīmā* were originally from Ban Tat Tong, given that it is a moated site. Those found at Ban Khum Ngoen and Wat Si Thammaram Temple may have been moved there at a later date. Alternatively, the site of Ban Khum Ngoen may have been a satellite site of Ban Tat Tong.

Apart from the one example of narrative art, and the one example of a Buddha-*stūpa* motif (discussed below), this workshop produced a variety of well-executed *stūpa-kumbha* motifs that then seem to have spread out into the surrounding sites in the cluster and beyond in the 8th and 9th centuries. Here again we see the idea of symbolic entrainment at play. These *stūpa-kumbha* images were more elaborate than in most other areas of the Khorat Plateau, with the exception of Cluster 6. They consist of an elaborate base similar in design to an ornate metal stand. Above this, there is a band of lotus petals, usually three in number; however, sometimes the floral design is more elaborate than this (Figs. 3.19 and 3.20). On top of this sits the *kumbha,* and a number of different foliate designs can sprout forth from it. In some incidences a double band of lotus petals is shown above the *kumbha*. In a further variant, the ornamental base can be replaced by a *kumbha* motif. In this case, we have what we can term a "double-*kumbha*" motif (Fig. 3.21).

The *stūpa* section of the motif can at times be shown with rings, most likely representing the *chattravali* of actual *stūpa*. The *stūpa* finial can take either trident-like forms or be shown as a wheel with four spokes, which may represent the *dharmacakra* motif. Five *stūpa-kumbha* motifs from the cluster are depicted with these wheel-shaped finials, while another two are shown with wheel designs midway up the *stūpa* (Figs. 3.22 and 3.23). In all examples bar one, the spokes of the wheel are depicted as diamond petal shapes moving out from a circular flower-like design in the centre similar to the *dharmacakra* from Ban Bua Simama and Ban Phan Lam from Cluster 3 (discussed previously). Furthermore, in two examples, the outer ring is decorated with a band of circular bead-like motifs similar to certain *sīmā* on Phnom Kulen (Figs. 4.18 and 4.19).

3.21 3.22 3.23

Ban Pueai Huadong and Muang Ngio

Two further sites can also be considered as part of the *stūpa-kumbha* iconographic sub-group – Ban Pueai Huadong and Muang Ngio. In addition, these two latter sites also have examples of the *dharmacakra* finial. The *sīmā* from the rest of the sites in this cluster, on the other hand, do not have *stūpa-kumbha* motifs and are instead carved with the more common axial *stūpa* motif.

Ban Pueai Huadong is located about 50 kilometres east of Ban Khum Ngoen. There are 48 *sīmā* at the site, 12 of which are decorated with *stūpa-kumbha* motifs. One of these *sīmā*, now kept at the Ubon Ratchathani National Museum, shows a *stūpa* emerging from a *kumbha* in the standard manner. However, near the top, a smaller *kumbha* is shown flanked by two birds, an addition that is not found anywhere else on the Khorat Plateau (Murphy 2010: Fig. 5.148). On a further *sīmā* from the site (Murphy 2010: Fig. 5.147), the *kumbha* is placed on an ornate stand and a *dharmacakra* motif is shown not as a finial but is instead placed about three-quarters of the way up the *stūpa* motif. These two examples indicate a degree of artistic licence was present at this site.

A similar example to this latter *sīmā* is also found at the site of Muang Ngio and suggests clear connections between the two locations. There are nine *sīmā* at this site, some of which have been excavated and left in situ.

Interpreting the *Stūpa* Motif

Given the profusion of *stūpa-kumbha* and axial *stūpa* motifs in Cluster 4, it seems apt to explore the possible meanings these symbols could have had for the Buddhist community of this area and on the Khorat Plateau in general. As a monument, a *stūpa* functions primarily as a reliquary. However, it also plays a significant role in religious pilgrimage and worship. As an integral component of the Buddhist architectural canon – it is an essential structure of monasteries throughout ancient India and Southeast Asia – it functions as a Buddhist symbol par excellence. It exists in various forms and media throughout the Buddhist world. And while the *stūpa* as an architectural structure has a more delimited and restricted scope of meaning, the *stūpa* as a symbol is polysemic.

Some of the earliest proposed meanings of the *stūpa* as symbol are in reference to the Great Stūpa at Sanchi. Alfred Foucher (2003), for instance, argues that as the earliest forms of the Buddha image were aniconic and that the artists at Sanchi used specific symbols to depict certain stages in the Life of the Buddha. The pipal tree represented the Enlightenment, the *dharmacakra* represented the first sermon, and the *stūpa* represented the *parinibbāna* and so forth. Susan Huntington (1990), however, rejects this idea and argues that the *stūpa*, pipal tree, and *dharmacakra* are representations of pilgrimage sites alone. In response,

Vidya Dehejia (1991) argues along similar lines to Foucher, illustrating that the *stūpa* possesses multivalent qualities.[21] This view is expressed by the majority of scholars working on Buddhism and is perhaps best represented in the works of Adrian Snodgrass (1985), who viewed *stūpa* and Buddha images as symbols with a surplus of meaning. The *stūpa* thus serves as an aniconic representation of the Buddha and is an object of worship in and of itself. This can be seen, for instance, at the rock-cut caves at Nasik in Maharastra. A *stūpa* image is shown being worshipped, depicted in relief on a panel on the rear wall of Vihāra III in the Gautamiputra Cave (Huntington and Huntington 1985: 170). At Amarāvati, the *stūpa* and the Bodhi tree are both shown as objects of veneration, again pointing to the fact that they represent aniconic forms of the Buddha.

The evidence for aniconic worship of *stūpa* images in the great Buddhist centres such as Sanchi and Amarāvati casts light on the *stūpa-kumbha* image on *sīmā*. This image, so prevalent among the Buddhist communities of the lower Chi River in particular, may also have functioned in this manner. Phasook Indrawooth (1999: 234), for instance, argues that *stūpa* worship was prevalent among the Dvāravatī of Central Thailand and proposes that this was brought by the Apara-mahavinaseliya sect, who could have been present in U Thong as early as the 3rd or 4th centuries. There is no clear evidence for this claim, however. It is based on Indrawooth's assertion that much of the Buddhist art, architecture, and beliefs in Dvāravatī came from Nagarjunakonda, where the Apara-mahavinaseliya sect was based (Indrawooth 1999: 234– 5). This sect did not believe in the worship of Buddha images but instead paid homage to, and built, *stūpa*. If a sect of a similar nature was present on the Khorat Plateau during the period in question, it may help explain the preference for *stūpa* images as opposed to Buddha images. And one *sīmā* mentioned above (Fig. 3.8) shows a figure worshipping a *stūpa-kumbha* image. However, it is impossible to establish the presence of this sect as there is no firm epigraphic, archaeological, or historical evidence to do so. Furthermore, numerous *sīmā* are found carved with Buddha images too. This would argue against the widespread presence of the Apara-mahavinaseliya sect. However, it may be possible that the idea of *stūpa* worship as advocated by this sect reached the Khorat Plateau by the 7th to 8th centuries and in some areas, such as Cluster 4, took hold and led to the preference of representing the Buddha by aniconic means.

The concept of Buddha as *stūpa* has also been proposed at Bagan (Shorto 1971). Harry Shorto argues that the arrangement of the *jātaka*

---

21   For a succinct summary and commentary on this debate, see Thompson (2011).

plaques at the Ananda Temple and the absence of the Buddha from them imply that the monument should be viewed as representing the Enlightened One. Furthermore, by the 15th century the plinths of *stūpa* were being referred to as *vajrāsana* (the throne of the Buddha) and the levelling of the platform to receive this structure parallels the language used in Pāli texts to describe the land that levels itself under the Buddha's feet (Shorto 1971: 77). An interesting linguistic observation refers to the term *mahādhātu*, which in Burmese and in Thai means both relic and *stūpa*. This in turn unites the idea of the Buddha and the relic (Shorto 1971: 79). It appears that by the Bagan period in Myanmar, the equating of the Buddha and the *stūpa* was well understood.

Figure 3.24: *Sīmā* with a *stūpa*-Buddha motif at Wat Sri Thammaram Temple, Yasothon town, Yasothon province, Thailand. 8th–9th centuries. Sandstone. Height: 184 cm; width: 80 cm; depth: 34 cm.

Snodgrass's seminal work on the *stūpa* and its multiple layers of meaning also provides a reference point for the investigation of the *kumbha*'s symbolic significance. Architecturally, the *kumbha* can be equated with the dome of a *stūpa*, the hemispherical structure from which the spire ascends. Buddhist texts have consistently referred to this aspect of the *stūpa* as either the *garbha* (womb or container), or the *anda* (egg) (Snodgrass 1985: 189). The dome is at once a microcosmos and a macrocosmos as it symbolises both the innermost point of the universe and at the same time its outermost reaches. The dome as the egg or womb also contains the world in its a priori state, waiting to come into being. As Snodgrass (1985: 190) states, "Viewed from without, the stūpa-Egg or stūpa-Womb is the progenitive source of manifestation, the procreative point whence the worlds are born, the most inward and central spring whence all life flows."

If the dome does indeed signify the wellspring of all existence, then its representation as a *kumbha* is a logical development. The overflowing vegetal motifs and the rows of lotus petals depicted issuing forth from many of the *stūpa-kumbha* motifs on *sīmā* perfectly encapsulates this abundant fertility and latent potential for creation. This symbolism is further emphasised when we consider the signification of the *stūpa* rising from the *kumbha*. As discussed previously, Ashley Thompson has highlighted the gendered pairing represented in this configuration. If the *kumbha* as *anda* is the centre of the universe, then the *stūpa* rising out from the point of creation is the axis-mundi par excellence, forming order out of chaos and orientating the universe, a fixed point anchoring down forces that are constantly in flux.

Seen from this aspect, the finial depicted on a number of *stūpa-kumbha* motifs from Cluster 4 in particular, now take on a new dimension. The terminus of the axis-mundi is represented in two ways: one as a trident, the other as a wheel. The trident instantly brings to mind the image of Śiva, destroyer and creator of universes, a fitting symbolism to surmount the pillar of creation. It also calls to mind, the *liṅga* – the aniconic phallic representation of Śiva. That this is a predominantly Hindu image should not be seen as problematic as there is plentiful evidence that Buddhism and Hinduism existed alongside each other at this period, with the former frequently appropriating and absorbing symbols from the latter. See, for instance, the 7th-century stele from Vihear Thom, Kampong Cham province, Cambodia, today housed at the National Museum of Cambodia where the trident of Śiva emergences from a *kumbha* pot (Ka. 1741; see Guy 2014: 160–2). This configuration bears a striking resemblance to *stūpa-kumbha* motifs.[22]

---

22   I would like to thank Ashley Thompson for bringing this to my attention.

The wheel finial with its four spokes and at times radiating lines of light, calls to mind the *dharmacakra*, the moment when the Law of the Buddha, the dharma, was put in motion. This too conjures up images of beginnings, of new universes coming into existence, and as such is a fitting emblem to be placed on top of the *stūpa*. The axis-mundi, which brings order to the universe, does so by the light of Dharma, the Law of the Buddha.

Finally, amongst all this, we return to the point of origin, the symbol of the Buddha itself and the moment of Enlightenment. As Snodgrass (1985: 195) points out, early Buddhism saw the egg as a prison that cracked open to release the awakened being. Just as the *stūpa* is an aniconic representation of the Buddha, the *kumbha* upon which it sits represents the point of origin from which the Buddha, by way of Enlightenment, broke free.

From this perspective, it is possible to propose a unified layer of symbolic meaning – the *stūpa-kumbha* motif as a representation of the Buddha. In depicting this motif, the Buddhist faithful were in effect worshipping the Buddha in all his aspects and meanings. This realisation materialises itself artistically in a *sīmā* from Wat Si Thammaram Temple, where the *stūpa-kumbha* motif is replaced by a *stūpa*-Buddha motif (Fig. 3.24). The Buddha is depicted seated cross-legged in meditation, with the spire of the *stūpa* with its numerous concentric circles, representing *chattravali*, rising from above his head. Vegetation and floral motifs flanking the Buddha may represent the Bodhi tree. In this *sīmā* the multiple layers of meaning coalesce, capturing in stone the impermanence and ephemeral nature of all things.

Like the image of the *stūpa* itself, the *stūpa-kumbha* motif represented on *sīmā* throughout the Khorat Plateau is possessed with a surplus of symbolism, a multivalence of meanings, with each component of the motif adding another layer and texture to the overall whole. In the most complete sense, the *stūpa-kumbha* represents the Buddha and all that his teachings encapsulate. In another aspect, the motif represents creation itself, from which arises the axis-mundi, the cosmic pillar. Whether the Buddhist communities who worshipped this image on *sīmā* saw in it all these layers are uncertain. However, we can say that in depicting this motif, they most probably saw it as an encapsulation of the Buddha and all he represented, and in this sense, they were carrying on the aniconic traditions of their Indian predecessors. This is further emphasised by the fact that they consciously chose to depict the *stūpa-kumbha* motif as opposed to an image of the Buddha. As evidence from other sites in the Khorat Plateau shows, if they had wished, they could have quite easily depicted a Buddha image.

The iconographic meaning of the axial *stūpa* can be unlocked when compared with that of the *stūpa-kumbha*. It too simultaneously represented the image of the axis-mundi as *stūpa*, the *stūpa* as the Buddha, and the Buddha as dharma. The Buddhist communities saw the *stūpa-kumbha* and axial *stūpa* motif as aniconic forms of the Buddha. However, as symbols have multiple layers of meaning, they may have subliminally seen much more in this image. The *kumbha* with its latent images of fertility may have spoken to them of the creation of universes and the reality of the Buddha's Enlightenment, while the *dharmacakra* finials would have touched on an innate human need to find order in the chaos of the cosmos.

Summary

Cluster 4 represents an extremely homogenous group in terms of its iconographic characteristics. Located along the lower part of the Chi River system close to the confluence with the Mun River, this cluster developed its own expression of the *sīmā* tradition and chose to depict *stūpa-kumbha* motifs as opposed to narrative art. The highly accomplished narrative scene from Ban Khum Ngoen further illustrates this point, evidencing that even though the artists of this area were well able to depict scenes such as the Life of the Buddha, they chose instead to embellish their *sīmā* differently. The profusion of *stūpa-kumbha* motifs in this region may reflect certain differences in the belief structure of the Buddhism present in this cluster or could perhaps reflect an urge to develop certain interregional identities vis-à-vis their counterparts further north along the Chi River system.

AN OVERVIEW OF BUDDHIST ART IN THE CHI RIVER

This chapter has charted the spread of Buddhist art into the upper and lower reaches of the Chi River system during the 7th to 11th centuries. While there is a profusion of sites within these clusters, the evidence for Buddhist art comes primarily from *sīmā*. There are no extant architectural remains surviving and very few examples of freestanding Buddha images. The art on the *sīmā* is also more restricted than in Cluster 1. There is limited narrative art and where it does occur, it is of lesser quality to that which we find at Muang Fa Daed. Instead, we see the predominance of the *stūpa-kumbha* motif. Inscriptional and stylistic evidence dates the majority of *sīmā* and Buddha images to the 8th to 9th centuries, though there are some examples that fall into the 10th to 11th centuries. This is consistent with evidence from the other areas of the Khorat Plateau discussed in this book.

The analysis of Clusters 2 to 4 also points towards the primacy of Cluster 1/Muang Fa Daed mandala in regard to the Chi River system. Located at the midpoint of this river system, there appears to have been an important Buddhist centre at Muang Fa Daed. The religion most likely spread westwards from here to Clusters 2 and 3 and southeastwards to Cluster 4 in the form of self-replicating modules of the *sangha*. However, the latter cluster, in particular, seems to have developed its own particular style and iconography, manifested in the *stūpa-kumbha* motif. Clusters 2 and 3, on the other hand, seem to have largely drawn on the art and iconography emanating from Muang Fa Daed.

Overall, it can be concluded that the Chi River system was the most prominent region in the Khorat Plateau regarding the *sīmā* tradition and the spread of Buddhist art in general. It has the highest proportion of both sites and *sīmā*, and exhibits the finest examples of carved *sīmā* in terms of artistic, iconographic, and aesthetic qualities. This and the previous chapter have shed light on the distribution of Buddhist art throughout the region. They have shown the extent to which it was present in the Chi River system in the 8th and 9th centuries and that Buddhism primarily spread along it and its tributaries. The religion developed in these lowland, alluvial plains where it took deep root and has continued to flourish to this day.

Chapter 4

THE MUN RIVER SYSTEM: ŚRĪ CANĀŚA AND BUDDHIST ART IN THE LOWER KHORAT PLATEAU

This chapter moves the focus southwards to the Mun River system. Here we encounter a number of overlapping spheres of influence – Dvāravatī in Central Thailand, Muang Sema in the upper western reaches of the Mun, and Khmer presence moving across the Dang Raek Mountain ranges from the south. All play a role in how far and wide Buddhist art circulates and

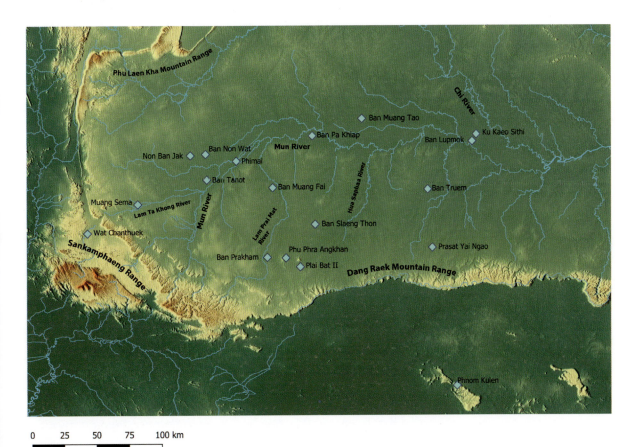

Map 10 Cluster 5: The Mun River system.

expresses itself. Muang Sema is strategically placed at the gateway to the Khorat Plateau and is the closest major settlement in the region to Central Thailand. As such, it shows strong affinities with certain aspects of Dvāravatī art and culture whilst maintaining its own identity, possibly as the centre of the kingdom of Śri Canāśa (Map 15). Further east along the Mun, we begin to encounter monumental bronze bodhisattva images, a phenomenon not seen in the Chi and Middle Mekong areas of the plateau. The Ban Tanod bodhisattva and the Prakhon Chai/Plai Bat II hoard all point to a sophisticated sculptural tradition in the Mun River. Is this, too, connected with the kingdom of Śri Canāśa? Possibly. And finally, what are we to make of two groups of *sīmā* on Phnom Kulen? Who facilitated their installation and who carved the stones? Is it possible that they received patronage or at the very least permission from King Jayavarman II (r. 802–850 CE) to do so? This chapter sets out to explore these questions through the rich and complex tapestry of evidence dispersed across this riverine and mountainous landscape.

From its source in the vicinity of Khao Khieo Mountain in the Sankamphaeng Range, the Mun River system winds its way eastwards across the entire breath of the southern part of the Khorat Plateau. Numerous tributaries originating in the Sankamphaeng and Dang Raek ranges to its south flow into it along its course. The terrain of the Mun River is high in the west and gradually becomes lower as it flows eastwards. Present-day conditions show significant seasonal differences with the monsoon causing distinct flood and non-flood seasons (Tian H, Yu GA, Tong L, et al. 2019). The Chi River is the largest tributary of the Mun, which in turn is the largest tributary of the Mekong River. The Mun was thus connected to two major waterways at its eastern end. Meanwhile, its western section was located close to the pass which gave access to Central Thailand.

The Mun River system was thus a key conduit for travel between Central Thailand, the Khorat Plateau, and the Mekong at its eastern end. It is along this river system that Buddhism spread into the southern part of the Khorat Plateau. However, the Mun River exhibits less evidence overall for Buddhist art than the Chi or Mekong. That being said, as the distribution analysis of the 18 sites designated as Cluster 5 illustrate, the religion had firmly established itself at a number of key locations in this region (Map 10; Table 8). These sites are closely tied to, and to a large extent, are dependent on the Mun River system and its tributaries. Apart from the sites of Ban Lupmok and Ku Kaeo Sithi in Si Sa Ket province, and Ban Truem and Prasat Yai Ngao in Surin province, the majority of sites are either in Buriram or Nakhon Ratchasima provinces (Maps 2, 10). Sites in this region are located further apart than those found in the Chi River system. The *sīmā* tradition is also much less prevalent in this river system than in the rest of the Khorat Plateau. From the 7th century onwards, much of the region to the south of the Mun River came under the sphere of Zhenla (Map 15), the capital of which was located at Īśānapura (modern-day Sambor Prei Kuk) in Central Cambodia.[23] Its first king, Citrasena-Mahendravarman (c. 550–611? CE), was known to have expanded his reach into the southern Khorat Plateau and installed a number of *liṅga* to stake his territorial claims (Dupont 1955: 56–7, 119–21; Lavy 2003: 26–7). This conquest was continued by his son and successor, King Īśānavarman I (616–637 CE) (Siribhadra and Moore 1992: 25), and the 8th-century brick-built temple of Prasat Phum Pon in Surin province is a tangible reminder of Zhenla's reach. However, as Michael Vickery has pointed out, these kings most likely never exerted direct control over the southern part of the Khorat Plateau. Instead, he sees the inscriptions set up as "records of exploratory probes rather than enduring conquests" (1994: 203).

Consequently, unlike in the Chi and Middle Mekong regions, Buddhism in the Mun River system had to compete much more directly with the Śaivism and Vaiṣṇavism practiced in Zhenla. That being said, the somewhat entrenched viewpoint in much scholarship on Southeast Asia that Buddhism and Hinduism could not mutually co-exist, is misleading (Revire 2016). In Central Thailand, for example, even though Buddhism was the more prevalent religion, there is evidence that Hinduism was also practised at numerous sites – U Thong, Si Thep, and Nakhon Pathom being three such locations (Revire 2016: 405–8). And as Johannes Bronkhorst (2011: 57–8) reminds us, assigning Brahmanism to the category of a religion is problematic: "In reality, Brahmanism represents primarily a social order. Only in this way can we make sense of the evidence from Southeast Asia, as well as of the evidence from South Asia." The evidence from Zhenla indicates that Śaivism, and to a lesser extent Vaiṣṇavism, dominated. However, Buddhism is still present to a limited degree. Furthermore, it is well known from South Asian contexts that kings such as the Ikṣvāku or Gupta Vākāṭaka dynasties could sponsor Buddhism, Śaivism, and/or Vaiṣṇavism. And as will be discussed below, Buddhism did make inroads into the heart of the Khmer lands, albeit briefly, as evidenced by the *sīmā* from Phnom Kulen.

The Khmer presence in the Mun River grew over time. By the 10th century, sites such as Muang Sema have clear evidence of Khmer occupation. This presence takes its most tangible form in the site of Phimai, Nakhon Ratchasima province. This 11th- to 12th-century temple conforms to standard Angkorian architectural norms. However, it was

---

23 It should be noted that the name Zhenla (also transcribed as Chenla) is derived from Chinese sources. This name, unlike Dvāravatī, has yet to be discovered in either the epigraphic record of Cambodia or Thailand. See Revire (2016: 396).

Buddhist in its religious persuasion, showing that the Khmer too followed Buddhism at certain times and places. This is perhaps unsurprising, given the religion's established presence on the Khorat Plateau.

The Mun River system also possesses several important findspots of bronze sculpture. The Prakhon Chai/Plai Bat II hoard from Buriram province is the most extensive and (in)famous. These spectacular bronzes represent a fusion between Khmer and Dvāravatī styles. It is likely that they were produced locally. The site of Ban Muang Fai in Buriram province, for example, may have been the location of a workshop for Buddhist sculpture, while the site of Ban Tanot in Nakhon Ratchasima province is the findspot for one of the largest and most impressive bronzes ever found in Thailand.

In comparison to the Chi River system, there is a marked absence of Buddhist narrative art from this region. Instead, the art consists of motifs such as *stūpa-kumbha*, axial *stūpa,* and *dharmacakra* motifs. The largest site in the Mun River system is Muang Sema in Nakhon Ratchasima province. It has the most numerous extant architectural remains of any site, as well as an 11-metre-long Buddha image in *mahāparinibbāna* posture (Fig. 4.3).

Buddhism would have spread along the Mun River system, particularly at the moated settlements located along its course. The Lam Ta Khong River, which merges with the Mun near modern-day Nakhon Ratchasima, may also have formed a vital communication route to Central Thailand. The site of Muang Sema was positioned on its course, affording it strategic control of the access to and from the Khorat Plateau. This site has the most evidence for Buddhist art and architectural remains in the Mun region and as a result, is the likely springboard from which this religion could have spread throughout the lower part of the Khorat Plateau and the Mun River system in particular.

MUANG SEMA AND ITS RELATED SITES: CENTRE OF THE ŚRI CANĀŚA MANDALA?

Muang Sema is a large moated site located on the Lam Ta Khong River, a tributary of the Mun River system, in Sung Noen district, Nakhon Ratchasima province. It covers an area of over 150 hectares (Moore 1988: 9) and shows ample evidence for the adoption of Buddhism. Perhaps the most impressive archaeological feature from this site is the 11-metre-long sandstone Buddha image lying in *mahāparinibbāna* posture (Fig. 4.3). A *dharmacakra* was also found in close vicinity to the Buddha image.

The distribution analysis indicates that Muang Sema appears to have held sway over a number of other sites in this region. Epigraphic evidence suggests it may have been the location of a kingdom known as Śri Canāśa/

The Mun River System: Śrī Canāśa and Buddhist Art in the Lower Khorat Plateau

Śrī Cānāśapura. Three inscriptions have been discovered to date which name this kingdom. The *New Tang Annals* (*Xin Tang Shu*) composed in the Song Dynasty also appear to mention it. Tatsuo Hoshino (2002: 27–8) proposes that the entity referred to as Jia Luo She Fu/Ge Luo She Fen corresponds to Śrī Canāśa, as this state was said to border Dvāravatī to its south and east. However, the reference to an eastern border does not appear to fit (Map 15). That being said, the accuracy of these accounts lacks a certain geographically precision. The description of Dvāravatī being located along Jia Luo She Fu's southern border does to a certain extent match the archaeological evidence.

This chapter proceeds to discuss the site of Muang Sema before exploring this possible location of Śrī Canāśa in greater depth. The site has been divided into three phases of occupation (Wangsuk 2000: iv). The earliest phase dates from the 4th to 5th centuries and can be considered a proto-Dvāravatī phase (Murphy 2016: 389–90). The second phase dates from the 6th to 9th centuries and represents the period in which Buddhist art and architecture appears and develops at the site. Phase three, from the 9th to 12th centuries shows evidence of growing Khmer presence, as indicated by the discovery of Buriram ceramics. Chinese Song Dynasty ware was also present, illustrating the site's connections to international trade routes during this period.

The site originally consisted of one moat, with the archaeological record showing that this phase dated to the 6th to 9th centuries. A second

Figure 4.1: Detail of fired brick *stūpa* "Monument 9" at Muang Sema, Sung Noen district, Nakhon Ratchasima province, Thailand. 8th–9th centuries.

Figure 4.2: Detail of the fired brick hemispherical threshold of the entrance to "Monument 4" at Muang Sema, Sung Noen district, Nakhon Ratchasima province, Thailand. 8th–9th centuries.

moat was added during the third phase when a Khmer temple was built at the centre of the settlement, the new external moat greatly increasing the area of the settlement (Wangsuk 2000: 33–126).

Excavations carried out by the Fine Arts Department of Thailand and the National Museum in 1980 focused on the area surrounding the *mahāparinibbāṇa* Buddha image. This is situated some 500 metres outside of the moat (Wangsuk 2000: 42–3). The excavations revealed foundations of a large building, 6.50 metres wide by 26 metres long. This building housed the Buddha image and appears to be an assembly hall. It is a two-roomed structure – the main room holds the Buddha image and a small room at one end most likely functioned as an antechamber.

Excavations in 1999 focused on nine monuments, seven of which were located within the moat, and two (Monuments 8 and 9) outside, at the northern end of the moat. Five of the interior monuments turned out to be small Dvāravatī-period *stūpa*, either four-sided or eight-sided in design, ranging from 6.12 by 6.40 metres to 6.70 by 10.90 metres in size. Monuments 8 and 9 also appear to be small *stūpa* (Fig. 4.1).

Monument 1 is the largest structure at the site and is situated roughly in the centre of the settlement. It measures 45 by 50 metres and has an entrance facing south and has been identified by Wangsuk as an assembly hall (2000: 44–6). Given its ground plan, this may be the case, but the surviving archaeological evidence is not sufficient to say so with any certainty. Monument 4, which measures 8.25 by 13.50 metres, was also identified by Khemica Wangsuk (2000: 45) as an assembly hall, again due

4.2

The Mun River System: Śrī Canāśa and Buddhist Art in the Lower Khorat Plateau

to its ground plan. However, she also notes that it is surrounded by *sīmā*. As *sīmā* can also demarcate an ordination hall, this building could also have fulfilled this function (Fig. 4.2).

The seven monuments located within the moat lie in close proximity to each other, none being further than 100 metres apart. The presence of two buildings, along with numerous *stūpa* located close to the centre of the site, illustrates that there was most likely a monastery situated in the centre of Muang Sema. Population estimates for Muang Sema put it at around 7,500 inhabitants, which in turn could support a monastic community of around 75 monks or perhaps more (Murphy 2015: 94). This is thus a sizable Buddhist presence, which is borne out by the archaeological remains at the site. For instance, the Buddha image in *mahāparinibbāṇa* is a remarkable piece of sculpture for this period, both in terms of its size and artistic execution (Fig. 4.3). The image has been fashioned out of at least seven separate sandstone blocks. These were placed on a base of stone blocks which have been built up on top of each other to form a core around which the Buddha image was constructed. The head of the Buddha image is made up of four separate stone slabs carved to create the characteristic Dvāravatī-style face and hair curls. Despite its somewhat fragmentary state, the arched eyebrows, oval-shaped eyes, and full lips can still be made out quite clearly. The head lies on the right arm, with the right hand tucked underneath and reappearing at the rear of the composition. This image immediately recalls the one at Phu Wiang (Fig. 3.17) and at Phu Bor (Fig. 2.25), the two other known

Figure 4.3: *Mahāparinibbāṇa* Buddha image at Muang Sema, Sung Noen district, Nakhon Ratchasima province, Thailand. 8th–9th centuries. Sandstone. Approximately 11 metres in length.

Figure 4.4: The Bo Ika inscription dating to 868 CE (K. 400). Sandstone. Height: 144 cm; width: 65 cm; depth: 27 cm. Phimai National Museum. Inventory number 39/89/2507.

examples on the Khorat Plateau from this period, both of which are located in the Chi River system. However, unlike the Muang Sema example, they are not executed in the round but are instead carved in relief into rockfaces on hillsides. Did the Muang Sema example act as inspiration for these images? Perhaps, and if so, this would be another example of symbolic entrainment taking place. However, we do not have the chronological precision to establish this. That being said, the iconographic message embedded in the Buddha in *mahāparinibbāna* must have also resonated amongst Buddhists from this site too.

Further evidence for the flourishing Buddhist artistic culture of Muang Sema can be seen in artefacts such as a *dharmacakra*, which was

found along with its pillar (*stambha*) and a possible base. This is one of the very few examples of a free-standing *dharmacakra* to be found outside of Central Thailand and indicates the close ties Muang Sema must have had with this region.

The evidence outlined above indicates that Muang Sema was a thriving settlement in the 7th to 9th centuries. It is possible that its ancient name was Śri Canāśa/Śrī Cānāśapura and/or that it was the centre of a kingdom of the same name (Hanwong 1991: 60). This can be inferred from three inscriptions, the most significant of which is the Bo Ika inscription (K. 400) found at Muang Sema dating to 868 CE (Fig. 4.4). More recently, archaeological evidence has been brought to bear on this issue with Charles Higham et al. (2020) arguing that there was a rapid transition from late Iron Age (500–600 CE) settlement types, as exemplified by Ban Non Wat and Non Ban Jak, to large regional centres such as Muang Sema, which they too identify as the location of Śri Canāśa (2020: 75–9).

On face A of the the Bo Ika inscription, it records in Sanskrit the donation of 20 water buffaloes, 50 cows and healthy calves, and 10 male and female slaves to the *sangha* from the glorious lord of Śri Canāśa to gain merit (Cœdès 1954: 83–5). We can assume that this community was based at a Buddhist monastery located at Muang Sema.

Face B of this inscription is an invocation to Śiva as supreme deity. It records the good deeds of a certain Amsadeva who installed a golden *linga*. Śri Canāśa meanwhile is also mentioned in an inscription found at Hin Khon (NM 31/ K. 389), 55 kilometres south of Nakhon Ratchasima. The inscription is in Sanskrit and has been dated on paleographic grounds to the 9th century. Hiram Woodward, however, disputes this and says it may date to the 7th century (2005: 100). The third piece of epigraphic evidence comes from an inscription found at Ayutthaya (K. 949). It dates to 937 CE and mentions a line of princes of Cānāśapura (Cœdès 1968: 122; 1996). How or why an inscription of this nature should turn up at Ayutthaya is uncertain. However, Peter Skilling (2020: 81) speculates that it may have been taken there during one of Ayutthaya's military campaigns into the region.

Two other inscriptions cast further light on the religious and political milieu of Muang Sema. The first, K. 1155 from Ban Phan Dung in Nakhon Ratchasima dating to 796 CE, evokes Śiva and records the installation of a Harihara and a Viṣṇu image and the offering of gifts (Kaeoklai 1987). As Nicloas Revire (2016: 413) notes, this is the earliest reference to Harihara in Thailand, though this god was popular in Zhenla at this period. The inscription then goes on to record the installation of a Buddha image in 825 CE. As with the Bo Ika inscription above, K. 1155 records both Hindu and Buddhist patronage.

A further but somewhat later inscription also follows this trend. Found nearby Muang Sema, K. 1141 is in Sanskrit and dates to 892 *śaka*

Figure 4.5: The head of a bodhisattva image found at Ban Tanot, Non Sung subdistrict, Nakhon Ratchasima province. 8th–9th centuries. Bronze. Height: 73 cm; width: 33 cm. National Museum Bangkok. Inventory number 01/684/2565.

or 970 CE (Estève 2009: 309–24). It mentions the deterioration of a Harihara image, which Revire (2016: 413–4) proposes is the same as that mentioned in K. 1155. Furthermore, it records the installation of a great *Śiva-liṅga* 131 years previously in 761 *śaka* or 839 CE, which was later reconsecrated by a provincial governor during the time of Jayavarman V (r. c. 968–1001 CE), along with an image of the Buddha through the "eye opening" ceremony (Estève 2009: 320–2).

These inscriptions show that Buddhist and Hindu images were installed before and after each other. They indicate that both religions co-existed at Muang Sema. The rulers of Śri Canāśa were thus engaged in similar practices as their counterparts in Central Thailand. The Hindu images most likely reflect their use in royal ideology, as rulers often styled themselves as avatars of Viṣṇu. The installation of a *liṅga* was also seen to be as much of a political statement as a religious one. All this being said, the overall corpus of archaeological remains from the site and surrounding area is predominantly Buddhist, suggesting that this religion was in the ascendency to a large degree.

Satellite Sites: Ban Tanot, Non Ban Jak, and Wat Chanthuek
The distribution analysis reveals three sites located within a 50-kilometre radius of Muang Sema that were most likely under its direct control, providing further evidence for its prominence in this region.

Ban Tanot is a modern village in Non Sung subdistrict, Nakhon Ratchasima province. It is located 50 kilometres northeast of Muang Sema. The 16 *sīmā* discovered at this site indicate that a *saṅgha* module must have been present here at some point. However, the site is best known as the findspot for a spectacular fragmentary bronze bodhisattva, now kept in the National Museum Bangkok (Fig. 4.5). This took place in 1961 when building work accidentally uncovered a brick *stūpa*, some votive tablets, and the aforementioned bronze sculpture (Boisselier 1967: 284–5). It is uncertain whether this bronze was originally produced at this site. However, as Jean Boisselier (1967: 284) notes, its large size would have made it difficult to transport.

Today only the head, three forearms, the right leg, and left foot remain. If other parts of the body also survived, they were not collected. Judging by the size of the head and the leg alone, the original image must have stood over 2 metres tall.[24] The head was sent to the Laboratoire de Recherche archéologique de Nancy, in France for restoration (Boisselier 1967: 285). It has the characteristic moustache, arched eyebrows, and

---

24   This sculpture has recently been reconstructed by the National Museum Bangkok and put back on display. It now stands at over 2 metres tall. The missing aspects such as the torso and certain parts of the limbs were modelled on the Ban Fai bodhisattva (Fig. 4.10).

jaṭāmukuṭa of a bodhisattva. Unfortunately, the central section of the *jaṭāmukuṭa* is missing (Boisselier 1967: Fig. 10), thus it is not possible to ascertain whether this bodhisattva represents Avalokiteśvara – identifiable by the Buddha Amitabha in his headdress – or Maitreya, identifiable by a *stūpa* in the headdress.

As can be discerned from the position of the legs, this sculpture was designed to stand upright, and with three surviving forearms, it is safe to assume it was a four-armed image. It appears to have been largely unattired, and likely represented the bodhisattva in an ascetic fashion. This mode of representation is the norm in the Khorat Plateau for large- and small-scale bronze bodhisattva figures. It can be seen in the Maitreya figure from Ban Muang Fai and numerous other examples from the Prakhon Chai/Plai Bat II hoard discussed below. On stylistic grounds this image dates to the 8th to 9th centuries and belongs to the larger corpus of the Khorat Plateau bronze tradition.

The site of Non Ban Jak is located 11 kilometres northwest of Ban Tanot. It is a medium-sized moated settlement, 360 metres in length and 170 metres wide. The total area of the site including the moats is 15 hectares. Excavations carried out to date have revealed an occupation sequence spanning the late Iron Age (400 CE) to about 800 CE (Higham et al. 2014). The only evidence for Buddhism discovered thus far at the site comes from a fragmentary miniature terracotta Buddha image about 7 centimetres high, seated in meditation. It is unfortunately missing its head (Ball 2019: Fig. 51). This find, the Dvāravatī-style pottery, and the proximity of the site to Ban Tanot strongly suggest that they were part of the same cultural, social, economic, and political milieu.

A detailed analysis of the ceramic assemblage undertaken by Helen Ball (2019) indicates that the populace fused local Iron Age pottery with incoming elements of Dvāravatī technology and style. This indicates that the population at the terminal Iron Age, proto-Dvāravatī, and Dvāravatī period proper had cultural contact with Dvāravatī in Central Thailand and gradually adopted and adapted the incoming technologies and styles as they saw fit (Ball 2019: 78–81). Ball proposes that this local pottery tradition be named "Mun River Dvāravatī Earthenware" to reflect this.

The cultural contact and new incoming technologies at Non Ban Jak may not have come directly from Central Thailand. They may have instead come via Muang Sema, given its position as the political and economic centre. This relationship would be consistent with the processes of symbolic entrainment. Further research and detailed comparisons between the ceramic assemblages of these two sites could prove fruitful in indicating if this is the case.[25]

---

25   At the time of publication, Helen Ball was undertaking PhD research that will

The site of Ban Non Wat lies in close proximity to the two aforementioned sites. It is 3 kilometres east of Non Ban Jak and about 11 kilometres northeast of Ban Tanot. Ban Non Wat is one of the most extensively excavated and studied prehistoric sites in Thailand, or anywhere in Southeast Asia for that matter. Its occupation spans the Neolithic to the proto-historic periods or 1750 BCE to the 5th century CE (Higham and Higham 2009). As such, its occupation ends a century or two before clear evidence for Buddhism in the region emerges. However, historic pottery discovered at the site has yet to be studied in detail (Ball 2019: 8). Its analysis may provide evidence for Dvāravatī-period occupation. Either way, the site indicates that this region of the Mun River system has a deep and rich history of occupation.

Ban Tanot, Non Ban Jak, and to a lesser extent, Ban Non Wat are three hinterland sites to the east of Muang Sema that appear to have come directly under its orbit. As mentioned previously, this conclusion has also been arrived at by Higham et al. (2020) in their analysis of the archaeological data from the latter two sites.

Looking west, there is one more site to consider. The site of Wat Chanthuek is based around Wat Chanthuek Temple in Chanthuek subdistrict, Pak Chong district, Nakhon Ratchasima province. It is located about 30 kilometres west of Muang Sema. An inscription (known as the Wat Chanthuek inscription) and fragments of four large stone Dvāravatī-style Buddha images were discovered in the temple grounds (Skilling 2020: 66, Figs. 1–9). The inscription is on a large red sandstone base and is now kept at the Phimai National Museum. It has a large open square at its centre designed to receive the tenon of a Buddha image. The statue, however, has never been located. The inscription is in Sanskrit language in Pallava script. There is agreement among the scholars who have read it that it dates to between the mid 6th to mid 7th centuries (Skilling 2020: 67). While the inscription is incomplete, Skilling (2020: 67) has proposed the following reading:

> *x x x x x -tava / sutā dvāravatī pateḥ /*
> *mūrttim asthāpayad devī / [śail]īn tāthāgatīm imām ||*
> ... daughter of the Lord of Dvāravatī ... the queen
> set up this [stone] image of the Tathagata.

Skilling interprets this to mean that the daughter of the lord of Dvāravatī married the ruler of a polity located in or near Wat Chanthuek, thus becoming queen. If this is the case, it may represent a marriage alliance between the kingdom of Śri Canāśa based at Muang Sema and that of Dvāravatī in Central Thailand. If so, it begs the question as to which

---

hopefully shed more light on these connections.

4.6

location the queen came from? Geographically, Lopburi would be the closest large-scale site, though Si Thep is also another contender. Or did she travel from U Thong or Nakhon Pathom to give her hand in marriage to seal an alliance between the lords of Central Thailand (Dvāravatī) and the Mun River (Śrī Canāśa) respectively?

Apart from the material discussed above, no evidence has come to light to date for a settlement at Wat Chanthuek. However, as it is located about 30 kilometres west of Muang Sema and is strategically placed along the pass that leads from the Khorat Plateau to Central Thailand, this would be an obvious spot to mark the extent of one's domain. Was this Buddha image with its inscription set up here to indicate that one was now entering the realm of Śrī Canāśa, the capital of which lay a day's march further to the east at Muang Sema? Unfortunately, we can only speculate

Figure 4.6: Seated Buddha image from Ban Muang Fai, Lam Plai Mat district, Buriram province, Thailand. 8th century. Sandstone. Height: 84 cm: width: 52 cm; depth: 25 cm. National Museum Bangkok. Inventory number 63/2510. Courtesy of Thierry Ollivier.

Figure 4.7: Seated Buddha image (headless), exact provenance unknown. 8th century. Sandstone. Height: 66 cm; width: 52 cm. Phimai National Museum. Inventory number 39/1/2536.

due to the paucity of both the epigraphic and archaeological record from both these regions. However, at the very least it tells us that there was a marriage alliance of some form between Central Thailand and a polity in the vicinity of Wat Chanthuek.

Taken as a whole, the material, architectural, and epigraphic evidence from Muang Sema and the sites in its vicinity indicate that it was the most important religious and political centre in the Mun River system from the 7th to 10th centuries. And while the evidence is not conclusive, it points to it being the prime candidate for the location of Śri Canāśa. Furthermore, the Bo Ika inscription shows the close relationship established between the *sangha* and the lay community. The resources needed to construct the Buddhist architecture and the *mahāparinibbāṇa* Buddha image would have called for substantial donations and patronage from the settlement's ruling elite and laity alike. This in turn indicates the wealth and resources available to this polity.

BUDDHISM ALONG THE CENTRAL AND EASTERN REACHES OF THE MUN RIVER SYSTEM

Archaeological and art historic evidence indicates that Buddhism also spread along the central and eastern sections of the Mun River system. And while there are no sites of the same size and scope as Muang Sema, some significant discoveries have been made. This section provides an overview of the key sites and evidence.

Ban Muang Fai

The moated site of Ban Muang Fai is located in Lam Plai Mat district, Buriram province. It is the source of some of the finest art ever discovered from the Khorat Plateau. This comes in the form of three stone Buddha images, two bronze bodhisattvas, and one bronze Buddha image. Despite this, the site has received very little attention in terms of archaeological excavations or research in general.

The most well-published image from this site is a seated Buddha in *bhūmisparśamudrā*, today housed at the National Museum Bangkok (Fig. 4.6). It is a perfect blend of Dvāravatī and Khmer styles, the former seen in the bow-shaped, connected eyebrows, the latter visible in the gentle smile and shape of the lips. It is one of the best examples of the Khorat Plateau aesthetic. An almost identical image is today housed in the Phimai National Museum (Fig. 4.7). Unfortunately, this latter piece is missing its head and its exact provenance is unknown. However, given the striking similarities, it must have come from the same site or at the very least, the same workshop or even artist. The postures of both are identical and the folds of the robe that fall over the left shoulder end in the exact same

The Mun River System: Śrī Canāśa and Buddhist Art in the Lower Khorat Plateau

Figure 4.8: Standing Buddha image possibly in double *vitarkamudrā* (right hand is missing) from Ban Muang Fai, Lam Plai Mat district, Buriram province, Thailand. 7th–8th centuries. Sandstone. Height: 115 cm; width: 34 cm; depth: 17 cm. National Museum Bangkok. Inventory number 323/2520. Courtesy of Thierry Ollivier.

Figure 4.9: Standing Buddha image in double *vitarkamudrā* from Ban Muang Fai, Lam Plai Mat district, Buriram Province, Thailand. 7th–8th centuries. Bronze. Height: 109 cm. National Museum Bangkok. Inventory number 01/681/2565.

Figure 4.10: Standing, four-armed bodhisattva from Ban Muang Fai, Lam Plai Mat district, Buriram province, Thailand. 8th–9th centuries. Bronze. Height: 137 cm. National Museum Bangkok. Inventory number 01/682/2565. Courtesy of River Books Bangkok.

4.9

The Mun River System: Śri Canāśa and Buddhist Art in the Lower Khorat Plateau

4.10

Figure 4.11: Standing Bodhisattva Maitreya from Ban Muang Fai, Lam Plai Mat district, Buriram province, Thailand. 8th–9th centuries. Bronze. Height: 62 cm. National Museum Bangkok. Inventory number 01/683/2565.

design. Perhaps, even more telling is the *cakra* motifs on both the hands and feet of the two images.

There seems no doubt therefore, that these two pieces are the creation of a single workshop or artist most likely based at Ban Maung Fai. This assertion is strengthened by the presence of two other Buddha images from this site, one in stone, the other in bronze (Figs. 4.8 and 4.9). Both are today kept at the National Museum Bangkok and bear the hallmarks of the Dvāravatī style. Both were also presumably in double *vitarkamudrā*; however, their left hands are now missing. Of particular interest is the palm of the right hand of the bronze image, as it also bears a *cakra* motif in the same design as the two seated stone Buddha images. It seems that this is a trademark motif of what could be referred to as the "Ban Fai workshop".

The technical and artistic heights this workshop reached can be illustrated by the two bodhisattva images recovered from the site (Figs. 4.10 and 4.11). The *stūpa* in the headdress of the smaller image identifies it as Maitreya, the Buddha of the future. The larger of the two images is a four-armed composition – though one of the arms is now missing – and stands over a metre tall. The bodhisattva is depicted in ascetic form. The only visible attire is a cord tied around its waist, which would have held its short robe in place. It has an elaborate *jaṭāmukuṭa* in which the four concentric coils of the upper part form an almost complete circle. Below this is a feature that is reminiscent of a doorway, which presumably enclosed a *stūpa* but is no longer clearly visible.

The second image is smaller in scale. It is two-armed though both arms are missing from just above the elbow. It stands in a very slight *tribhaṅga* posture. Its *jaṭāmukuṭa* is less elaborate than its larger counterpart and the *stūpa* is depicted more conventionally. These two bodhisattva images share many similarities in terms of style and production technique with the numerous Khorat Plateau bronzes that have been found throughout the region. There has been much debate and speculation as to the origins of these images and this discussion will be explored in more depth below in relation to the Prakhon Chai/Plai Bat II hoard. However, it seems that these images could have been produced locally. As with the seated stone Buddha images from this site, they provide fine examples of the artistic heights that the Khorat Plateau aesthetic reached during this period.

Images of this quality could only be produced by highly skilled artisans operating out of an established workshop. It stands to reason that the local rulers and/or lay community at this settlement were actively engaged in Buddhist religious practices, most likely of a Mahāyāna persuasion, given the presence of the two bodhisattva figures. The ability to produce such high-quality bronze and stone images indicates a considerable degree of patronage and support, as this would require a considerable amount of

144 Buddhist Landscapes: Art and Archaeology of the Khorat Plateau, 7th to 11th Centuries

Figure 4.12: *Sīmā* with a four-armed bodhisattva, its face remodelled in modern concrete. Wat Phu Phra Angkhan temple, Phu Phra Angkhan, Chaloem Phra Kiat district, Buriram province, Thailand. 8th–9th centuries. Sandstone. Height: 174 cm; width: 91 cm; depth: 18 cm.

local resources such as bronze, stone, and wood (for heating the furnaces for smelting). At present, there is no archaeological evidence to back up the existence of a workshop. However, intensive survey work and/or excavations could potentially help considerably in furthering our understanding of this important site.

Phu Phra Angkhan

Phu Phra Angkhan is located close to the Lam Plai Mat River, in Buriram province. Fifteen *sīmā* were discovered at this hilltop site, twelve of which depict Buddha/bodhisattva images. These *sīmā*, located close to a Khmer

4.12

temple that dates from circa 10th to 13th centuries, provide further evidence for Mahāyāna Buddhist practices in the area.

Only one image still has its original face (Fig. 4.12) and it appears that the rest of the *sīmā* have been reworked on at least three separate occasions. Standard *stūpa* and *stūpa-kumbha* motifs are depicted on one side of the *sīmā*. This presumably represents the first and oldest carving on these stones, stylistically datable to the 8th to 9th centuries. At a later stage the images on the reverse side of the *sīmā* were carved. One *sīmā* seems to represent a Buddha image, but the rest were carved as bodhisattvas in *tribhaṅga* posture with conical headdresses and lotuses in their right hands. Their robes are depicted with the characteristic Khorat Plateau *drapé-en-poche*. However, the triangular flaring is more rounded than 8th- and 9th-century examples.

No Na Paknam (1986: 70) proposes that these images were carved during the late 12th to early 13th centuries as they are in the Bayon style. He argues that they reflect the presence of Mahāyāna Buddhism entering the region. However, there has been one further recent re-working, which unfortunately has made the identification of these images somewhat problematic. The faces of all the images save one have been remodelled with cement, making it impossible to ascertain what the originals may have looked like. In many cases the lotus flower has also been remodelled. Wings also seem to have been added to a number of the images, perhaps in the misunderstanding that they represented *deva* images.

Three of the *sīmā* have also been smothered in thick gold paint, which again poses interpretative challenges. One *sīmā*, however, still has the original lotus clasped in the right hand. The face, however, has unfortunately been completely remodelled. It appears that the bodhisattva images represent Avalokiteśvara, perhaps in his manifestation as Padmapāṇi (Paknam 1986: 70).

The Phu Phra Angkan group represents an interesting example of how *sīmā* can be re-carved and re-designed over time to suit the prevailing religious winds of change. Furthermore, these *sīmā* are still actively worshipped today – 12 of them have been set up to form a *sīmā* boundary, while the other three have been placed in a separate building as objects of worship.

Ban Pa Khiap and Ban Prakham

The moated site of Ban Pa Khiap is located on the Mun River in Buriram province. There are 46 *sīmā* at this site, making it the largest number of any location in this river system. From this we can assume that there would have been a Buddhist monastery here. Twenty of the *sīmā* have *stūpa-kumbha* motifs in shallow relief while another five depict axial *stūpa*. None show any evidence of narrative art. One *sīmā*,

Figure 4.13: *Sīmā* with *dharmacakra* surmounted by a truncated *stūpa-kumbha* motif. At Wat Pho Yoi Temple, Ban Prakham, Pakham district, Buriram province, Thailand. 8th–9th centuries. Sandstone. Height: 68 cm; width: 64 cm; depth: 12 cm.

however, has an image of a Buddha depicted on one side, but it is now quite badly eroded.

The site of Ban Prakham in Buriram province is noteworthy in that a *sīmā* found at the local temple has a *dharmacakra* motif depicted on it (Fig. 4.13). Unlike the other two known examples from the Khorat Plateau (Figs. 3.15 and 3.16), the example from Ban Prakham is in higher relief and is not sitting on a *stambha* or *stūpa* of any kind. Instead, there is a truncated *stūpa-kumbha* motif emerging from the top of the *dharmacakra* and the wheel consists of 12 diamond-shaped petals. A fully formed flower in bloom, presumably representing the lotus, is shown at its centre. The closest parallels to this are on a number of *sīmā* found at Phnom Kulen discussed below.

Surin, Si Sa Ket, and Ubon Ratchathani

Moving eastwards into Surin, Si Sa Ket, and Ubon Ratchathani provinces respectively, the evidence for Buddhism thins considerably. This, as discussed previously, is most likely due to the much stronger Zhenla and later Angkorian presence in this part of the Mun River system. The 7th- to 8th-century site of Prasat Phumphon in Surin would have been a centre

The Mun River System: Śrī Canāśa and Buddhist Art in the Lower Khorat Plateau

of Zhenla in this area (Siribhadra and Moore 1992: 85). In the case of Prasat Yai Ngao in Surin province, evidence for both the presence of Buddhism and Hinduism exist side by side as *sīmā* are located nearby this Khmer temple (Fig. 4.14). It is most likely that the site was first Buddhist, before being supplanted by Hinduism in a move that was perhaps as much political as it was religious.

There are two sites in Si Sa Ket province with evidence for Buddhism. One, Ban Lupmok, has four fragmentary *sīmā*. The other, Ku Kaeo Sithi, was recently excavated by the Fine Arts Department. It is a small, four-sided brick structure with stairways in the middle of each of its sides.

Figure 4.14: *Sīmā* with axial *stūpa* motif possibly in situ at Prasat Yai Ngao Temple, Ban Chop, Sangkha district, Surin province, Thailand. 8th–9th centuries. Sandstone.

These stairways have hemispherical thresholds at their base similar in design to those seen at Muang Sema. The architecture of this monument suggests that it most likely functioned as a *stūpa*. A few fragmentary *sīmā* were found in its vicinity, one of which has an inscription, which as far as I know has not been read at the time of this publication.

Finally, there is a group of *sīmā* at Wat Su Phatthanaram Worawihan Temple in Ubon Ratchathani town. They are carved with *stūpa-kumbha* motifs and were most likely collected from the surrounding region by the small museum located in its grounds. However, it is unclear from which sites they have been collected.

Plai Bat II: The Prakhon Chai Hoard

In 1964 one of the most important caches of bronze sculptures anywhere in Southeast Asia was supposedly discovered. Initial reports in the *Illustrated London News* (28 August 1965: 37) stated that villagers had unearthed the material in an abandoned temple and that the findspot was somewhere along the Thai-Cambodian border. Three years later Jean Boisselier (1967) stated that the location was Prakhon Chai, a district in the southern part of Buriram province and that the temple in question was Prasat Lom Thom. The discovery, consisting of numerous large bronze bodhisattva and Buddha images dating to the 7th to 9th centuries, was subsequently named the Prakhon Chai Hoard. The material was smuggled out of Thailand and quickly found its way onto the international art market and over time entered the collections of museums and private collectors worldwide.[26] The findspot remained unquestioned for many years despite the fact that both the modern town and district of Prakhon Chai had little to no known archaeological or historic significance. In 2002 the late Emma Bunker, a former board member and consultant to the Denver Art Museum and long-time consultant for auction houses such as Sotheby's, wrote an article in *Arts of Asia* calling this into question. Bunker (2002) argued that the findspot had nothing whatsoever to do with Prakhon Chai and was instead located in the precincts of a ruined 10th-century Khmer temple called Plai Bat II. This temple is located on Khao Plai Bat hill, near Yai Yaem village, in the district of Lahan Sai, Buriram province, 40 kilometres southwest of the town of Prakhon Chai (Bunker 2002: 108). Bunker states that she

---

26   Prakhon Chai bronzes have ended up in institutions such as the Metropolitan Museum of Art, New York; The Asia Society, New York; the Norton Simon Museum, Pasadena; the Kimbell Art Museum, Fort Worth, Texas; and the Museum of Asian Art, San Francisco; amongst others. The Kimbell Art Museum piece has an accession number (AP 1965.01), indicating that it was acquired in 1965 and is thus indicative of the speed with which this material was smuggled out of Thailand and sold on the art market. For a full list, see Bunker (2000: appendix A).

The Mun River System: Śrī Canāśa and Buddhist Art in the Lower Khorat Plateau

discovered the true whereabouts of the hoard when she visited the site in May 2001 and spoke to villagers (2002: 110, fn. 12). However, she provides no information about how she knew to visit this particular village in the first place. Was it just serendipity or did she have access to information not available to the scholarly community at large? Bunker had a long professional relationship with the late Douglas Latchford, a disgraced collector and art dealer who at the time of his death in 2020 was under investigation in the United States for antiquities smuggling of both Thai and Cambodian material. Bunker and Latchford also co-authored a number of self-published books on Latchford's collections (Bunker and Latchford 2004, 2008, 2011).[27]

On 1 December 2022, *Denver Post* investigative journalist Sam Tabachnik published a series of newspaper articles that confirmed what many had already suspected.[28] Much of his conclusions drew on research carried out by Tanongsak Hanwong, a founding member of *Sam-Nuk Sam-Roi Ong/Reminiscing the 300 Buddhas,* a grassroots organisation that campaigns for the repatriation of the Plai Bat II material. Since 2014, they have carried out numerous interviews with villagers from the surrounding areas in an attempt to reconstruct the extent, nature, and sequence of looting at Plai Bat II. This movement effectively harnessed the power of social media to put pressure on government officials and the Fine Arts Department of Thailand to act (Phanomvan 2021). Progress, however, is slow and many hurdles – both legal and political – stand in their way. One can only hope that they are eventually successful in this endeavour to bring back the bronzes to the Khorat Plateau.

Based on *Sam-Nuk Sam-Roi Ong*'s work, it is now clear that Douglas Latchford was directly involved in the pillaging of this site.[29] Not only that, he was the main buyer of this material and funder of this illicit operation. Furthermore, the *Denver Post* investigation unequivocally showed that Bunker had a working relationship with Latchford from at least the late 1970s and perhaps as early as 1972 or before. This then was how Bunker knew where to look and was able to name the actual findspot as Plai Bat II, and not Prakhon Chai. She worked closely with Latchford

---

27   See the investigative journalism on this matter at: https://chasingaphrodite. com/tag/douglas-latchford/.

28   See: https://www.denverpost.com/2022/12/01/emma-bunker-douglas-latchford-cambodian-art-denver-art-museum/, https://www.denverpost. com/2022/12/01/denver-art-museum-stolen-asian-relics-cambodia-thailand-emma-bunker/.

29   In 2014 I accompanied Tanongsak Hanwong on his first trip to Plai Bat II and we made initial inquiries with the local villagers in regard to the looting. I revisited in September 2022 and conducted an interview with Tanongsak Hanwong on his research in the intervening years in which he kindly shared with me his findings to date and the role of Latchford in the looting.

for most of her career, and often provided expert opinion and authentication of unprovenanced, problematic, and even stolen Southeast Asian pieces that were circulating on the international art market.[30] She was thus deeply implicated in the trade in illicitly exported material from Thailand and Cambodia.

According to Bunker's account – which is impossible to verify as she does not provide any documentary evidence to substantiate it – after a particularly heavy rainstorm, local villagers found several large slabs of laterite some 15 metres or so from the main shrine. These became visible as the rain washed away the topsoil. Removing the slabs, the villagers reportedly found eight to nine Buddha and bodhisattva figures wrapped in textiles (2002: 110). This latter details casts doubt on the veracity of the account as it is highly unlikely that textiles would survive intact for this length of time. The villagers – which, it should be noted, are also unnamed and therefore makes it impossible to corroborate Bunker's account – go on to claim that these sculptures ranged in size from 50 to 142 centimetres in height. Numerous other smaller figures were apparently also found around the pit itself.

Several months after the discovery, it was claimed that over 200 more smaller and cruder images were uncovered within the temple itself. Bunker, however, is more sceptical about this claim, stating that the number may be an exaggeration, and the whereabouts of these pieces have never been satisfactorily ascertained. It should also be noted that the art market is awash with supposed Prakhon Chai sculptures, many of which are forgeries. It would thus be in dealers' interests to keep alive rumours of such a large cache being found as a way to explain their bulging inventories. Bunker states that she attempted to reconstruct what she thinks is the original group of sculptures based on her research in the international art world. However, it now seems likely that she was able to do so based on privileged information she could obtain via her relationship with Latchford.

The sculptures themselves are a spectacular find. This makes that fact that they were not recovered in a controlled archaeological excavation and instead dispersed worldwide all the more tragic. The majority are four-armed bodhisattva figures of either Avalokiteśvara (Fig. 4.15) or Maitreya (Fig. 4.16, 4.17), though there are also a number of Buddha images and one ascetic figure, the latter now in the Brooklyn Museum (acc. no. 83.120). The bodhisattvas are attired in an ascetic fashion – their hair arranged in a *jaṭāmukuṭa*, and their bodies devoid of any ornamentation

---

30   See: https://www.denverpost.com/2022/12/01/emma-bunker-douglas-latchford-cambodian-art-denver-art-museum/, https://www.denverpost.com/2022/12/01/denver-art-museum-stolen-asian-relics-cambodia-thailand-emma-bunker/.

The Mun River System: Śrī Canāśa and Buddhist Art in the Lower Khorat Plateau

Figure 4.15: Four-armed Bodhisattva Avalokiteśvara. Reportedly found at Plai Bat II Temple, Lahan Sai district, Buriram province, Thailand. 8th century. Bronze with high tin content inlaid with silver and black glass or obsidian in eyes. Height: 142 cm; width: 58 cm; depth: 39 cm. Rogers Fund 1967. Acc. no: 67.234. Metropolitan Museum of Art, New York, USA. The Metropolitan Museum of Art/Art Resource/Scala, Florence.

Figure 4.16: Four-armed Bodhisattva Maitreya. Reportedly found at Plai Bat II Temple, Lahan Sai district, Buriram province, Thailand. 8th century. Copper alloy with inlays of silver and black stone. Height: 95 cm; width: 36 cm; depth 27 cm. Asia Society, New York: Mr and Mrs John D. Rockefeller 3rd Collection, 1979.63. Asia Society/Art Resource, NY/Scala, Florence.

Figure 4.17: Four-armed Bodhisattva Maitreya. Reportedly found at Plai Bat II Temple, Lahan Sai district, Buriram province, Thailand. 8th century. Bronze. Height: 123 cm; width: 51 cm; depth: 32 cm. AP 1965.01. Kimbell Art Museum, Fort Worth (TX), USA. Kimbell Art Museum, Fort Worth, Texas/Art Resource, NY/Scala, Florence.

The Mun River System: Śrī Canāśa and Buddhist Art in the Lower Khorat Plateau

or clothing apart from a short lower garment. One is instantly reminded of the bronze sculptures discovered at Ban Tanot and Ban Muang Fai and the bodhisattva depicted on the *Mahānāradakassapa-jātaka* from Ban Kut Ngong (Fig. 3.5). Overall, there is a stylistic homogeneity to these pieces and Bunker argues, as do I, that they represent a distinctive Khorat Plateau aesthetic.

As discussed throughout this book, Khorat Plateau aesthetics and motifs manifest themselves in numerous examples in a variety of forms

4.17

and media. The most prevalent is the *sīmā* tradition. The other most significant form, I would argue, is this corpus of bronzes, which also includes the sculptures from Ban Tanot and Ban Muang Fai. In these works, there is a blending of Dvāravatī and Khmer characteristics in a way that makes them distinctive to this region. Two of the finest examples are in the Asia Society, New York (acc. no. 1979.63) and the Kimbell Art Museum (acc. no. AP 1965.01) respectively (Figs. 4.16 and 4.17). Both examples are masterful depictions of the bodhisattva Maitreya. His benevolent face has a gentle smile, and his upper lip is topped by a thin moustache – a Khmer feature that is found on nearly all the known examples of this group of sculptures. The *jaṭāmukuṭa* is depicted as a graceful bundle of matted locks hanging in loops. Below this, the hair is depicted in straight vertical lines pulled taut from a border along the forehead into the topknot above.

The lower garment is always shown clasped in place by a narrow cord that extends around the waist and on some examples, such as the Asia Society piece, is gracefully knotted in front. The lower garment is short, extending only as far as the upper thighs. At times its folds are creased into an anchor-shaped design reminiscent of pre-Angkorian examples, or in the case of the Asia Society piece, folded in a similar fashion to examples on figures depicted on *sīmā* (Fig. 2.6).

A number of bronze Buddha images were also recovered from the hoard. They show strong stylistic affinities with images found throughout the Khorat Plateau, whether they be in stone or bronze. As with the example from Ban Muang Fai, two of the known examples are shown in double *vitarkamudrā*. One is in a private collection (Bunker 2002: Fig. 1) and the other is at the Metropolitan Museum of Art, New York (acc. no. 1982.220.5). They have the same sense of frontality common to most Dvāravatī Buddha images and the robes are depicted in the familiar diaphanous fashion. The outer robe falls in a u-shaped pattern; the inner robe gently flares outwards. The Metropolitan Museum example sports a thin moustache along its upper lip in a similar style to the bodhisattva images.

Stylistically, the majority of these bronzes belong to the 8th to 9th centuries, though some, such as the Avalokiteśvara at the Asian Art Museum, San Francisco (acc. no. B65B57), may date to the late 7th century (Chutiwongs and Patry Leidy 1994: 38). Buddhism in general thrived on the Khorat Plateau from the 7th to 9th centuries. The *sīmā* tradition provides clear evidence for this, as does the overall archaeological and epigraphic evidence. It is within this context then that we must view these bronzes. They flourished as part of the wider tradition of Buddhism in the region. Given the gracefulness of their execution and the sublime nature of their composition, the Prakhon

Chai/Plai Bat II bronzes in many ways represent the finest expression of the Khorat Plateau aesthetic.

The prevalence of bodhisattva images in the hoard makes it clear that Mahāyāna or perhaps Vajrayāna Buddhism was being practised to some extent on the Khorat Plateau during the 7th to 9th centuries. More specifically it appears that a cult of asceticism had developed. This is reflected in the fact that all the bodhisattvas are depicted in an ascetic fashion. This tallies with the bronzes from Ban Tanot and Ban Muang Fai, which are depicted in the same way. Further afield in Central Thailand, at the cave of Khao Thamorat about 15 kilometres from Si Thep, there is further evidence for the worship of the bodhisattva Maitreya. At least two images of this bodhisattva have been carved into the rock face, one of which has a *jaṭāmukuṭa* of very similar style to those found on the Khorat Plateau (Guy 2014: cat. 148). There also are depictions of bodhisattva from the Dvāravatī site of Khu Bua in Western Thailand (Guy 2014: cat. 146). However, these are crowned and bejewelled and are therefore more indictive of another tradition from peninsular Thailand, where bodhisattva figures are shown in a more princely and regal fashion.

Where then were the Prakhon Chai/Plai Bat II bronzes cast? Their style and technical consistency point towards a highly developed workshop. Overall, they do not conform to the pre-Angkorian styles of Cambodia, though there are some close examples from the 8th-century temple of Ak Yum at Angkor.[31] The presence of Dvāravatī-style Buddha images amongst the hoard indicates it is to the Khorat Plateau that we must turn. There is no evidence at Plai Bat Hill or the surrounding area for a moated settlement, so it is unlikely that they were forged in the vicinity of the findspot. The site of Ban Muang Fai lies approximately 60 kilometres north and is the obvious contender. Alternatively, the site of Ban Tanot is about 80 kilometres to the northwest, while Muang Sema is further still at 140 kilometres to the northwest. Any of these sites could have been home to the possible workshop. Given its size and importance, Muang Sema would seem like the obvious choice. The presence of bronze sculpture at Ban Muang Fai also means it cannot be overlooked either. However, until archaeological evidence locates the presence of such a workshop at any of the above sites, the matter must remain one of speculation.

---

31   As a result of the work carried out by the Cambodian Government Restitution Team led by Bradley J. Gordon, reports have come to light that Latchford also sourced similar material in Cambodia, referring to them as "Srivichai" bronzes (pers. Comm. Bradley J. Gordon 9 October 2022). It may therefore be possible that some bronzes labelled "Prakhon Chai" in museum collections worldwide may in fact be from Cambodia. Further research needs to be carried out to establish if this is in fact the case.

A related part of the puzzle is why were these sculptures hidden at the 10th-century temple of Plai Bat II in the first place? If the accounts given in Bunker (2002) are to be believed, then it indicates that they were ritually buried. Given the date of the temple, the images must have been interred sometime in or after the 10th century. The most logical explanation would seem to relate to the growing presence of the Khmer on the Khorat Plateau. By the 10th century, the Khmer were the political masters of this region. Being primarily *Śaivite*, this religion would have eclipsed Buddhism as the official form of worship. Were the bronze bodhisattva and Buddha images from the region collected up and ritually interred by the Khmer rulers? This would explain their location in such a temple. However, Vajrayāna Buddhism continued to be practised at Phimai, so this indicates that Buddhism and Hinduism did co-exist at this period on the Khorat Plateau.

The bronze Avalokiteśvara from Ban Tanot was also discovered in a *stūpa*, again suggesting that it had been ritually deposited. Bronzes are highly portable, and it would thus have been easy enough to collect them up and move them quite some distance. In comparison, objects such as *sīmā* and life-size stone Buddha images were heavy and cumbersome, explaining why they, on the other hand, stayed put to a greater extent.

Whatever the reasons for them being hidden away, the Prakhon Chai/Plai Bat II hoard represents one of the most significant collections of bronzes anywhere in Southeast Asia.

Phnom Kulen

While the Prakhon Chai/Plai Bat II hoard speaks to one form of interconnectivity between the Khorat Plateau and the Khmer, two *sīmā* sites located on Phnom Kulen provide another window into this relationship. This sacred mountain is located about 20 kilometres northeast of Angkor. The Khorat Plateau lies about 90 kilometres further north across the Dang Raek Mountain range. Phnom Kulen is widely considered to be the birthplace of the Angkorian Empire. This occurred under the reign of King Jayavarman II, who in 802 CE conducted the *devaraja* ritual and thus consecrated himself as king (Cœdès 1968: 97–9). The presence of *sīmā* at this location raises a number of questions. How did they come to be set up at the heart of what was then the Khmer Empire? Who brought the tradition here? How were they received in a predominantly Śaivite environment? Inscriptions and stone or bronze Buddha images do illustrate that Buddhism was being practised in Cambodia in the 7th and 8th centuries. However, there is scant evidence for the period spanning the 8th to 11th centuries (Filliozat 1981).

The presence of *sīmā* at Phnom Kulen illustrates the extent to which traditions and belief systems travelled during this period. Buddhism, it seems, was able – to a limited extent – to function alongside the predominantly state-sponsored Śaivism. The *sīmā* are located at two sites, Peam Kre and Don Meas, and were first recorded by J. Boulbet and B. Dagens (1973). They described several of the more ornately carved *sīmā* and provided plans, photographs, drawings, and descriptions within a broader inventory of archaeological sites at Phnom Kulen. Both sites have *sīmā* set up in pairs (16 slab type *sīmā* at each). Many of the stones are ornately carved with *stūpa-khumba*, *dharmacakra*, and a number of unique designs, with a few portraying intricate scenes and narratives.

The *sīmā* were still in situ when Boulbet and Dagens surveyed them. Since then, the sites have unfortunately been looted and almost all the stones have been disturbed and moved (Latinis and Murphy 2017). At least one *sīmā*, depicting Gaja Lakṣmī, has disappeared. Fortunately, however, most of the stones still remain. To the best of my knowledge, apart from this group of *sīmā* on Phnom Kulen, there are no other examples in Cambodia prior to the 13th to 14th centuries. Many of the motifs on the *sīmā* from Phnom Kulen depict *dharmacakra* and/or *stūpa-kumbha* motifs. These designs thus have their origins in the *sīmā* of the Khorat Plateau. This is clear from the proliferation of the *stūpa-kumbha* motif and *sīmā* in general. There are three examples of the *dharmacakra* motif depicted on *sīmā* from the Khorat Plateau that also serve to illustrate this point. As discussed previously, they come from the sites of Ban Prakham, Ban Bua Simama, and Ban Phan Lam (Figs. 3.15, 3.16, 4.13).

According to Boulbet and Dagens (1973: 43–7), all bar two of the *sīmā* from Phnom Kulen had *dharmacakra* motifs. They have the same diamond-shaped leaves radiating out from a central flower as the three examples from the Khorat Plateau (Fig. 4.18). However, at Phnom Kulen the overall design is more elaborate, with the rim of the wheel being decorated with either one or two bands of small circular motifs. Furthermore, the wheels themselves are sometimes flanked by elaborate foliage or flame-like patterns enveloping the *dharmacakra* (Fig. 4.19). On other examples, the *dharmacakra* spokes are depicted as thin lines, giving them the appearance of an actual wheel (Fig. 4.20).

On certain examples from Phnom Kulen, the *dharmacakra* is placed on a *stūpa-kumbha* motif. In some cases, the *kumbha* are depicted with vegetation flowing forth and ending in volute-type designs reminiscent of those found on the spokes of three-dimensional *dharmacakra* from Central Thailand. In these cases, the *dharmacakra* appear to be emerging from the mouth of the *kumbha* pot along with the floral motifs.

On one particular *sīmā*, the *kumbha* pot is flanked by a lion and a boar. On a further example, a monkey is shown climbing up the side of the pot (Fig. 4.18). The fact that the *stūpa-kumbha* motif is present alongside, or at times as part of the *dharmacakra* motif, illustrates that the artists responsible for the carving of these *sīmā* were extremely familiar with the existing motifs from the Khorat Plateau (Fig. 4.21). Robert Brown further suggests that the *cakrastambha* and *stūpa-kumbha* motifs have become conflated on the Phnom Kulen *sīmā*. He points out that this feature is also found on silver plaques discovered in Maha Sarakham province (1996: 93–5).

Given that these motifs originated in the Khorat Plateau, we can infer that a group of Buddhist monks and craftsmen decided to move from this region, most likely in the vicinity of the Mun River, and settled on Phnom Kulen. Recent archaeological research can shed further light on this. LIDAR (Light Detecting and Ranging) survey work carried out in 2012 and 2015 has revealed the city of Mahendraparvata, the 8th- to 9th-century capital of the Khmer civilisation, in much greater detail (Chevance 2015; Evans 2016; Chevance et al. 2019). This research indicates that this urban centre covered an area of about 40 to 50 square kilometres. Both *sīmā* sites are within this zone, and it appears that one of the sites, Peam Kre, was located about 200 to 300 metres away from an

Figure 4.18: In situ *sīmā* with *dharmacakra* motif and elaborate *kumbha* on stand with a monkey climbing up the right side. Peam Kre, Phnom Kulen, Cambodia. 8th–9th centuries. Sandstone. Height: 140 cm; width: 80 cm; depth 24 cm.

Figure 4.19: Detail of a *sīmā* with *dharmacakra* motif. Peam Kre, Phnom Kulen, Cambodia. 8th–9th centuries. Sandstone.

architectural structure today called the Banteay Site. Archaeological excavations carried out by Jean-Baptiste Chevance from 2009 to 2012 indicates that it is highly likely that this structure was the palace of Jayavarman II (Chevance 2015). The excavations show that it is a complex, large-scale, quadrangular site spanning 615 by 400 metres and made up of earthworks, embankments, and platforms. There is a hierarchy of spaces governed by the arrangement of platforms. They included a brick building and important built structures surrounded by multiple earth levees. The absence of a temple structure further argues for this site's function as a palace and civic centre (Chevance 2015: 315–8). This identification has been further confirmed by the radiocarbon dates obtained, which correspond from the 8th to first half of the 9th century, with occupation ceasing by the late 9th century (Chevance 2015: 292, 296, 308, 313, 319–20). This date range encompasses the reign of Jayavarman II (c. 802–835 CE) (Chevance et al. 2019: 1307).

Mapping and test excavations carried out in 2015 by APSARA National Authority and the Nalanda-Sriwijaya Centre, Archaeology Unit, Singapore indicate that Don Meas was built atop a rock outcrop. It has a commanding view of the valley and floodplains below. Peam Kre was built close to an existing stream at the base of the hill. The archaeological team also surveyed a *sīmā* quarry adjacent to the Don Meas site (Latinis and Murphy 2017). Two unfinished or rejected *sīmā* stone blanks were partially carved out of sandstone outcroppings with the marks of the quarrying techniques still clearly visible. The pottery record recovered at these sites led the team to conclude that, like the Banteay palace site, the *sīmā* sites were abandoned by the mid 9th century or earlier.

These recent archaeological discoveries are key to explaining the presence of *sīmā* at Phnom Kulen. The proximity of these sites to the palace indicates that Buddhist monks may have set up a monastery here during this period, or at the very least, sites of pilgrimage. It is likely that these monks, aware of the presence of a powerful new kingdom ruled from Mahendraparvata atop Phnom Kulen, set out from the Khorat Plateau and headed south to found a new monastery. There was a growing Khmer presence in the Mun River valley from as early as the 7th century, with the incursions of Mahendravarman and his son Īśānavarman I (Vickery 1994: 202–4). Routes of communication and travel were therefore well established and thus the movement of monks and artisans would have been easily achievable.

That two groups of *sīmā* were established on Phnom Kulen indicates that the Buddhist monks were initially successful in gaining the support of perhaps the king (possibly Jayavarman II), or at the very least, the local populace and elites. This could indicate support for the practice/ideology of merit, as opposed to an endorsement of Buddhism per se (Bronkhorst

Figure 4.20: *Sīmā* with *dharmacakra* motif and elaborate *kumbha* on stand. Don Meas, Phnom Kulen, Cambodia. 8th–9th centuries. Sandstone.

Figure 4.21: Fragmentary *sīmā* with a *stūpa-kumbha* motif. Peam Kre, Phnom Kulen, Cambodia. 8th–9th centuries. Sandstone. Height: 96 cm; width: 60 cm; depth: 27 cm.

2011; Revire 2016). However, it appears that in the end the Buddhist monks could not compete with the dominant Śaivism of the Khmers. When the capital shifted down to Angkor in the 9th century, there is no evidence to suggest that the Buddhist monks went with it.

On a final note, there is also a Buddha image carved into the rockface in *mahāparinibbāṇa* posture atop Phnom Kulen. Smitthi Siribhadra (2009: 25 n. 3) proposes that this is contemporary with the *sīmā* at Don Meas and Peam Kre. Located in the modern Preah Ang Thom Temple, it is reminiscent of the examples found in the Khorat Plateau and may be part of this same tradition. However, dating this *mahāparinibbāṇa* image is problematic, as it has been heavily remodelled over time – a not uncommon practice as this book has indicated elsewhere. Given this, it is impossible to ascertain the date of this image with any certainty.

Phimai

The site of Phimai provides a further example of interaction between Buddhism on the Khorat Plateau and Khmer culture. The site is located on the Mun River at the confluence of two of its tributaries, about 25 kilometres east of Ban Tanot. It was the epicentre of Khmer power in the region with the powerful Mahīdharapura Dynasty said to have come from

4.20

this area (Cœdès 1929; Woodward 2005: 147). The temple complex at its heart practised Vajrayāna Buddhism.

The temple has been restored and as it stands today reflects its early 12th-century form. There is, however, evidence for an earlier brick structure underneath which probably dates to the 11th century (Woodward 2005: 150). Furthermore, archaeological excavations have shown that Phimai was inhabited from the late prehistoric period onwards, indicating that while the Khmer town of Vimayapura, as ancient Phimai was known, dates to the 11th to 12th centuries, the site itself has a longer history of occupation.

The main image at Phimai (the lord Vimaya) is now lost but was probably a *nāga*-protected Buddha (Woodward 2005: 149). The principal deities in the central sanctuary were Samvara, Vairocana, a crowned Buddha, and Vajrapani. Hevajra and Vajrasattva are also present (Conti 2014: 385–9). A further bronze Buddhist deity, now housed in the

4.21

National Museum Bangkok, may have also come from the site and represents a form of Trailokyavijaya. This identification is based on its posture of *pratyālidḥa* (a type of dance pose) in *vajrahumkaramudrā* (Woodward 2005: 154 and PL. 46a).

It is also worth keeping in mind that Phimai was a syncretic temple with Hindu themes represented on the outer decoration of the main sanctuary and Buddhist themes depicted on the inner. The four interior lintels, for instance, have Buddhist subject matters. The defeat of Mara is shown on the southern lintel, the northern lintel depicts Vajrasattva, while the outer main southern entrance depicts a dancing Śiva. This mixing of imagery and religious persuasions may also go some way in explaining the Buddha images in *vitarkamudrā* on the western lintel (Woodward 2005: 154). The diaphanous U-shaped robe so prevalent on Dvāravatī Buddhist imagery throughout the Khorat Plateau has here given way to a more Khmer-style depiction – the lower half of the robe has a central pleat which wraps around the waist of the Buddha. These double *vitarkamudrā* Buddha images represent a fusion of the Khorat Plateau style that flourished in the region from the 7th century onwards with the incoming Khmer artistic modes that became established from the 10th century onwards. One final interesting development is that these Buddhas are now crowned. It is argued by Woodward (2005: 146, 156) that this form of crowned Buddha originated at Phimai and from here spread throughout the Khmer Empire.

Phimai is unique in the Khorat Plateau for being the only known settlement dedicated to a Vajrayāna form of Buddhism. This sets it apart from both the Buddhism of the Khorat Plateau in general, and from the religious persuasions of Angkor, which were primarily Śaivite. The reasons for its adoption of Vajrayāna Buddhism remain unclear. However, its location in a region which had been Buddhist for at least 400 years before its founding must have been a major factor. Its proximity to the former Muang Sema/Śri Canāśa mandala would have provided a conducive environment within which different forms of Buddhist doctrine could flourish.

SUMMARY

The Mun River system was an important conduit along which Buddhism spread into the southern part of the Khorat Plateau. In doing so, it inevitably ran up against Hindu forms of worship that were also making their way into the region due to the growing presence and dominance over time of the Khmer. This led to Buddhism being checked to a certain degree along the Mun River system. However, as we have seen with Phnom Kulen, the Buddhism practised in the Mun River system did manage to make inroads, albeit eventually unsuccessful, into the heart of the Khmer lands.

The most important site within the river system was Muang Sema and it was most likely the centre of the Śri Canāśa mandala. It controlled the settlements in its direct hinterlands and vicinity and most likely exerted control over the sites along the Mun River system. Strategically located in the southwest corner of the Khorat Plateau, it acted as the gateway to the region, regulating access to and from Central Thailand. This pivotal position allowed it to prosper and grow. It formed alliances through marriage with the powerful rulers of Dvāravatī in the Chao Phraya River basin and supported some of the largest Buddhist foundations anywhere in the Khorat Plateau. Only Muang Fa Daed in the Chi River system rivals it in terms of the size and scale of the Buddhist art and architectural remains.

The Mun River system is also notable for its Buddhist bronze tradition, the likes of which is found nowhere else in the Khorat Plateau. The Prakhon Chai/Plai Bat II bronzes, as well as those found at Ban Muang Fai and Ban Tanot, all point to the existence of a highly skilled atelier somewhere in the region. This in turn, indicates the level of support Buddhism had acquired by the 8th century. Considerable investment and resources would have been needed to produce bronzes of such beauty and quality. This points to Muang Sema and the kingdom of Śri Canāśa as the source of this tradition.

Overall Buddhism spread and flourished in the Mun River system over the course of the 7th to 9th centuries. Esoteric forms such as those represented by the ascetic bronze bodhisattvas of Prakhon Chai /Plai Bat II and Ban Muang Fai, or that which later manifested itself in Phimai, found room for expression alongside the Pāli-anchored forms of Buddhism which dominated the region at this time.

Chapter 5

THE MIDDLE MEKONG: BUDDHIST ART FROM VIENTIANE TO WAT PHU

From its source in the Tibetan Plateau, the Mekong River traverses China before flowing through the heart of mainland Southeast Asia. As it does so, tributaries begin to join it on its east and west banks, increasing its flow considerably. The largest of these are the Chi and Mun river systems. They merge just west of Ubon Ratchathani and join the Mekong at a bend in the river about 70 kilometres east of this city and 40 kilometres northwest of Pakse in Laos. From here the Mekong River makes its way down through Southern Laos and into Cambodia where the modern-day capital Phnom Penh hugs its western banks. It finally discharges into the South China Sea via the Mekong Delta, just south of modern-day Ho Chi Minh City. For centuries it has connected these cities and regions geographically, economically, and culturally and these factors continue to play out today in complex geopolitical configurations.

This chapter, however, restricts itself to investigating a stretch of the Lower Mekong basin from Vientiane in the north to Wat Phu Champassak in the south in the 7th to 11th centuries (Map 11). In discussing this Middle Mekong section of the river, the chapter will explore its Buddhist art and architecture through three distinct geographical clusters. Of particular interest is Cluster 6 – the area around Vientiane province of Laos and Nong Khai/Udon Thani provinces of Thailand (Maps 2, 4 and 12). The evidence here is situated within a variety of landscapes both upload and lowland. Within these locations, Buddha images, *sīmā* with narrative art and *stūpa-kumbha motifs*, and a handful of inscriptions build up a picture of the Buddhist practices present.

Further downriver, we find more evidence from a group of sites around That Phanom and the Se Bang Fai River (Cluster 7). Here Buddhism existed side by side with Hinduism to a large extent. And moving further downstream again to Savannakhet town and Phra That Phon, we encounter the southernmost cluster of sites (Cluster 8) on this river system. Below this, the archaeological evidence from the eastern bank of the Mekong is almost exclusively Khmer Hindu remains. However, there is a small amount of Buddhist material at the Khmer centre of Wat

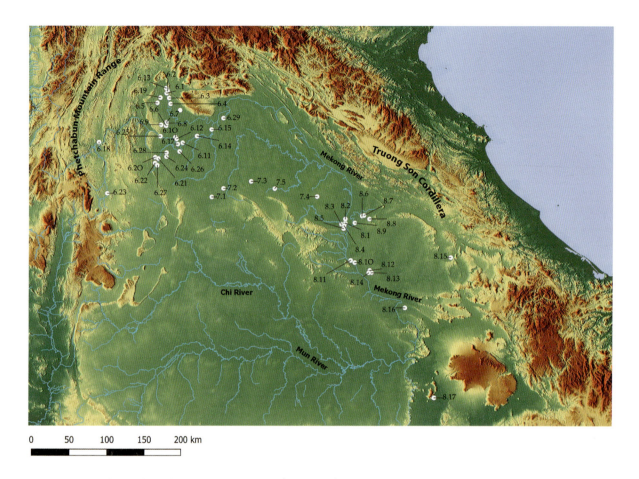

Map 11 Sites in the Middle Mekong group. See Table 3 (p. 224–225) for the corresponding site names.

Phu, illustrating once again that as at Phnom Kulen, Buddhism was practised to a lesser degree alongside Śaivism.

Overall, the Middle Mekong shows a less uniform distribution pattern than the Chi or the Mun. Most of the sites are located either close to the Mekong River or on tributaries of it. Fifty-one sites have been identified in the Middle Mekong group (Table 3; Map 11), out of which three clear clusters can be discerned (Clusters 6, 7, and 8). As with the Chi and Mun rivers, the majority of these sites closely follow the course of the river and/or a number of its tributaries, once again emphasising the important role waterways and trade routes played in the dissemination of Buddhism.

CLUSTER 6: VIENTIANE AND ITS HINTERLANDS

Cluster 6 spans the areas of modern-day Vientiane province in Laos and Nong Khai, Loei and Udon Thani provinces in Thailand and has 29 sites in total

The Middle Mekong: Buddhist Art from Vientiane to Wat Phu

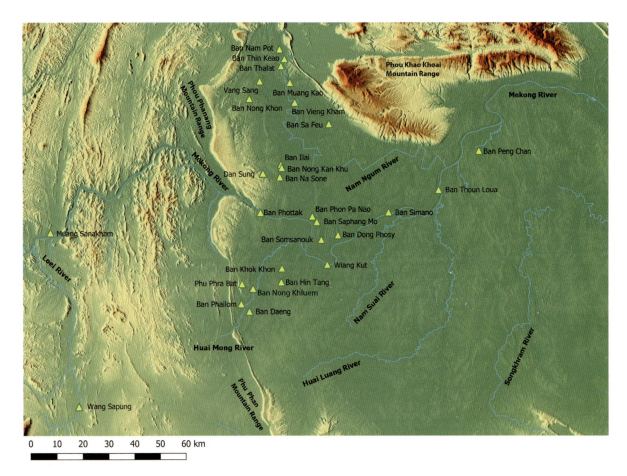

Map 12 Cluster 6.

– the largest amount of any of the clusters (Maps 2, 12; Table 9). The modern-day city of Vientiane is located on a bend on the northern side of the Mekong River. Beyond it lies a plain that is enclosed to its east and west by two mountain ranges – the Phou Khao Khoai and Phou Phanang respectively. The plain is bisected by the Nam Ngum River, which flows southwards from the northern uplands before turning sharply eastwards just before Vientiane and joining the Mekong River somewhat further downstream. The sites within Vientiane province are located in and around Vientiane city itself or along the course of the Nam Ngum River, with the exception of Dan Sang, which is located in the Phou Phanang range. South of the Mekong the land is generally flat – apart from the area around Phu Phra Bat discussed below – with some hilly areas along the banks of the river.

The distribution analysis illustrates that sites in Cluster 6 (Map 12) show significant correlation in terms of geographical proximity, style, and iconography of Buddhist art. Chronologically, the evidence spans the 7th to 11th centuries. The sites are located on a number of different rivers: the Mekong which flows east–west through the cluster, the Nam Ngum River which flows southwards from Northern Laos before joining the Mekong, the Loei River which flows north into the Mekong, and the Huai Mong River that flows from Ban Phue northwards, joining the Mekong near the modern-day city of Nong Khai.

Vientiane and the Nam Ngum River

In his study of Vientiane and its surrounding area, Michel Lorrillard (2008, 2010–2011, 2014) identifies numerous locations of Buddhist remains from the 7th to 9th centuries. His work builds on that of Pierre-Marie Gagneux, who carried out surveys in the region in the late 1960s and early 1970s (Gagneux 1972). Many of the sites are located along the Nam Ngum River. Perhaps the most significant of Gagneux's finds was a Buddha image and an inscription found in Wat Pho Seng Arun Temple in Ban Thalat village, approximately 60 kilometres north of Vientiane. In 2004, nine *sīmā* were unearthed at this temple, one of which is decorated with a *stūpa-kumbha* motif (Lorrillard 2014: 45).

The Buddha image and inscription from Ban Thalat are today kept at Wat Ho Phra Keo Temple in Vientiane city (Figs. 5.1 and 5.2). The inscription is in Mon language and has been read by Emmanuel Guillon (1974). He dates it on palaeographic grounds to the 7th century. It consists of 14 lines inscribed into one face of the stone only. It commemorates the meritorious donation by a certain Lord Wanna of five to six pairs of buffaloes, six to seven pairs of cows, and a number of slaves to a monastery.

The Buddha image is carved from a somewhat friable local sandstone. As a result, the face is quite badly eroded, the area around the jaw and chin having flaked away completely. This makes it difficult to discern what its original facial features would have looked like. However, its *uṣṇīṣa* and hair curls are still visible and the overall rendering of the body, robe, and feet all bear the hallmarks of the Dvāravatī style. The outer robe, for instance, has a diaphanous quality to it and terminates in the characteristic U-shaped design, while the undergarment flares out gently on both sides. Stylistically it dates to the 7th to 8th centuries. Given that the inscription also dates to circa 7th century, the two pieces are mostly likely contemporaneous.

A number of other *sīmā* and Buddha images have been discovered at Ban Thin Keao, a village on the opposite bank of the Nam Ngum to Ban Thalat. The Buddha images are fragmentary but do appear to date from the Dvāravatī period (Lorrillard 2014: 42–4, Figs. 2–5). It seems then that they and the pieces from Ban Thalat all belong to the same ancient settlement and perhaps the very monastery mentioned in the inscription.

More *sīmā* have been discovered at the site of Ban Muang Kao, 10 kilometres downstream from Ban Thalat. One, today kept at That Luang, has a *stūpa-kumbha* motif (Fig. 5.3) similar in design to those found in the Chi River and Cluster 4, in particular. Further downstream, *sīmā* have also been discovered at Ban Vieng Kham and Ban Nong Khon. Lorrillard (2014: 52) has recorded nine *sīmā* at the modern temple of Ban Nong Khon, six of which have axial *stūpa* motifs.

Excavations carried out at Ban Vieng Kham by Anna Karlstrom between 2003 and 2004 turned up a number of Dvāravatī-period *sīmā* (Karlstrom et al. 2005). She concluded that while the *sīmā* themselves were Dvāravatī period in date, the site itself dated to the 17th to 18th centuries (Karlstrom 2009: 170). This indicated that the *sīmā* had been re-used at that time. Several have *stūpa* and *stūpa-kumbha* motifs while others have only lotus bands at their base (Karlstorm 2009: 134–6).

Figure 5.1: Buddha image from Ban Thalat, Vientiene province, today kept at Wat Ho Pra Keo Temple, Vientiane city, Laos. 7th–8th centuries. Sandstone.

Figure 5.2: Inscription from Ban Thalat, Vientiene province, today kept at Wat Ho Pra Keo Temple, Vientiane city, Laos. 7th century. Sandstone.

5.1

5.2

Figure 5.3: *Sīmā* with a *stūpa-kumbha* motif from Ban Muang Kao, Vientiane province, Laos. Today kept at That Luang, Vientiane. 8th–9th centuries. Sandstone. Height: 150 cm; width: 50 cm; depth: 20 cm.

About 15 kilometres north of Vientiane city, both *sīmā* and Buddha images have been discovered at a group of sites – Ban Na Sone, Ban Ilai, Ban Nong Kan Khu, and Dan Sung. The latter site will be discussed in some detail later in this chapter. As for the other three sites, nine *sīmā* have been discovered at Ban Na Sone, seven as recently as 2005 (Fig. 5.4). One appears to have Khmer script on it, but the letters are largely illegible. Another *sīmā* has a variant of the *stūpa-kumbha* motif (Lorrillard 2014: 57–8). A few kilometres away at Ban Nong Khan Khu, two more *sīmā* with *stūpa* designs were discovered, as was a large, eroded Buddha head over 40 centimetres in height (Lorrillard 2014: Fig. 12). Its body, however, has not been discovered. The village of Ban Ilai lies a few kilometres north of Ban Nong Khan Khu. Here nine *sīmā* still remain standing in situ around an earthen mound. Given the close proximity of these three villages, it is likely that the material discovered there is all part of one

Figure 5.4: A number of *sīmā* discovered at Ban Na Sone, Vientiane province, Laos have been gathered up and stored at a local shelter.

overall settlement where Buddhism took hold. The site of Dan Sung further supports this hypothesis (see below).

A number of artefacts have come to light in Vientiane city that further attests to the presence of Buddhism. There are several *sīmā* with narrative art while others have *stūpa-kumbha* motifs. At Wat Ban Phon Pa Nao Temple, one *sīmā* appears to depict the *Vidhurapaṇḍita-jātaka* (Lorrillard 2014: 61–2, Fig. 30). Another *sīmā* (Fig. 5.5) from Ban Dong Phosy, but today kept at Wat Ho Phra Keo, may depict a bodhisattva in royal ease posture (*lalitāsana*). This posture is depicted in a very similar fashion to that on a *sīmā* from Ban Phan Lam in the Chi River system (Fig. 3.14). The figure appears to be holding a *vajra* in his left hand. If so, it may indicate that it is Indra. However, given the lack of other details and identifying traits, it is impossible to identify for certain who is being represented. There is an eight-line inscription on the upper third of this *sīmā* and while it is not legible in its entirely, the term "*śrī dharmarājā*" (a

5.6

king who rules in accordance to dharma, the teachings of the Buddha) has been read by Christian Bauer (cited in Lorrillard 2014: 63–4).

Two more *sīmā* that are today also kept at Wat Ho Phra Keo Temple, but originally come from Ban Saphang Mo, have narrative art. One (Fig. 5.6) is fragmentary, but three figures, all seated, are clearly visible – one on top and two below. The figure on top is seated in *vajrāsana*. However, the top of the *sīmā* is no longer present and the section of this image from the crown of his head upwards is missing. It is thus impossible to establish

Figure 5.5: *Sīmā* from Ban Dong Phosy, Vientiane province today kept at Wat Ho Pra Keo Temple, Vientiane city, Laos. 8th–9th centuries. Sandstone.

Figure 5.6: Fragmentary *sīmā* from Ban Saphang Mo, Vientiane province with an unidentified narrative scene. Today kept at Wat Ho Pra Keo Temple, Vientiane city, Laos. 8th–9th centuries. Sandstone. Height: 70 cm; width: 50 cm; depth: 12 cm.

5.5

Figure 5.7: Fragmentary *sīmā* from Ban Saphang Mo, Vientiane province showing the Courting of Amarā from the *Mahāummagga-jātaka*. Vientiane city, Laos. 8th–9th centuries.

whether he had the conical headdress of a bodhisattva or an *uṣṇīṣa* of the Buddha. If it were the former, this would likely indicate a *jātaka* tale; if the latter, it would most likely indicate a Life of the Buddha episode. The figure appears to be wearing a necklace of some sort, which would point towards him being a bodhisattva. However, his hand is in *vitarkamudrā*, which is suggestive of the Buddha. The *vitarkamudrā* in this instance is depicted somewhat differently than the examples seen in the Chi River system. Instead of the right hand facing fingers upwards, palm facing outwards, in this depiction the fingers are facing sideward. The figure to the bottom left seems to be a king of some kind due to his conical

headdress. The figure to the right is possibly his queen or an attendant. Unfortunately, their faces are defaced but the "king's" arms are clearly placed together in *añjalimudrā* (both hands pressed together in prayer), paying respect to the Buddha/bodhisattva. If this is a Life of the Buddha scene, it may represent the Buddha preaching to King Bimbisara or his father, such as that found at Muang Fa Daed (Fig. 2.10).

The other *sīmā* from Ban Saphang Mo appears to depict an episode from the *Mahāummagga-jātaka* showing the Courting of Amarā (Fig. 5.7). Four examples of this have been found in the Chi River system (Figs. 3.4 and 3.13). However, as Lorrillard (2014: 66) points out, if this is in fact so, then the figures have been reversed in this case – Amarā is shown on the left and Mahosadha on the right. There is also an inscription on the upper section that is presumed to be in Mon but appears to be illegible (Lorrillard 2014: 66).

The material reviewed so far indicates that the area stretching from Ban Thalat in the north to Vientiane city in the south shows ample evidence for the adoption of Buddhism in this area from the 7th century onwards. The discussion now turns to three mountaintop sites to further illustrate the nature of Buddhism in this cluster.

Pilgrimage and Mountaintop Retreats: Phu Phra Bat, Dan Sung, and Vang Sang

Evidence for Buddhist art in mountaintop locations comes from three sites in this cluster: Phu Phra Bat, Dan Sung, and Vang Sang. They show strong similarities with each other in terms of the selection and utilisation of their natural landscapes and represent a distinctive manifestation of Buddhist art that emerged in this area of the Khorat Plateau.

The Phu Phan range are low hills that straddle the Khorat Plateau in a northwest to southeast direction, stretching from Mukdahan province to Udon Thani province. Near its terminus in the northwest, we find the site of Phu Phra Bat in Ban Phue district, Udon Thani province. Today the mountain range is covered with hardwood forest, which was most likely also the case during the Dvāravatī period. The site covers an area of about 10 square kilometres, is at an average height of 320 to 350 metres above sea level, and rises 120 to 160 metres above the plain below. There is evidence for both prehistoric and Dvāravatī-period habitation (Chutiwongs 2000: 48). The site has numerous rock shelters, many of which have prehistoric wall paintings. The evidence for Buddhism comes in the form of *sīmā* and Buddha images carved into the rock face (Fig. 5.8). There is also a *buddhapāda* (footprint of the Buddha) – hence the name of the site – but it is from a later date and enclosed by a *stūpa* built in 1920. There are approximately 40 *sīmā* still present at Phu Phra Bat spread out over 23 sites. Originally, however, there must have been more,

Figure 5.8: Buddha image carved into the rockface at Phu Phra Bat, Ban Phue district, Udon Thani province, Thailand.

as evidenced by the remains of holes still visible today carved into the base of the exposed rock floor into which *sīmā* would have been slotted.

The sites are spread out across the top of the mountain range, suggesting there was a sizable monastic community here during the Dvāravatī period. Prior to their use as Buddhist sites, these shelters were used by prehistoric inhabitants. Due to natural erosion, many of the rock shelters have quite unusual shapes that seem to defy gravity. They are somewhat mushroom-like, slender in the middle with wide, overhanging tops. Nandana Chutiwongs has suggested that these rock formations may have been chosen by Buddhist monks not only for their practical value to provide shelter, but also for their mystical appeal (2000: 43). The rock shelters have been adapted for habitation with little use of permanent building material such as brick.

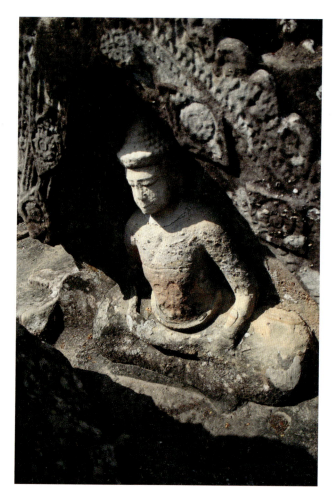

The placement of *sīmā* around many of these structures could have been an attempt to "Buddhisise" these formerly animistic prehistoric locations (Fig. 5.9). Here we thus observe that *sīmā* during this period were used for demarcating spaces other than monastic buildings. The most remarkable rock shelter is known today as Usa's Tower. A brick structure has been built into this natural rock formation to create a small chamber, with one door and two windows (Fig. 5.10). It was accessible by ladder and most likely functioned as a monk's cell. Many of the other rock shelters have also been modified to form suitable places for meditation. Usually their floors would have been levelled and smoothed, or their roofs dug out to allow for a person to stand within the shelter. Some were large enough to accommodate up to 10 monks at a time.

In the same vein, a seat for meditation has been carved out of the natural rock in a shaded spot at the edge of a cliff. It has views of the plains below, providing an ideal environment for spiritual contemplation (Chutiwongs 2000: 46). Given the number of rock shelters present, and the fact that each could hold between two to ten monks, there could have

Figure 5.9: In situ *sīmā* placed around a rock shelter at Phu Phra Bat, Ban Phue district, Udon Thani province, Thailand. 8th–9th centuries.

Figure 5.10: Rock shelter known as "Usa's Tower" at Phu Phra Bat, Ban Phue district, Udon Thani province, Thailand.

5.10

potentially been up to a hundred monks at this site at any given time. The site of Phu Phra Bat represents some of the best evidence anywhere in Southeast Asia for a 1st millennium CE monastic forest community.

The presence of naturally occurring rock formations suitable for remodelling into habitats, a plentiful water supply, ample forest cover, and the relative isolation of the hilltop, all made Phu Phra Bat an ideal choice for those withdrawing from society in the quest for spiritual enlightenment. Connection with the lowland Buddhist communities would still have taken place. There were numerous Buddhist sites along the river systems in the area directly surrounding the Phu Phan Mountain range. And as discussed above, there were substantial Buddhist communities on the northern side of the Mekong too. The monks from these communities could have spent time in retreat at Phu Phra Bat,

The Middle Mekong: Buddhist Art from Vientiane to Wat Phu

particularly during the rainy season. Pilgrimage to Phu Phra Bat by the lay community was also a likely activity. Further evidence for these connections can be seen in the sites of Dan Sung and Vang Sang in Vientiane province.

The site of Dan Sung shares many similarities with Phu Phra Bat, albeit on a somewhat smaller scale. It is located approximately 50 kilometres to the north of Phu Phra Bat, in close proximity to the sites of

Figure 5.11: Buddha images with modern gold leaf paint located under a rock shelter at Dan Sung, Vientiane province, Laos. 8th–9th centuries.

Ban Na Sone, Ban Ilai, and Ban Nong Kan Khu discussed above. The mountain range on which it is situated has an average height of 290 metres and, as with Phu Phra Bat, natural erosion has created rock formations that can be readily converted into shelters. The site was first reported by Suzanne Karpelès (1949), who ascribed the art to the Lopburi period. It was Gagneux, however, who made the connection that it was in fact "Mon", by which he means in the Dvāravatī style (1977).

The site can be divided into northern and southern sections. They lie about 150 metres apart (Lorrillard 2014: 53). The first rock shelter (no. 12) in the southern section has a meditating Buddha image carved into the rockface flanked by two motifs. These motifs are covered in modern plaster and it is thus difficult to ascertain what they may represent. Karpelès thought they may have been lotus flowers, as does Lorrillard (2014: 53), and this seems to be the most plausible suggestion. The second rock shelter (no. 11) has a further group of Buddha images carved into the rock face. They have been modified with modern plaster, but the faces appear to still be original. Four standing Buddha images are located within the rock shelter itself. However, once again, their original features are masked by the application of modern plaster (Fig. 5.11). There is also a Buddha in high relief, but only the head and forearms are original (Lorrillard 2014: 55). At the northern end of this rock shelter, there are two rectangular features carved into the base of the rock. It appears they were used as slots for the tenon of a Buddha image or a *sīmā* in a similar fashion to those seen at Phu Phra Bat.

Six *sīmā* have so far been discovered around rock shelter 11, one of which has a seven-line inscription. The first three lines appear to be in post-Pallava script, while the remaining four seem to be in Khmer characters from the Angkor period and are thought to date to the 9th to 10th centuries with the language appearing to be Sanskrit (Lorrillard 2014: 56). This date range generally corresponds to the Buddhist sculpture at the site, as they are Dvāravatī in style but also exhibit a certain degree of Khmer traits, such as the moustache and wider, more squarish faces.

Dan Sung thus shares many similarities with Phu Phra Bat. Both are in mountain foothills, have numerous Buddha images carved into the rock face, have *sīmā*, and have made use of natural geological formations as rock shelters. Stylistically the Buddha images from Dan Sung are similar to those found at Phu Phra Bat. However, a number of them also show some Khmer features and may thus be somewhat later in date, circa 9th to 10th centuries.

The site of Vang Sang is approximately 40 kilometres north of Dan Sung and about 10 kilometres southwest of Ban Thalat. Unlike Dan Sung and Phu Phra Bat, it is not on elevated terrain but instead is located at a large rock outcrop at a bend on the banks of the Nam Cheng River.

Numerous Buddha images have been carved into this rockface. It was first published by Charles Batteur (1925) and subsequently by Karpelès (1949), Gagneux (1977), and Lorrillard (2014). The Buddha images most certainly date to the late Dvāravatī period, but as Lorrillard (2014: 49–50) points out, some of them have been significantly altered in the 20th century. However, the four Buddhas seated in meditation carved into the northern rockface appear to be untouched. The largest of them is in *vitarkamudrā* (Fig. 5.12). Another Buddha is located in the rockface next to them, separated by a crevice. It appears that the images would have been covered by an awning or shelter of some kind, as there are mortises carved above them into the rock face at certain points. It is most likely that a wooden roof was constructed by slotting beams into them (Lorrillard 2014: 50).

Figure 5.12: Buddha images carved into the rockface at Vang Sang, Vientiane province, Laos. 9th–10th centuries.

The two large seated Buddha images in the opposite corner were restored with cement in 1957 on account of them being badly eroded. Photographs taken in 1933, however, reveal their original features (Lorrillard 2014: 51, Fig. 15). Their facial features are similar to the five Buddha images on the north face. Overall, the style of the images at Vang Sang is similar to those found at Dan Sung. Their angular faces and thicker coiffures also indicate a degree of Khmer stylistic traits and place them from the. 9th to 10th centuries.

All three sites – Phu Phra Bat, Dan Sung, and Vang Sang – have very similar characteristics. They were located in upland areas and shaped and modified the natural environment to suit their spiritual needs and purposes. It is unlikely that this is a coincidence; instead it seems clear that they were all part of a common Buddhism practice of creating locations to retreat from society. All three sites were located close to lowland Buddhist communities, suggesting that they could have been used for the rainy season retreat. They would also have been formed as pilgrimage sites by Buddhist monks and laity alike. As with Phu Wiang, Phu Bor, and Phu Kao Putthanimit in the Chi River system, we once again see Buddhist practitioners shaping both their physical and cognitive environments by inscribing Buddhist imagery and symbolism into the landscape.

Ban Phailom and Ban Nong Khluem

Two of the most significant sites in this cluster are Phra Putthabat Bua Ban Temple in Ban Phailom and Wat Non Sila Temple in Ban Nong Khluem. These sites, located within 10 kilometres of each other, are close to the Huai Mong River in Ban Phue district, Udon Thani province. As will be shown below, they were clearly connected, and it appears that the same group of artists worked at both sites.

The *sīmā* at these two sites were by and large still in situ when they were excavated in 1998 by the Fine Arts Department (FAD 1998a). The excavations clearly showed that at both locations the *sīmā* had been set up to demarcate ritual space. At Ban Nong Khluem, 22 *sīmā* were erected in a rectangular pattern. However, it is unclear if all were still in situ. At Ban Phailom, on the other hand, 24 *sīmā* were placed in a rectangular pattern in three concentric rows which expanded in size from the centre outwards. The two sites illustrate that the number of *sīmā* employed to form a boundary at any given site could vary and could be more than 20 in some cases. No evidence for a structure was found in the centre of the areas demarcated by the *sīmā*, suggesting that it was either built of perishable materials or that there was no structure present in antiquity.

The *sīmā* tradition that flourished at these two sites dates to c. 11th to 12th centuries and was a fusion of Khmer artistic styles and the local Buddhist tradition that had established itself in the region from around the 7th to 8th centuries onwards. The scenes depicted on the *sīmā* have by and large lost any aspects of the Dvāravatī art style and instead resemble the figurative artwork of Khmer temple lintels (Kingmanee 1998b). However, the content – *jātaka* and Life of the Buddha scenes – remains consistent with that of the *sīmā* tradition of the preceding centuries.

The supposition that Khmer lintels formed the template for the artwork on these *sīmā* is further strengthened by observations made by Hiram Woodward (1997: 78). He points out that the Khmer-style Buddha images that first appear at Phimai were depicted without monastic robes and that their chests are shown bare with a characteristic Khmer lower garment wrapped around their waists. The crowns shown on their heads were also directly inspired by those found on Khmer Hindu images. It appears that the Khmer artists, initially unfamiliar with the iconographic characteristics of the Buddha, chose to depict him using the templates available to them – that of Hindu temple imagery. The Buddha and bodhisattva images on the *sīmā* at Ban Phailom and Ban Nong Khluem are also shown bare-chested with Khmer-style crowns. This points towards the handiwork of craftsmen familiar with the decorated lintels of the numerous Khmer temples on the Khorat Plateau. A number of examples are now discussed to illustrate this.

The Sāma-jātaka

This *jātaka* has been identified on one *sīmā* (Fig. 5.13) from Ban Nong Khleum by Kingmanee (1998b: 44–6). It depicts the moment Sāma is struck by an arrow from King Piliyakkha's bow (Cowell 1978: Vol. VI, 38–52). The arrow is clearly visible, piercing his right side and exiting through the left. The posture of King Piliyakkha indicates a sense of movement. His right hand raised behind his head signifies the arrow's release. Sāma is shown wearing a Khmer-style crown and King Piliyakkha has a lower garment in the Khmer fashion. The pleating at the thighs is particularly indicative of this.

The Suvannakakkata-jātaka

This *jātaka* (Fig. 5.14), on a *sīmā* from Ban Nong Khluem, has been identified by Kingmanee (1996: 133–8; 1998b: 46–7). It is the only known example of this *jātaka* from anywhere in the Khorat Plateau during the period covered by this study. In this tale the Buddha was reborn as a farmer and he befriended a golden crab that lived in a pond in one of his fields (Cowell 1978: Vol. III, 183–6). He used to keep him in his garment while tending his fields. A crow that nested in a tree nearby desired to eat the eyes of the bodhisattva and enlisted the help of a snake. The snake lay in wait and when the bodhisattva eventually passed by, bit him on the leg. The bodhisattva fell and the crow descended on him. As it

Figure 5.13: Detail of a *sīmā* depicting the *Sāma-jātaka* from Wat Non Sila Temple, Ban Nong Khleum, Ban Phue district, Udon Thani province, Thailand. 11th century. Sandstone. Height: 334 cm; width: 75 cm; depth: 48 cm.

Figure 5.14: Detail of a *sīmā* depicting the *Suvannakakkata-jātaka* from Wat Non Sila Temple, Ban Nong Khleum, Ban Phue district, Udon Thani province, Thailand. 11th century. Sandstone. Height: 176 cm; width: 74 cm; depth: 35 cm.

was about to peck out his eyes, the crab emerged from the garment and grabbed both the crow and the snake by the neck, thus saving the bodhisattva. Knowing they would attempt this again, the crab crushed both animals with its claws. The crab and the crow are understood to be earlier births of Ānanda, a top disciple of the Buddha, and Devadatta, a disciple who became his nemesis.

This *sīmā* shows this very episode. Depicted on its base, the *sīmā* shows the bodhisattva exposed, lying on his back after being struck by the snake. The crow is perched on his body, hoping to pluck out his eyes. The crab is shown appearing from the bodhisattva's garment, catching both the snake and the crow in its claws. The artist has also cleverly chosen to incorporate the *stūpa* motif into the overall composition with the body of the snake shown wrapped around it. This episode also appears on reliefs from the 8th- to 9th-century temple of Candi Mendut in Java, where once again the crab is shown grasping the snake and crow. Marijke Klokke (1993: 159–60) suggests either the Pāli *jātaka* or an early Indian *Pañcatantra* text as possible sources.

The Temiya-jātaka

This *jātaka* has been identified by Kingmanee (2006) on one *sīmā* from Ban Nong Khluem (Murphy 2010: Fig. 5.12). It depicts Temiya in the centre of the composition and the charioteer crouching to the left. Temiya carries a spade in his right hand and lifts his left hand above his head as if to protect himself. The chariot is depicted to the right of Temiya, identifiable by the horse to the far right and the spoked wheel shown just

above the bodhisattva's left foot. Temiya is adorned with a Khmer crown and lower garment.

The Buddha's Return to Kapilavastu

This scene has been identified on one *sīmā* apiece from Ban Nong Khluem and Ban Phailom (Murphy 2010: Figs. 5.75 and 5.76), which both show very similar compositional arrangements. Both possibly depict the Buddha seated with his wife and son; however, the identification is tentative. Both *sīmā* depict the Buddha at the centre, seated cross-legged on a throne in *vajrāsana*. There is a female figure to the left of the Buddha; to the right of the Buddha are two other figures, one of which appears to be a child sitting on the knee or back of the other figure. It is possible that the child is Rāhula and the female figure is Yaśodharā.

The Buddha

One *sīmā* apiece from Ban Nong Khluem and Ban Phailom appear to show the Buddha seated cross-legged in *vajrāsana* at the bottom centre, flanked by Indra to the right and Avalokiteśvara or Maitreya to the left (Murphy 2010: Figs. 5.100 and 5.101). Kingmanee (1998b: 38) suggests that the *sīmā* from Ban Phailom represents the Buddha, Indra, and the Buddha's mother. The figure to the right holds a *vajra* and thus could be Indra. However, the figure to the left holds a lotus flower and is thus unlikely to be the Buddha's mother. Perhaps she is instead Padmapāṇi, the female form of Avalokiteśvara. If this is the case, the figure on the right may not be Indra but the bodhisattva Vajrapāṇi, the protector of the

5.14

Buddha who holds a *vajra* as his attribute. Comparisons can be made with Candi Mendut in 10th-century Java, Indonesia. At this temple, the Buddha is flanked by Avalokiteśvara to the left and Vajrapāṇi to the right. This appears to be a more likely identification.

A number of other *sīmā* from these two sites appear to show either the bodhisattva Avalokiteśvara or Maitreya seated with a lotus flower in his right hand. The remaining *sīmā* appear to show generic Buddha images or perhaps episodes from the Life of the Buddha. In these cases, the Buddha is seated cross-legged on a throne, flanked by attendant figures.

It appears that a community of monks settled around the sites of Ban Nong Khluem and Ban Phailom in the 10th or 11th centuries. This group and their artists managed to fuse the Buddhist content of the region with the stylised and refined forms of Khmer art and in doing so, created a distinctive and original aesthetic.

Stūpa-kumbha Motifs

A number of sites in Cluster 6 have *sīmā* with elaborate *stūpa-kumbha* motifs. The site of Wang Sapung in Loei province, in particular, has some noteworthy examples. It is located on the Loei River, a tributary of the Mekong. The *sīmā* from this site are situated at local temples in two of the surrounding villages. What is remarkable about the 35 *sīmā* present here is that 28 of them have the *stūpa-kumbha* motifs (Fig. 5.15). The quality and quantity of these depictions point towards the existence of a skilled group of craftsmen who were extremely familiar with the iconographic components of this motif. *Sīmā* depicting almost identical *stūpa-kumbha* designs are also found in Ban Muang Kao and Muang Sanakham in Vientiane province, illustrating the close link between these two areas.

In terms of style, the *stūpa-kumbha* from Loei and Vientiane provinces can at times be more elaborate than those found at sites such as Ban Tat Tong and Ban Khum Ngoen in Cluster 4. It may be that they represent a later phase in the development of this motif.

Summary

The area encompassed by Cluster 6 provides clear evidence for Buddhist art on both sides of the Mekong River spanning the period of the 7th to 11th centuries. Narrative art is present, albeit to a much lesser extent than in the Chi River system, and many *sīmā* have elaborate *stūpa-kumbha* motifs. Some stone Buddha images survive as do a number of inscriptions, such as that from Ban Thalat. The sites of Phu Phra Bat, Dan Sung, and Vang Sang indicate a tradition of withdrawing to mountaintops for meditation and also pilgrimage, and this in turn inscribed Buddhism into the surrounding natural landscape. With the growing Khmer presence in the 10th century, the area retained its Buddhist faith, albeit with a new aesthetic, as seen in the sites of Ban Phailom and Ban Nong Khleum.

Given the considerable amount of evidence for Buddhist art concentrated around Vientiane and its hinterlands, it is likely that a polity of some form which supported Buddhism existed in this area. Hoshino (2002: 40–1), in his study of the *New Tang Annals*, points out that Wendan had two vassals to its north, Dao Ming and Can Ban. He suggests Can Ban refers to the site of Sri Thep and that Dao Ming was located in

Figure 5.15: *Sīmā* with a *stūpa-kumbha* motif from Wat Phathsimaram Temple, Wang Sapung district, Loei province, Thailand. 8th–9th centuriees. Sandstone. Height: 170 cm; width: 73 cm; depth: 30 cm.

Fig. 5.16: Detail of inscription K. 981 on a cylindrical *sīmā* from Wat Si That temple, Ban Don Kaeo, Ban Chiang Haeo subdistrict, Kumphawapi district, Udon Thani province. 7th–early 8th centuries. Sandstone. Length: 114 cm; diameter: 55 cm. National Museum Khon Kaen. Inventory number 17/34/2517.

the area around Vientiane province (Map 15). He hypothesises that Dao Ming was a Chinese rendering of the Thai *thao muang*, meaning vassal state. They were also said to have no salt, which given its preponderance in the Chi River system, would place this vassal state north of that. Given the archaeological evidence and site distribution in Cluster 6, it is certainly possible that this area was in fact the Dao Ming referred to in Chinese texts, as no other locations appear possible. The presence of the term *śrī dharmarāja* on one *sīmā* from Vientiane provides further tantalising evidence of this possibility. However, to date no inscription has been discovered bearing a name of a kingdom from the 7th to 9th centuries, nor has any settlement been located – though it is possible that the modern footprint of Vientiane city is concealing it. Further archaeological research in this area may in time cast more light on the name and characteristics of this polity.

CLUSTER 7: UDON THANI AND THE SAKHON NAKHON BASIN

There are a few sites in the upper north-eastern corner of the Khorat Plateau lying just north of the Phu Phan range that have evidence for Buddhist art. However, it is much scarcer than in other areas of the Khorat Plateau. Of these, Ban Don Kaeo and Ban Chiang are Dvāravatī-period moated sites. Three further sites – Ban Ma, Ban Ta Wat Dai, and Ban Panna in Sakhon Nakhon province – also have evidence for Buddhism. Unlike the other clusters, there are no particular unifying features in the five sites that make up Cluster 7 (Map 13; Table 10). As

The Middle Mekong: Buddhist Art from Vientiane to Wat Phu

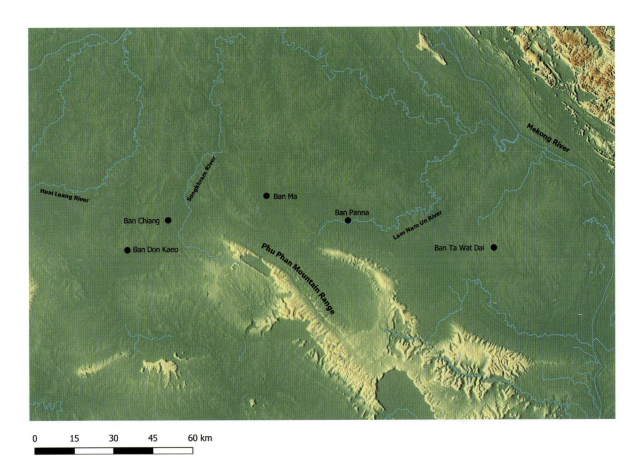

Map 13 Cluster 7.

such, it is more a convenient geographical grouping for discussion purposes.

The most important location in this group is Ban Don Kaeo, in Ban Chiang Haeo subdistrict, Kumphawapi district, Udon Thani province. It is a large moated site, almost 2 kilometres in diameter at its widest point. Ten *sīmā* were found here and are today kept at Wat Si That Temple. One has a two-line inscription (K. 981) (Fig. 5.16). It was first reported in 1963–1964 during the Archaeological Salvage Expedition led by William G. Solheim and Chester Gorman (Solheim and Gorman 1966: 158–9). It has a fragmentary Sanskrit inscription in Pallava script which has been translated by George Cœdès (1964: 159–60). He dated it to circa 7th to early 8th centuries CE. It has been transliterated as follows:

(1) [...] māyo   yatir vviprādipūjitaḥ
śilām imām asau saimīṃ   sthāpayām āsa bhikṣubhiḥ

(2) [...] ne   śucisaṃvatsare śake
daśame caitraśukle bhūt   sīmeyaṃ saṅghasammatā

Cœdès' French translation reads, "[...] cet ascète honoré par les brahmanes a érigé cette pierre tenant l'office de borne, avec les bhikṣu." Piriya Krairiksh (1974a: 41) translated this into English as "[...] this ascetic honoured by the Brahmans erected this stone having the function of boundary stone with the Bhikkhus [sic]." However, Peter Skilling (pers. comm.) proposes a revised reading of this inscription that downplays the role of the Brahmins:

(1) [Name or epithet] the renunciant venerated by Brahmins and others caused this stone in the form of a boundary by the monks to be established.

(2) [Year in words] the tenth day of the bright half of Caitra, this boundary was agreed by the Saṅgha.

Skilling interprets this to indicate that brahmins were present, but do not appear to have conducted the consecration. This indicates their presence alongside Buddhists during the 7th to 8th centuries. However, as Johannes Bronkhorst (2011: 64) has pointed out, "Respect for Brahmins in South and Southeast Asia should not be confused with 'conversion' to Brahmanism."

Three other *sīmā* from this site are similar typologically. They are cylindrical in shape, more so than the normal octagonal type found elsewhere in the Khorat Plateau. Ban Panna in Sakkon Nakhon province also provides epigraphic evidence for Buddhism. One *sīmā* has a two-line inscription in post-Pallava script, Old Mon language, dated paleographically to the 9th to 10th centuries. Kongkaew Wiraprajak's reading of the inscription states that members of the Mipa Suraya family donated doors and windows to build a new temple (2007: 51). The other *sīmā*, today kept at Khon Kaen National Museum, has a *stūpa-kumbha* motif with the inscription written vertically to the right of it. It too is in Old Mon language (Hunter 2013: 182, 197, 376–81).

The site of Ban Ma in Sawang Deang Din district of Sakhon Nakhon province presents another example of how Khmer stylistic traits fused with the local Buddhist *sīmā* tradition. Unfortunately, this *sīmā* was stolen in 1981 and has not been recovered. However, photographic evidence for this *sīmā* shows two scenes from the *Ramayana*. One side depicts the episode where Sītā is kidnapped by Viradha, while the other side is thought to depict Kuberu, the guardian god of the north, who is also the protector of sacred space (Suksavasti 1991: 105). While this *sīmā* is no longer present, it does provide an example of how Khmer traditions did not replace those already in existence in the Khorat Plateau, but instead blended with them.

The site of Ban Ta Wat Dai in Sakhon Nahkon province has a group of *sīmā* which may possibly be in situ. They are located at Wat Klang Sri Chiang Mai Temple, beside the ruined foundations of a Khmer monument. These *sīmā* are similar to those found throughout the Khorat Plateau during the 8th to 9th centuries, two of which have *stūpa-kumbha* motifs. The remaining 13 have axial *stūpa* motifs. As with Ban Ma, this site shows that Khmer culture often occupied sites that were previously inhabited by Buddhist communities.

CLUSTER 8: FROM THAT PHANOM TO PHRA THAT PHON

Cluster 8 has 17 sites in total divided into two groups located along a roughly 65-kilometre north–south stretch of the Mekong River (Table 11). This starts in the locality of That Phanon in Nakhon Phanom province, Thailand, and ends around Phra That Phon, a *stūpa* some 35 kilometres southeast of Savannakhet town in Laos (Map 14). The first group consists of nine sites located on both sides of the Mekong River. The second group consists of seven sites located on the eastern side of the Mekong. Four are in close proximity to Phra That Phon, while the other two are outliers and located at a considerable distance away.

This section of the Mekong is largely defined by the Truong Son Cordillera/Annamite Mountain range. It is located directly to the east of the river and as a result, there are often only narrow stretches of lowland between it and the banks of the Mekong. However, from Nakhon Phanom to Savannakhet, the mountains recede somewhat, leaving a lowland basin within which most of the sites discussed on the east bank are located. The west bank by comparison is flatter, but does include the southernmost section of the Phu Phan range, which means that certain areas are at a higher elevation.

The evidence from this cluster is exclusively from *sīmā*. None have narrative art on them, though many have axial *stūpa* or *stūpa-kumbha* motifs. They represent the most easterly spread of this tradition and the Mekong River and its tributaries played a key role in its dissemination. South of Phra That Phon, the archaeological record predominantly reflects Khmer culture. This is particularly the case from the site of Huan Hin down to Wat Phu (Lorrillard 2010–2011). However, as will be discussed below, there is some evidence for Buddhist art at this latter site.

That Phanon and Its Surrounds

Stūpa in Northeast Thailand and Laos are usually referred to as *phra that* or *that* for short. They have their own architectural form and can be found dotted throughout the Khorat Plateau. The body of a *phra that* is designed as an angular lotus bud. This usually stands on a low lotus base surmounted by a square pedestal. A further elongated lotus design forms the spire which is topped by an umbrella-shaped finial. The term comes from the Pāli word *dhātu* (relic). Most were built from the 14th century onwards and many of them are either located at sites that were occupied during the 7th to 9th centuries or have artefacts from this period located nearby or incorporated into their architecture. As such, they represent a continuation and intertwining of Buddhist traditions in the region. There are often local Buddhist myths and legends attached to these monuments or the associated Dvāravatī-period material. As such, they act as hubs of local forms of knowledge on the region's Buddhist past.

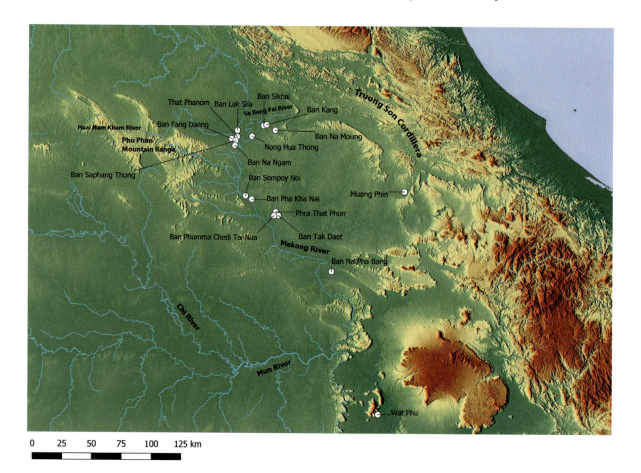

Map 14 Cluster 8.

The most well-known *phra that* is Phra That Phanom in Nakhon Phanom province. Phra That Phanom as it stands today is 57 metres tall, ornately decorated with stucco and gold – the umbrella alone weighs a full 16 kilograms of this precious material. Dating a *phra that* precisely can be difficult due to the constant renovations, extensions, and sometimes complete dismantling and subsequent reconstruction. Local Buddhist myths also play their part. The hill that That Phanom rests on, for instance, is said to have not only been visited by the Buddha himself, but also Kakusandha, Koṇāgamana, and Kassapa, the three Buddhas of the three corresponding previous ages (Pruess 1976: 6). The *phra that* is believed to have been built shortly after the Buddha's death and his breastbone is said to be enshrined within. Historically, however, evidence for Buddhism at the site itself seems to be no earlier than the 7th to 10th centuries, and the monument did not seem to come to prominence until the 16th century when it was renovated at the behest of King Setthathirath of Lan Xang. The present structure dates to 1976, having been rebuilt after it collapsed in a rainstorm in August 1975.

Architecturally, the many smaller *phra that* found throughout the Khorat Plateau are based stylistically on That Phanom. Local myths also interweave the smaller *phra that* into larger Buddhist narratives, with many of them also claiming to contain corporeal relics of the Buddha. In some instances, such as at Ban Muang Phrai in Roi Et Province, the 7th- to 9th-century *sīmā* at the site are incorporated into the mythology. Locals explain that at some point in the distant past, these boundary stones were originally destined for That Phanom; however, for some reason they never reached their intended destination and ended up in Ban Muang Phrai instead.[32]

Phra that make up a unique and distinctive architectural feature in the modern religious landscape of the Khorat Plateau. They can often be found incorporated into themes regarding the arrival of Buddhism into the region either by being woven into Buddhist legends or by association with artefacts such as *sīmā*. In a number of cases, such as at Muang Fa Daed, they are actually built on top of ruined foundations of Dvāravatī-period *stūpa*, further emphasising the enduring ties between Buddhism, past and present.

Of the nine sites that make up the subgroup, five are located in That Phanom district on the western back of the Mekong, in close proximity to the Huai Nam Kham River. The other four sites are on the eastern bank of the Mekong located along the Se Bang Fai River. The Huai Nam Kham and the Se Bang Fai rivers enter the Mekong on opposite banks

---

32 This instance of local lore was recorded by the author in 2008 based on an interview with the villagers and monks at Ban Muang Phrai while conducting fieldwork.

within 2 kilometres of each other, facilitating ease of access between all the sites in this group.

At That Phanom, four *sīmā* have been placed at each of the four corners of the inner terrace. Three are octagonal type and one is slab type. Typologically these *sīmā* date to the 7th to 8th centuries and are very similar in design and dimensions to those found at Ban Don Kaeo, and it is possible that they were gathered up from here and installed at That Phanom. The other possibility is that there may have been a Dvāravatī-period site located here, though to date there is no clear archaeological evidence for this. Alternatively, the *sīmā* may have been brought here from one of the other four sites in its vicinity. Further detailed archaeological surveys of these sites and the surrounding area may provide clearer answers to these questions.

The four sites on the eastern bank of the Mekong – Ban Sikhai, Ban Kang, Ban Na Mouang, and Nong Hua Thong – are all are located along the Se Bang Fai River. The sites are grouped close together and several of the *sīmā* have the *stūpa-kumbha* motif depicted on them (Lorrillard 2008: 171, Fig. 6). They show strong similarities with those found in Yasothon in Cluster 4 and Loei and Vientiane provinces further north in Cluster 6.

Nong Hua Thong is the most significant site in this group. Archaeological excavations and a chance discovery of silver repoussé plaques from this site point towards it being an important ancient settlement during the 7th to 10th centuries (Hawixbrock 2009; Lorrillard 2010–2011: 241–4). It is located on the east bank at a bend in the Se Bang Fai River. The site is enclosed by dual linear earthen embankments, making it generally rectilinear in shape. It appears to stretch up to 2 kilometres in length from top to bottom. The site was first noted by Henri Parmentier (1954: 136), but it was not until 2008 that it began to receive renewed attention. On 24 April of that year a villager accidently uncovered a trove of archaeological material while digging foundations (Lorrillard 2010–2011: 243–4). These objects were reportedly contained in an earthenware jar. There were several pieces of gold and silver jewellery and a number of silver dishes. Two of the dishes had Khmer inscriptions, while a third had one in Sanskrit (Lorrillard 2010–2011: Figs. 30–32). These were read by Claude Jacques at the request of the late Mr Thongsa Sayavongkhamdy, Director of the Heritage Department, Ministry of Information, Culture and Tourism of Lao PDR. The Khmer inscriptions were given inventory numbers K. 1262 and K. 1263. They were engraved on the edge of the dishes and date from the 9th century (Lorrillard 2010–2011: 243). Jacques dated the inscription in Sanskrit on the third dish to the 8th century. It mentions the donation of land, slaves, cattle, and money to maintain the cult of Śiva.

In 2009 a rescue excavation was conducted by Viengkeo Souksavatdy, Deputy Director of the Heritage Department, Ministry of Information, Culture and Tourism of Lao PDR, and Christine Hawixbrock, an archaeologist attached to the École française d'Extrême-Orient (EFEO). It recovered over 116 objects including box covers, a pitcher, bowls, a candlestick, vases, three silver repoussé plaques, gold leaf, and stone and glass beads amongst other items. The three repoussé plaques all appear to have Hindu iconography (Fig. 5.24). One shows a male figure holding a rosary flanked by two kneeling figures clasping lotuses. John Guy has suggested that the central figure may represent Kubera (2020: 58–60). Another plaque shows a female figure standing on a lotus, holding a lotus in her left hand. She is flanked by two kneeling women and may represent Lakṣmī (Lorrillard 2010–2011: 243). The third plaque depicts a female deity of some kind framed by a floral arch. The plaques are reminiscent of those found at Maha Sarakham province (Diskul 1973). Further examples of plaques of this nature have been discovered at Si Thep, in Central Thailand, albeit in gold (Guy 2014: 243–4).

Despite being predominantly Hindu, two Dvāravatī-period *sīmā* with *stūpa* motifs were also discovered, indicating that Buddhism was practised at this site too. Nong Hua Thong is by far the largest known site in this group, and the cluster for that matter. Its exact nature and period of occupation are still unclear. However, given its key strategic position and the finds that have come to light to date, it appears to have been an important settlement where Hindu and Buddhist ideologies co-existed. It could also be the political centre of the sites in this group. Once again, the work of Hoshino (2002: 48–50) on the Chinese sources may shed some light on this. He identifies mention of a Chinese prefecture on the Mekong called Changzhou. As late as 791 CE, it was under direct control of the provincial government located at Hanoi (2002: 49) (Map 15). By studying the geographical information provided, Hoshino argues that this prefecture was located in the vicinity of Nakhon Phanom/Tha Kheak. If this is in fact the case, then Nong Hua Thong would seem to be the best candidate. That being said, there is little to no archaeological evidence suggesting Chinese presence here. It is more likely the case that the polity in this vicinity was ruled by the local populace and had a local name, but was in some form of tributary arrangement with Hanoi. However, as is the case with Wendan and Dao Ming, no definitive conclusions can be made until such time as epigraphic evidence is found indicating the names of these polities/settlements.

The other three sites in this cluster are located about 15 kilometres inland from Nong Hua Thong. Ban Sikhai and Ban Kang are about 2 kilometres apart and given their proximity, it is likely the *sīmā* from these two villages are from the same ancient settlement. The *sīmā* at Ban Sikhai are located at the local temple, Wat That Nimit. There are six of them, discovered in July 2000. The nine *sīmā* at Ban Kang were discovered in a paddy field in January 2009 (Lorrillard 2010–2011: 246). Ban Na Moang is about 10 kilometres east of these sites and eight *sīmā* were found lying in the ground, largely buried. They have now been placed in a shelter. Quite a few of the *sīmā* from these three sites have *stūpa-kumbha* designs on them reminiscent of those found in Yasothon province.

The evidence from the nine sites discussed in this group indicates that Buddhism had spread on both banks of this stretch of the Mekong River. On the right bank at least, it seems to have co-existed with Hinduism, as seen by the finds from Nong Hua Thong. The *sīmā* conform most closely in shape and motifs to those from Cluster 4, suggesting that Buddhism may have spread into this area from the lower reaches of the Chi River.

Moving downstream to the second group, the evidence comes from two sites just south of Savannakhet town and two more sites that cluster around the *stūpa* of Phra That Phon. The sites of Ban Pha Kha Nai and Ban Sompoy Noi are located on the banks of the Mekong about 15 kilometres south of Savannakhet. They have a few *sīmā* with axial *stūpa* motifs, but apart from that there is no other evidence present.

There are a number of Dvāravatī-period *sīmā* set up around the monument at Phra That Phon, but it is uncertain when this occurred and where they are from. However, stylistically they are similar to those discovered at the nearby sites of Ban Tak Daet and Ban Phumma Chedi Tai Nua and most likely came from one of the two (Lorrillard 2010–2011: 234). Ban Phumma Chedi Tai Nua is 2 kilometres southwest of Phra That Phon. The *sīmā* were discovered in the middle of a rice field around a small earthen mound. It appears that they were set up at the cardinal and subcardinal points and were therefore most likely in situ (Lorrillard 2010–2011: 235–7). Most of the *sīmā* are carved with the axial *stūpa* motif.

Ban Tak Daet is located a further 2.5 kilometres southeast of Ban Tai Phumma Chedi (and just 2 kilometres south of the That Phon). The *sīmā* were found in a forest temple nearby. One of them is 3.05 metres in height and 92 centimetres in width, making it the largest found in Laos to date (Lorrillard 2010–2011: 237) and one of the biggest on the Khorat Plateau in general. It has a *stūpa-kumbha* motif similar to those found in Cluster 4.

Finally, there are two outlying sites. The first, Muang Phin, is located 130 kilometres due east of Savannakhet, at the entry to the Lao Bao pass. Eight *sīmā* with axial *stūpa* designs have been discovered here (Lorrillard 2010–2011: 232). This is the furthest east any *sīmā* from this period has been discovered. The Lao Bao pass was an important route for trade and travel between the Khorat Plateau and the Cham culture on the other side of the Annamite Mountain range (also known as the Annamese/Truong

Son Cordillera). As I have shown elsewhere (Murphy 2019), artists who carved *sīmā* on the Khorat Plateau moved between here and sites in Champa, such as Mỹ Sơn and Đồng Dương, during the 8th to 9th centuries. They most likely took this route to do so. It is therefore not unsurprising to find *sīmā* in this location.

The final site, Ban Na Pha Bang, lies about 65 kilometres south of Savannakhet and 12 kilometres east from the Mekong. Five *sīmā* with axial *stūpa* motifs have been discovered here, one of which has a *stūpa-kumbha* design (Lorrillard 2010–2011: Fig. 14). Further south than this, there is no known evidence for Buddhism in the 7th to 10th centuries apart from that found at the site of Wat Phu.

The Wat Phu complex is located in Champassak province, Southern Laos, on the right bank of the Mekong. It is primarily known for its Khmer temple sanctuary located on the slopes of a mountainside, and the 5th-century Devānīka inscription which commemorates the city's founding. The peak of the mountain that overlooks the sanctuary and city is known as the Liṅgaparvata owing to its characteristic shape. It is considered to be a natural *liṅga* and has been worshipped since at least the 5th century. Śiva, in his earliest manifestations in Southeast Asia, often appeared as a *liṅga*. This was prevalent among the Khmer of Zhenla, and its first ruler Citrasena-Mahendravarman (c. 550–611? CE) is known to have erected a number of them in the Dang Raek Mountain range associated with his conquest of territory (Dupont 1955: 56–7, 119–21; Lavy 2003: 26–7).

The site has thus long been considered as one of the earliest and most important Śaivite religious complexes of the Khmer. However, more recently a limited degree of evidence has come to light for Buddhism also being present at the site in the 7th to 8th centuries. Excavations carried out at a part of the ancient settlement known as Nong Vienne in 1996 and 1998 by the French Archaeological Mission to Laos, in cooperation with the Division of Archaeology of the Lao PDR Ministry of Information and Culture, turned up two structures that appear to be *stūpa* (Santoni 2008: 98–100). Two circular brick foundations, each about 25 metres in diameter, were discovered side by side. This is unusual, as *stūpa* are not usually placed in such a configuration on the Khorat Plateau. The structures do not have stairways at their cardinal points either, a common architectural feature in most *stūpa* of the Khorat Plateau. Despite this, it is hard to imagine what other use these monuments may have had.

The Buddhist nature of the two monuments is further supported by the discovery of a number of examples of Buddhist sculpture. A fragmentary Buddha image and a Buddha seated in meditation at the Wat Phu site museum come from a private collection. Two other Buddha heads come from Ban Wat Lakhon, a site within the vicinity of Wat Phu.

The findspot of a further Buddha head at the museum is uncertain but most likely came from the area. This Buddha head, with its thick hair curls, hemispherical *uṣṇīṣa*, and overall facial features, bears the characteristics of the 7th to 8th centuries. Given its scale, it most likely belonged to a roughly life-size, or somewhat smaller, standing or seated Buddha image. The two other Buddha heads from Ban Wat Lakhon are similar in style, with one bearing close similarities to a Buddha head currently on display at the Metropolitan Museum of Art (acc. no. 2005.512).

One of the two fragmentary images from the private collection depicts the Buddha in meditation. All that remains of the other Buddha image is the section from the upper thighs to the feet and its base (Lorrillard 2010–2011: Fig. 13). However, this is enough to indicate that this image was a Buddha seated in *bhadrāsana* (legs pendant). Stylistically it can be dated to the 7th to 8th centuries and bears similarities with others of its type found in Southern Vietnam and the Dvāravatī culture of Central Thailand (Revire 2011). The Buddha in *bhadrāsana* is often associated with royal iconography and is suggestive of patronage from these quarters.

There are a number of parallels between the Buddhist evidence at Wat Phu with that found at Mahendraparvata (Phnom Kulen). As discussed in Chapter 4, Buddhism was present at this ancient capital of the Khmer, even though it was predominantly Śaivite. It most likely received patronage from the Khmer elite and perhaps even its kings. This may also have been the case at Wat Phu, as here too Buddhist remains have been found in the midst of one of the most important centres of Khmer Śaivism. Given its close proximity and ease of access to the lower Chi and Mun rivers, as well as the sites further north in Cluster 8, it is very likely that Buddhist monks from sites in these locations travelled to Wat Phu in an attempt to inculcate the teachings of the Buddha there. Furthermore, Buddhism was also present in 7th- to 8th-century Cambodia, both in Zhenla and what was formally Funan in the Mekong Delta of what is today Vietnam. A number of fine Buddhist sculptures have been recovered that indicate this. An Avalokiteśvara from Rach Gia (MG5063) in the Mekong Delta, today housed at the Musée Guimet and a standing Buddha image (Ka. 1589) from southern Kampong Speu province in Southern Cambodia, today at the National Museum, Phnom Penh, are both cases in point, as are a number of other images from these regions (Guy 2014: 93–105, 196, 232–4). It is therefore possible that the Buddhism practised at Wat Phu arrived from the south. Here monks from the Khorat Plateau may have linked up with their brethren from Zhenla to promote the religion. However, as with Phnom Kulen, it seems that while they may have initially been successful in establishing a presence, Buddhism at Wat Phu did not take hold and only reappeared many centuries later.

SUMMARY

For millennia, the Mekong River and its tributaries have functioned as some of the most important waterways of mainland Southeast Asia. This river system facilitated the movement of peoples, goods, and ideas, connecting them with cultures and communities along its course. Buddhism too spread along its banks. The highest concentration is located around Vientiane province of Laos and Nong Khai/Udon Thani provinces of Thailand. Here Buddha images, *sīmā* with narrative art and *stūpa-kumbha* motifs, and a handful of inscriptions attest to this. The area also developed the clearest evidence for the tradition of mountaintop retreats anywhere on the Khorat Plateau. Based around the sites of Phu Phra Bat, Dan Sung, and Vang Sang, these sites shared this tradition with those of Phu Wiang in Cluster 3 and Phu Bo and Phu Kao Putthanimit in Cluster 1.

Cluster 6 was located at the far north of the Khorat Plateau. Here it could flourish largely unencumbered by the Śaivism of Zhenla and later, Angkor. However, Buddhism did not spread any farther upriver. North of Vientiane marks the limit of the Khorat Plateau and the start of the mountainous uplands. Buddhism did not spread to these higher climes until many centuries later.

Buddhism, however, did manage to take hold in areas of the Mekong where Hinduism was also present. The group of sites around That Phanom and the Se Bang Fai River, in particular, highlight this. Here Buddhism existed side by side with Hinduism, as evidenced by the site of Nong Hua Thong. Moving further downstream, it also found a footing south of Savannakhet town, around Phra That Phon. However, below this the eastern bank of the Mekong becomes primarily Hindu in its religious orientation, best encapsulated by the Khmer politico-religious centre of Wat Phu. There too, Buddhism prevailed to a lesser degree but was finally eclipsed completely by Śaivism.

Chapter 6

BUDDHIST LANDSCAPES OF THE KHORAT PLATEAU

The motivation for this book grew out of a number of unanswered questions, or more precisely, out of history that I didn't know. For instance, what was the nature and extent of early Buddhist art on the Khorat Plateau? How did it shape and in turn become shaped by the cultures, societies, and environments that it encountered? What precisely was the *sīmā* tradition? How did it function, where did it originate, what can its artwork tell us? Why did it emerge and proliferate so extensively in this region? I also wanted to challenge the perspective of most of the

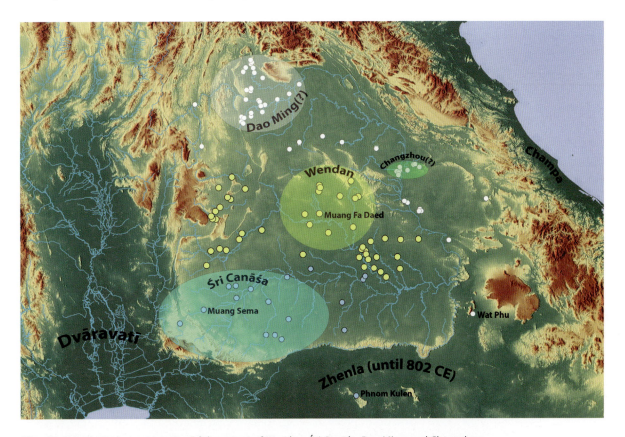

Map 15 Hypothetical reconstruction of the extent of Wendan, Śrī Canāśa, Dao Ming, and Changzhou.

previous scholarship, which viewed the Khorat Plateau as a periphery between the Dvāravatī culture of the Chao Phraya basin to its west and that of the Zhenla and later Angkor civilisations to its south and southeast.

Could the Khorat Plateau alternatively be seen as a region in its own right? And was it possible to reconstruct the Buddhist landscapes of the Khorat Plateau? A key issue of the book has been the recontextualisation of the Buddhist material and visual culture back into the physical and cognitive landscape of the Khorat Plateau. This has grown out of theories of historical ecology and landscape archaeology. Doing so has facilitated an analysis of distribution patterns of this material coupled with art historic/visual analysis of the evidence and allowed for a number of conclusions to be drawn.

First, the evidence was divided into three distinct groups (the Chi, the Mun, and the Middle Mekong river systems) and eight separate clusters. It revealed that Cluster 1 in the Chi River system, and the site of Muang Fa Daed in particular, was the most prominent area on the Khorat Plateau in regards to Buddhist art. Cluster 6 in the Middle Mekong also has significant evidence for Buddhist art. In the Mun River system, the site of Muang Sema stands out as another key centre for Buddhist art. However, overall, the religion did not flourish as strongly in this river system as it did in the Chi and Middle Mekong, most likely as a result of the strong Khmer presence.

By analysing the available evidence, this book concludes that Buddhism moved into the Khorat Plateau along the major river systems and developed primarily in the lowland, alluvial plains. This occurred from the 7th century onwards, peaking in the 8th to 9th centuries. In the 10th to 11th centuries its artwork fused with that of the Khmer as they moved in and asserted control over the region. Buddhism was still practised at this time, but it appears that the *sīmā* tradition, so prevalent in the 8th to 9th centuries, waned under this influence. Centres of power also shifted, with Phimai becoming the major settlement on the Khorat Plateau in the 12th century. However, it too maintained the tradition of Buddhism albeit in a Vajrayāna form.

Turning back to the 7th to 9th centuries, Buddhism during this period centred particularly around Cluster 1 in the Chi River system, Muang Sema in the Mun River system, and Vientiane in Cluster 6 in the Middle Mekong. In Chapter 2, I posit the idea of a Muang Fa Daed mandala. This, I argue, had direct control over Cluster 1. It most likely had control over Clusters 2, 3, and 4 as well, which were probably in a tributary arrangement of some kind. The reach of Muang Fa Daed, be it cultural, artistic, or political, seems to have spread beyond the Chi River system too. It was also in contact with the Cham culture to its east and Dvāravatī of Central Thailand to its west (Murphy 2019). Given its prominence, it may be the polity of Wendan referred to in Chinese texts (Map 15).

In the Mun River system, the epigraphic evidence points to an entity known as Śri Canāśa. I argue in Chapter 4 that this was most likely centred around the site of Muang Sema. This mandala would have exerted direct control over the sites in its vicinity and perhaps all or most of them along the Mun River. As the Wat Chanthuek inscription illustrates, it was also closely connected to Central Thailand, controlling the pass to and from the Khorat Plateau. It also seems prominent enough to be recorded in the *New Tang Annals*, which referred to it as Jia Luo She Fu.

While Muang Fa Daed and Muang Sema provide clear evidence for Buddhist/political centres in the Chi and Mun respectively, the evidence from the Mekong is not as forthcoming. That said, the area around Vientiane and the Nam Ngum River and the sites on the southern side in Udon Thai, Loei, and Nong Khai provinces strongly suggest that a political centre is located here. The mention of *śrī dharmarājā* on a *sīmā* from Vientiane also hints at this, as do the Chinese sources that mention a vassal state of Wendan called Dao Ming. While there is perhaps not enough evidence to date to posit a "Vientiane mandala", there must have been an ancient settlement somewhere in this area that controlled this stretch of the Mekong River. The existence of a well-developed tradition of mountaintop retreats and centres for pilgrimage, as evidenced by Phu Phra Bat, Dang Sun, and Vang Sang, also indicates that Buddhism was flourishing in this region and further points toward there being a political and economic centre in the vicinity that could support such a community. However, at present the archaeological evidence is neither conclusive nor robust enough to draw definite conclusions.

The recontextualisation of the Buddhist visual and material culture back into the physical and cognitive landscape allowed for a number of patterns to emerge. Regarding *sīmā*, narrative art is restricted to a handful of key locations, predominantly in Clusters 1, 2, and 6. As indicated in the above discussion, this form of art is closely tied to Muang Fa Daed and Vientiane respectively. This is unsurprising as it is only at sites of this size that established workshops/schools could develop. The axial *stūpa* and *stūpa-kumbha* motifs, on the other hand, were much more widely spread and are more representative of the artwork of the *sīmā* tradition. Cluster 4, and to a lesser extent Cluster 6, emerge as centres of this iconographic tradition.

Differences also emerge in the types of Buddhist material culture encountered in the three river systems. As mentioned, the Chi River system sees a proliferation of *sīmā* with high-quality Buddhist narrative art. However, Buddha images carved in the round in stone or bronze are almost completely absent from the archaeological record, except for the roughly hewn examples from Ban Khon Sawan. However, Buddha images are found carved in relief into rockfaces and on votive tablets, as well as on the repoussé examples from Maha Sarakham. Were Buddha images in the round made instead from wood or bronze and do not survive? This would seem to be the most plausible explanation, but they are conspicuous by their absence all the same.

The Mun River system, in contrast, does not have a great deal of evidence for *sīmā*. However, there is greater evidence for Buddha and bodhisattva images in stone and bronze. The sophisticated bronze working tradition seen at Plai Bat II and the bodhisattva from Ban Tanot mark it out from the other two river systems. And while there are *sīmā* at Muang Sema, there is also a *dharmacakra*. In some senses, Muang Sema thus represents a fusion of characteristics between Central Thailand and the Khorat Plateau. This can be explained by its key location in relation to both regions.

The situation in the Mekong is more mixed. There are both Buddha images and *sīmā* with narrative art, but the distribution is more uneven and the craftsmanship is of a somewhat lower calibre. However, it did develop an elaborate form of the *stūpa-kumbha* motif, visible at many of the sites throughout the Middle Mekong that matched that of Cluster 4 in terms of style and composition.

The recontextualisation of the Buddhist visual and material culture also furnishes clear evidence for what can be termed "Khorat Plateau aesthetics and motifs". Art on *sīmā* provides some of the best representations of this. For instance, the narrative art usually portrays episodes against a blank background, and the robes of figures are at times depicted with a *drapé-en-poche*. The *stūpa-kumbha* motif, which is found throughout the Khorat Plateau but particularly in the Chi River, also develops its own stylistic and iconographic traits not found in Central Thailand. The tradition of Buddha images carved into hill and mountainsides in *mahāparinibbāṇa* is also a distinctive motif of the Khorat Plateau, as is the tradition of large-scale bronze Buddha and bodhisattva images that are found throughout the Mun River system. These latter bronze images fuse both Dvāravatī and Khmer stylistic elements with those of the Khorat Plateau.

This book has proposed that a number of workshops were in existence during this period and as such represent the locales where the Khorat Plateau aesthetic and motifs emerged. They most likely functioned as restricted centres of diffusion (Brown 1994). The first and most prolific was at Muang Fa Daed, with Ban Nong Hang acting as a satellite workshop. The second, in Cluster 2, was the site of Ban Kut Ngong, but it was on a smaller scale than the latter two. However, it too produced a number of highly accomplished compositions. The site of Ban Khon Sawan is also a possible candidate for a workshop. However, the artwork on the *sīmā* from this site is of a lesser quality than the previous three as the scenes are executed in lower relief.

A workshop of a different kind emerged in Cluster 4 based around the sites of Ban Tat Tong and Ban Khum Ngoen. It developed a form of the *stūpa-kumbha* motif, as opposed to narrative art or Buddha images. In the 10th to 11th centuries a workshop appears to have emerged based around the sites of Ban Nong Kluem and Ban Phailom in Cluster 6 and managed to fuse Dvāravatī narrative modes with Khmer stylistic conventions. In the Mun River system, there may have been a workshop at Ban Muang Fai that specialised in large bronze images. Alternatively, it may have been located at Muang Sema or somewhere closer to Plai Bat II. While the evidence to date makes it impossible to pin down its exact location, it produced some of the finest Buddhist art anywhere in Southeast Asia.

Reviewing the material, visual, and epigraphic evidence allows us to begin to distinguish the forms of Buddhism being practised at this time, as well as which texts and oral traditions may have been in circulation. The results, however, were not wholly conclusive with no one form or sect of Buddhism coming to the fore. That being said, the sometimes close connections between episodes of the Life of the Buddha and *jātaka* depicted on *sīmā* and the Pāli *Nidana-katha* leads to the assumption that these were most likely the texts used. However, the presence of oral traditions cannot be underestimated, nor can the possibility that different textual sources could have had very similar renditions of *jātaka* and Life of the Buddha tales. Sites in Clusters 1 and 2 may thus have practised a form of what we today understand as Theravāda Buddhism. However, it should be kept in mind that the Sanskrit tradition also had its own collection of the past lives of the Buddha, the *avadāna*, and their presence cannot be discounted. The depiction of the *khakkharaka* on two *sīmā* may also show evidence for the Mūlasarvāstivāda sect (Revire 2009). This Sanskrit-based form of Buddhism was present in Magadha in the Middle Ganges basin from the 7th century onwards. However, as noted previously, the *khakkharaka* was not exclusive to this group and thus does not indicate only one form of Buddhism.

The possible association with *stūpa* worship has led Phasook Indrawooth (1999: 234) to suggest the presence of the Apara-mahavinaseliya sect who were active in Nāgarjunakonda from the 3rd century. However, once again, many if not all forms of Buddhism recognised the *stūpa* as one of the key symbols of the religion, so it cannot be used to pinpoint one particular sect.

Mahāyāna and Vajrayāna Buddhism were also present to a certain extent. This is seen in the Mun River system in the bronze bodhisattva images that have been discovered in this area. In the 10th to 11th centuries, bodhisattvas begin to appear on *sīmā* in Ban Nong Kluem and

Ban Phailom, suggesting that Mahāyāna Buddhism was being introduced by the Khmers.

Considering the wide geographical range and a timespan of over 400 years (7th to 11th centuries), it is also unlikely that there was only one form of Buddhism present at any given time. Given the independent modularity of Buddhism, it seems likely that the Buddhist traditions present had a degree of fluidity and drew inspiration from a wide variety of texts, ideas, sects, and patrons that they encountered throughout their development.

In regard to *sīmā*, the tradition of using large stone boundary markers to demarcate sacred and ritual Buddhist space appears to have originated on the Khorat Plateau. Buddhist texts require certain areas to be consecrated and clearly marked by *nimitta*, and while other regions may have used natural features such as rocks, streams, lakes, or trees, on the Khorat Plateau this requirement was fulfilled by *sīmā*. This tradition begins in the 7th century, reaching its height in the 8th to 9th centuries. It continues to develop in the 10th and 11th centuries, then expands in later centuries to all regions where Theravāda Buddhism takes hold and becomes one of its defining features. It was during the 8th to 9th centuries that the majority of the narrative art was created and the tradition began to spread out and cover the entire region. It flourished in the Chi River system, particularly in Clusters 1, 2, and 4, and more specifically at the site of Muang Fa Daed. It also took hold in the Middle Mekong and Mun River systems. The *sīmā* tradition represents a unique phenomenon of the Khorat Plateau and is one of the key features of the Khorat Plateau aesthetic.

By recontextualising the evidence for Buddhism, it is clear that it was primarily a lowland phenomenon which spread along the courses of the existing river systems. During this period, it does not seem to have reached the highland areas of Laos. As rivers such as the Chi, Mun, and Mekong were major trade, transport, and communication routes, this to a certain extent explains Buddhism's profusion in these areas. Furthermore, Buddhist monks needed patronage to thrive and develop and would have been drawn to the large moated sites that were also located and dependent on the major river systems. Buddhism in the Chi is usually found in conjunction with this form of settlement. Buddhism also spread to smaller communities and more isolated areas, and in the absence of clearly defined sites or remains of religious buildings, *sīmā* provide the primary evidence for its presence. In addition, the tradition of mountaintop retreats and pilgrimage sites is best evidenced by Phu Phra Bat in Cluster 6 and Phu Bor and Phu Wiang in Clusters 1 and 3.

In considering the question of the interaction between religion and society within the context of the Khorat Plateau, it is clear that the two are mutually interdependent. Both are defined by and define the other to a certain degree. Buddhism takes root on the Khorat Plateau with the support, both economic and spiritual, of the societies and cultures it encountered. The *sangha* aided in the advancement of these urban centres. They brought with them writing systems and sophisticated forms of ritual and symbolism. Added to that was the offer of deeper and more profound cosmological and philosophical principles, as well as practical guidance for worldly issues.

However, not everything on offer was of a purely spiritual nature and political concerns also played a role. The interaction between rulers and the *sangha* has a long history and local elites would have been quick to realise the legitimising potential of Buddhism. To settle and flourish, Buddhism needed monasteries which were often founded and sustained through donations from both the lay community and, in particular, the elite of society. Likewise, by doing so, these individuals had their status validated by the local *sangha*. Glimpses of this process can be gleaned from inscriptions throughout the Khorat Plateau, which were often donative in nature. Furthermore, the fact that Buddhism flourished at large moated sites such as Muang Fa Daed and Muang Sema, points to a considerable degree of support and integration into those societies.

As the *sangha* spread throughout the region, Buddhism began reshaping both the cognitive and physical landscape. As Buddhist architecture arose and *sīmā* began to be set up, society began to conceptualise its surroundings in terms of the teachings and concepts of this religion. At the same time, Buddhism was also being transformed and began to absorb and express local characteristics. Over time, Buddhism and the traditions of the Khorat Plateau became subsumed into each other so that today they are both part of the region's distinctive culture. As it has been clearly demonstrated throughout this book, the Khorat Plateau is a distinct region in its own right and not a derivative of Khmer or Dvāravatī culture.

Much remains to be discovered about the beginnings and development of Buddhism in Southeast Asia. Questions surrounding the exact date of its arrival from South Asia, its impact on the societies and cultures it encountered, and the various texts that may have been in circulation still arouse debate, discussion, and enquiry. This book provides one such case study. The recording, analysing, and recontextualising of the material and visual culture of Buddhism have provided a greater understanding of the nature and extent of this religion on the Khorat Plateau. It has done so through the monumental *sīmā* carved with *jātaka* tales, the crumbling *stūpa* remains, the bodhisattvas cast in bronze, and the reclining Buddhas etched into mountainsides that overlook the Buddhist landscapes of the Khorat Plateau. They are, it seems, permanent reminders of the impermanence of all things.

BIBLIOGRAPHY

Arthur, Chris. 2000. "Exhibiting the Sacred". In *Godly Things: Museums, Objects and Religion*, edited by Crispin Paine, 1–25. Leicester: Leicester University Press.

Aymonier, Étienne. 1876. *Géographie du Cambodge*. Paris: Leroux.

——. 1895–1897. *Voyage dans le Laos*. Paris: Leroux.

Balée, William. 2006. "The Research Program of Historical Ecology". *Annual Review of Anthropology* 27: 75–98.

Ball, Helen. 2019. *A Pottery Rim Form and Petrographic Analysis. Dvāravatī in Northeast Thailand in the Proto-historic Period: Technologies and Culture Transfer from Central and North Thailand seen in the Archaeological Ceramics*. Unpublished BA thesis. College of Arts, Society and Education, James Cook University, Australia.

Baptiste, Pierre and Thierry Zéphir (eds). 2009. *Dvāravatī: aux sources du bouddhisme en Thailande*. Paris: Réunion des musées nationaux.

Batteur, Charles. 1925. "Sculptures rupestres au Laos". *Bulletin de l'École française d'Extrême-Orient* 25, no. 1: 203–4.

Bauer, Christian. 1991. "Notes on Mon Epigraphy". *Journal of the Siam Society* 79, no. 1: 31–83.

Baxandall, Michael. 1992. *Patterns of Intention: On the Historical Explanation of Pictures*. New Haven: Yale University Press.

Blagden, C.O. 1928. "Mon Inscriptions Section II – The Mediaeval Mon Records: No. XII, The Inscriptions of the Kalyāṇīsīmā, Pegu". *Epigraphia Birmanica* 3, no. 2: 75–290.

Boisselier, Jean. 1967. "Notes sur l'art du bronze dans l'ancien Cambodge". *Artibus Asiae* 29, no. 4: 275–334.

Boulbet J. and B. Dagens. 1973. "Les sites archéologiques de la région du Bhnam Gulen". *Arts Asiatiques* XXVII: 1–130.

Bronkhorst, Johannes. 2011. *Buddhism in the Shadow of Brahmanism*. Leiden, Boston: Brill.

Brown, Robert. 1994. "'Rules' for Change in the Transfer of Indian Art to Southeast Asia". In *Ancient Indonesian Sculpture*, edited by Marijke J. Klokke and Pauline Lunsingh Scheurleer, 10–32. Leiden: KITLV Press.

——. 1996. *The Dvāravatī Wheels of the Law and the Indianization of Southeast Asia*. Leiden: E.J. Brill.

——. 1997. "Narrative as Icon: The Jātaka Stories in Ancient Indian and Southeast Asian Architecture". In *Sacred Biography in the Buddhist Traditions of South and Southeast Asia*, edited by J. Schober, 64–111. Honolulu: University of Hawaii Press.

Bunker, Emma C. 2002. "The Prakhon Chai Story: Facts and Fiction". *Arts of Asia* 32, no. 2: 106–25.

Bunker, Emma C. and Douglas A.J. Latchford. 2004. *Adoration and Glory: The*

Golden Age of Khmer Art. Chicago: Art Media Resources.

——. 2008. *Khmer Gold: Gifts for the Gods*. Chicago: Art Media Resources.

——. 2011. *Khmer Bronzes: New Interpretations of the Past*. Chicago: Art Media Resources.

Champa, Yuangcharoen and Mitem Thoem. 1985. "Charuekbaisemawatnonsilaphutthasattawatti14 [A 14th-century BE Inscription on a Sīmā Stone from Wat Non Sila Temple]". *Silpakorn* 29, no. 4: 83–9 (in Thai).

Cherry, Deborah. 2013. "The Afterlives of Monuments". *South Asian Studies* 29, no. 1: 1–14.

Chevance, Jean-Baptiste. 2015. "Banteay, palais royal de Mahendraparvata". *Aséanie* 33: 279–330.

Chevance, Jean-Baptiste, Damien Evans, Nina Hofer, Sakhoeun Sakada, and Chhean Ratha. 2019. "Mahendraparvata: An Early Angkor Period Capital Defined through Airborne Laser Scanning at Phnom Kulen". *Antiquity* 371: 1303–21.

Chirapravati, Pattaratorn. 1997. *Votive Tablets in Thailand, Origin, Styles and Uses*. Kuala Lumpur: Oxford University Press.

——. 1999. "Buddhist Votive Tablets and Amulets from Thailand". In *Art from Thailand*, edited by Robert Brown, 79–92. Mumbai: Marg Publications.

Chutiwongs, Nandana. 2000. "Phu Phra Bat: A Remarkable Archaeological Site in Northeast Thailand". *Journal of the Siam Society* 88: 42–52.

——. 2009. "Le bouddhisme à Dvāravatī et à Hariphunchai". In *Dvāravatī: aux sources du bouddhisme en Thaïlande*, edited by Pierre Baptiste and Thierry Zéphir, 59–74. Paris: Réunion des musées nationaux.

Chutiwongs, Nandana and Denise Patry Leidy. 1994. *Buddha of the Future: An Early Maitreya from Thailand*. Singapore: The Asia Society Galleries. New York: Sun Tree Publishing.

Cœdès, George. 1928. *Les collections archéologiques du Musée National de Bangkok*. Ars Asiatica Series, vol. 12. Paris and Brussels: G. Van Oest.

——. 1929. "Nouvelles données chronologiques et généalogiques sur la dynastie de Mahidharapura". *Bulletin de l'École française d'Extrême-Orient* 29: 289–330.

——. 1954. *Inscriptions du Cambodge Vol. VI*. Paris: E. de Boccard, 1937–1966.

——. 1964. *Inscriptions du Cambodge Vol. VII*. Paris: E. de Boccard, 1937–1966.

——. 1968. *The Indianized States of Southeast Asia*. Honolulu: East-West Centre Press.

——. 1996. "Une nouvelle inscription d'Ayuthya". *Prachumsilacharuek* IV, no. 117: 216–20.

Conti, Pia. 2014. "Tantric Buddhism at Prasat Hin Phimai: A New Reading of Its Iconographic Message". In *Before Siam: Essays in Art and Archaeology*, edited by Nicolas Revire and Stephen A. Murphy, 374–95. Bangkok: River Books & The Siam Society.

Cowell, Edward B. 1978. *The Jātaka or Stories of the Buddha's Former Births*. Six volumes. Delhi: Cosmo Publications.

Crumley, Carole L. 2015. "New Paths into the Anthropocene: Applying Historical Ecologies to the Human Future". In *The Oxford Handbook of Historical Ecology and Applied Archaeology*, edited by Christian Isendahl and Daryl Stump, 1–18. Oxford: Oxford University Press.

Dehejia, Vidya. 1991. "Aniconism and the Multivalence of Emblems: Another Look". *Ars Orientalis* 21: 45–66.

Diffloth, Gerard. 1984. *The Dvaravati Old Mon Language and Nyah Kur*. Bangkok: Chulalongkorn University Print House.

Diskul, Subhadradis. 1956. "Mueng Fa Daed. An Ancient Town in Northeast Thailand". *Artibus Asiae* 19, no. 3/4: 362–67.

———. 1973. "Phaenngernsamaithawarawadisuengkhutkhonphoptiamphoekantharawichaichangwatmahasarakham [Dvāravatī Silver Plaques Found in Kantharawichai District, Maha Sarakham Province]". *Borankadi* 5, no. 3: 302–14 (in Thai).

Dumrigon, Surapol. 2006. *Paendin Isan* [The Land of Isan]. Bangkok: Muang Boran Publishing House (in Thai).

Dupont, Pierre. 1955. *La Statuaire Préangkorienne*. Ascona: Artibus Asiae, Supplementum XV.

———. 1959. *L'Archeologie Mone de Dvāravatī*. Paris: École Française d'Extrême-Orient.

———. 2006. *The Archaeology of the Mons of Dvāravatī*. Translated with updates, additional figures, and plans by Joyanto K. Sen, two volumes. Bangkok: White Lotus.

Estève, Julia. 2009. *Étude critique des phénomènes de syncrétisme religieux dans le Cambodge angkorien*. Unpublished PhD dissertation. École Pratique des Hautes Études, Paris.

Evans, Damian. 2016. "Airborne Laser Scanning as a Method for Exploring Long-term Socio-ecological Dynamics in Cambodia". *Journal of Archaeological Science* 74: 164–75.

Feinman, G.M. and J. Marcus. 1998. *Archaic States*. Santa Fe: School of American Research Press.

Filliozat, Jean. 1981. "Sur le Çivaisme et le Bouddhisme du Cambodge". *Bulletin de l'École française d'Extrême-Orient* 70: 59–99.

Fine Arts Department. 1959. *Plan and Report of the Survey and Excavations of Ancient Monuments in Northeast Thailand*. Bangkok: Fine Arts Department (in Thai and English).

———. 1969–1971. *Concluding Report of the Excavations of Ancient Monuments at Muang Fa Daed Sung Yang*. Unpublished departmental report dated 13 March 1971.

———. 1973. *Laengborankadiprathetthai* [List of Registered Ancient Monuments throughout the Kingdom]. Bangkok: Fine Arts Department (in Thai).

———. 1990. *Laengborankadiprathetthailemsi* [List of Registered Ancient Monuments throughout the Kingdom Volume 4]. Bangkok: Fine Arts Department (in Thai).

———. 1998. *Baisemaklumphraphuthabatbuabanamphoebanpheuchangwatudonthani* [A Group of *Sīmā* Stones from Phraphuthabatbuaban, Ban Pheu District, Udon Thani Province]. Bangkok: Fine Arts Department (in Thai).

———. 2007. *Uthayanprawatisatsrithep* [Si Thep Historical Park]. Bangkok: Fine Arts Department (in Thai).

Foucher, A. 2003. *The Life of the Buddha, According to the Ancient Texts and Monuments of India*. Translated by Simone Brangier Boas. New Delhi, India: Munshiram Manoharlal Publishers Pvt. Ltd.

Gagneux, Pierre-Marie. 1972. "Vers une révolution dans l'archéologie indochinoise: le Buddha et la stèle de Thalat, Vientiane". *Bulletin des Amis du Royaume Lao* 7–8: 83–105.

———. 1977. *Les sites anciens de la plaine de Vientiane (viie–ixe siècles)*. Rapport pour le service des monuments historiques du Laos (not paginated).

Gaston-Aubert, Jean-Pierre. 2010. "Nāga-Buddha Images of the Dvāravatī Period: A Possible Link between Dvāravatī and Angkor". *Journal of the Siam Society* 98: 116–50.

Giteau, Madeleine. 1969. *Le bornage rituel des temples bouddhiques au Cambodge.* Paris: École Française d'Extrême–Orient.

Griffiths, Arlo. 2014. "Early Indic Inscriptions of Southeast Asia". In *Lost Kingdoms: Hindu-Buddhist Sculpture of Early Southeast Asia*, edited by John Guy, 53–7. New York: Metropolitan Museum of Art; New Haven: Yale University Press.

Guillon, Emmanuel. 1974. "Recherches sur quelques inscriptions Môn". *Bulletin de l'École française d'Extrême-Orient* 61: 339–48.

Guy, John (ed.). 2014. *Lost Kingdoms: Hindu-Buddhist Sculpture of Early Southeast Asia.* New York: Metropolitan Museum of Art; New Haven: Yale University Press.

——. 2020. "Making Sense of Dvāravatī". In *Defining Dvāravatī: Essays from the U Thong International Workshop 2017,* edited by Anna Bennett and Hunter Watson, 48–63. Chiang Mai: Silkworm Books.

Hanwong, Thanongsak, 1991. "Phranonwatdharmachakrasemaram [A Sleeping Buddha at Wat Dharmachakrasemaram]". *Silpakorn* 34, no. 6: 60–75 (in Thai).

Hawixbrock, Christine. 2009. "Rapport de fouilles [à Nong Hua Thong], 29 mars-6 avril 2009". Unpublished report. École française d'Extrême-Orient.

Hendrickson, Mitch. 2010. "Historic Routes to Angkor: Development of the Khmer Road System (Ninth to Thirteenth Centuries AD) in Mainland Southeast Asia". *Antiquity* 84: 480–96.

Hidalgo Tan Suwi Siang, Noel. 2014. *Painted Sites, Sacred Sites: An Examination of Religious Syncretism in Southeast Asia through Rock Art Site Usage Volume 1.* Unpublished PhD thesis. The Australian National University.

Higham, Charles and Thomas Higham. 2009. "A New Chronological Framework from Prehistoric Southeast Asia Based on a Bayesian Model from Ban Non Wat". *Antiquity* 83: 125–44.

Higham, Charles and Rachanie Thosarat. 1998. *Prehistoric Thailand: From Early Settlement to Sukhothai.* Bangkok: River Books.

Higham, Charles, Judith Cameron, Nigel Chang, Christina Castillo, Sian Harcrow, Dougald O'Reilly, F. Petchey, and Louise Shewan. 2014. "The Excavation of Non Ban Jak, Northeast Thailand: A Report on the First Three Seasons". *Journal of Indo-Pacific Archaeology* 34: 1–41.

Higham, Charles, Bryan Manly, and Jorge Alberto. 2020. "From Late Prehistory to the Foundation Of Early States in Inland Southeast Asia: A Debate". *Journal of Indo-Pacific Archaeology* 44: 52–79.

Horner, I.B. 1951. *The Book of the Discipline (Vinaya Piṭaka).* Six volumes. London: Luzac & Co.

Hoshino, Tatsuo. 2002. "Wen Dan and Its Neighbors: The Central Mekong Valley in the Seventh and Eighth Centuries". In *Breaking New Ground in Lao History: Essays on the Seventh to Twentieth Centuries*, edited by M. Ngaosrivathana and K. Breazeale, 25–72. Chiang Mai: Silkworm Books.

Huntington, Susan L. 1990. "Early Buddhist Art and the Theory of Aniconism". *Art Journal* 49: 401–7.

Huntington, Susan L. and John C. Huntington. 1985. *The Art of Ancient India: Hindu, Buddhist, Jain.* New York and Tokyo: Weatherhill.

Indorf, Pinna. 1994. "The Precinct of the Thai Uposatha Hall [BOT], A Southeast Asian Spirit World Domain". *Journal of the Siam Society* 82: 19–54.

Indrawooth, Phasook. 1999. *Thawarawadi: kansueksachoengwikhaochaklaktangthangborankadi* [Dvāravatī: A Critical Study Based on the Archaeological Evidence]. Bangkok: Silpakorn University (in Thai).

——. 2001. *Raingankankhutkonmueangfadaetsongyangamphoekamalasai changwatkalasin* [Report on the Excavation at Mueang Fa Daet Song Yang, Kamalasai District, Kalasin Province]. Bangkok: Silpakorn University (in Thai).

Indrawooth Phasook, Krabuansang Sinchai and Narkwake Payao. 1991. "Muang Fa Daed Song Yang: New Archaeological Discoveries". In *Récentes Recherches en Archéologie en Thailande: Deuxième Symposium Franco–Thai*, edited by Universite Silpakon, 98–111. Bangkok: Silpakorn University.

Isendahl, Christian and Daryl Stump. 2015. "Introduction: The Construction of the Present through the Reconstruction of the Past". In *The Oxford Handbook of Historical Ecology and Applied Archaeology*, edited by Christian Isendahl and Daryl Stump, 1–18. Oxford: Oxford University Press.

Jacques, Claude and Philippe Lafond. 2007. *The Khmer Empire: Cities and Sanctuaries Fifth to the Thirteenth Centuries*. Bangkok: River Books.

Jayawickrama, N.A. 1990. *The Story of Gotama Buddha, the Nidana-katha of the Jātakatthakatha*. Oxford: The Pāli Text Society.

Kaeoklai, Cha-em. 1987. "Charuekphrasiwatsasangthewarupaksonpallawaphasasansakrit [The Inscription of Phra Srivatsa Installing Images of Gods: Pallava Script, Sanskrit Language]". *Silpakorn* 31, no. 5: 91–6 (in Thai).

——. 2001. "Charuekphraphutthasaiyanphuwiang [Inscription on a Reclining Buddha Image from Phu Wiang]". *Silapakorn* 44, no. 3: 57–61 (in Thai).

Karlstrom, Anna. 2009. *Preserving Impermanence. The Creation of Heritage in Vientiane, Laos*. Studies in Global Archaeology 13, Uppsala: Uppsala University.

Karlstrom, Anna, Kanda Keosopha, and Bounheuang Bouasisengpaseuth. 2005. *Viengkham and Say Fong Archaeological Excavations 2003–2004*. Uppsala: Uppsala University.

Karpelès, Suzanne. 1949. "Les grottes sculptées de la province de Vientiane, vestiges de l'art de Lavapuri". *Bulletin des Amis du Laos* 4: 141–8.

Kawaguchi, Keizaburo and Kazutake Kyuma. 1977. *Paddy Soils in Tropical Asia: Their Material Nature and Fertility*. Monographs of the Center for Southeast Asian Studies, Kyoto University. Honolulu: The University Press of Hawaii.

Kermel-Torres, Doryane. 2004. *Atlas of Thailand: Spatial Structures and Development*. Chiang Mai: Silkworm Books.

Khunsong, Saritpong. 2009. "L'art rupestre". In *Dvāravatī: aux sources du bouddhisme en Thailande*, edited by Pierre Baptiste and Thierry Zéphir, 229–33. Paris: Réunion des musées nationaux.

Kieffer-Pülz, Petra. 1993. *Die Sima: Vorschriften zur Regelung der buddhistischen Gemeindegrenze in älteren buddhistischen Texten*. Berlin: Reimer.

Kingmanee, Arunsak. 1996."Baisemasalakphap 'suwannakakakata-jadok' chakwatnonsilaatwararam [Suvannakakkatajātaka on a Bai *Sīmā* of Wat Non Sila-atwararam]". *Muang Boran* 22 no. 2: 133–8 (in Thai).

——. 1997a. "Phapsalakruang 'bhuridattachadok' bonbaisemachakmueangfadaetsong-yangchangwatkalasin [Bhūridattajātaka on the Carved *Sīmā* in Kalasin]". *Muang Boran* 23, no. 4: 104–9 (in Thai).

——. 1997b. "Phapsalakbonbaisemachakwattrairongamphoekhonkaen-changwatkhonkaen [*Sīmā* of Devadhamma Jātaka at Wat Trairong, Khon Kaen Province]". *Muang Boran* 23, no. 1: 148–54 (in Thai).

——. 1998a. "Baisemasalakphap 'Temiyachadok' tiphrathatyadumueangfadaetamp-hoekamalasaichangwatkalasin [*Sīmā* Carved with the '*Temiyajātaka*' at Phra That Yadu Stūpa, Mueang Fa Daet, Amphoe Kamalsai, Changwat Kalasin]". *Silpakorn* 41, no. 5: 56–7 (in Thai).

——. 1998b. "Kansueksadanprawatisatsilpakhongbaisemaklumphraphuthabatbuaban [Study of the Art History of a Group of *Sīmā* Stones from Phraphuthabatbuaban]". In *Baisemaklumphraphuthabatbuabanamphoeban-pheuchangwatudonthani* [A Group of *Sīmā* Stones from Phraphuthabatbuaban, Ban Pheu District, Udon Thani Province], 26–53. Bangkok: Fine Arts Department (in Thai).

——. 2001. "Baisemasalakphapphuthaprawat 'Animisjaydi' chakchangwatyasothon [The Boundary Marker with *Animisa Jetiya* Scene from Yasothon]". *Muang Boran* 27, no. 4: 68–73 (in Thai).

——. 2002. "Baisemasalakphap 'sanulaktaenbangprasudikongphraphutthathong' [A Symbol Representing the Birth of the Lord Buddha Carved on a *Sīma* Stone]". *Silpakorn* 45, no. 1: 78–87 (in Thai).

——. 2006. "Baisīmā 'temiyachadok' chakwatnonsilaasvararam [*Sīmā* Stone Carved about the Scene of '*Temiyajātaka*' at None Sila–asvararam Temple]". *Silpakorn* 49, no. 4: 43–56 (in Thai).

——. 2007. "Baisemasalakphap 'phraphuttachaonangnueanak (phraphuttarupnakaparok)' chakbannongpan amphoekamalasaichangwatkalasin [*Sīmā* Presenting the Carving of the 'Buddha Sitting under the Nāga Hood' from Ban Nong Pan in Kommalasai District of Kalasin Province]". *Silpakorn* 50, no. 2: 58–69 (in Thai).

Klokke, Marijke J. 1993. *The Tantri Reliefs on Ancient Javanese Candi*. Leiden: KITLV Press.

Knapp, A. Bernard and Wendy Ashmore. 1999. "Archaeological Landscapes: Constructed, Conceptualized, Ideational". In *Archaeologies of Landscape: Contemporary Perspectives*, edited by Wendy Ashmore and A.B. Knapp, 1–33. Oxford: Blackwell Publishers.

Krairiksh, Piriya 1974a. "Simas with Scenes from the Mahānipāta-Jātakas in the National Museum at Khon Kaen". In *Art and Archaeology in Thailand*, 35–100. Bangkok: Fine Arts Department.

——. 1974b. *Buddhist Folk Tales Depicted at Chula Pathon Chedi* [*Phutthasasanatichedichulapathon*]. Bangkok: Prachandra Printing Press (in English and Thai).

——. 2012. *The Roots of Thai Art*. Bangkok: River Books.

Lam Pao Project. 1978. *Land-Use and Socio-Economic Changes under the Impact of Irrigation in the Lam Pao Project Area in Thailand*. London: School of Oriental and African Studies, University of London.

Latinis, D. Kyle and Stephen A. Murphy. 2017. "Sīmā Stones and Mountain Palaces from the Dawn of Angkor". *NSC Highlights* 6, Sept.–Nov.: 7–9.

Lavy, Paul. 2003. "As in Heaven, So on Earth: The Politics of Viṣṇu, Śiva and Harihara Images in Preangkorian Khmer Civilisation". *Journal of Southeast Asian Studies* 34, no. 1: 21–39.

Layton, Robert and Peter Ucko. 1999. "Introduction: Gazing on the Landscape and

Encountering the Environment". In *The Archaeology and Anthropology of Landscape*, edited by Peter Ucko and Robert Layton, 1–20. London and New York: Routledge.

Lorrillard, Michel. 2008. "Pour une géographie historique du bouddhisme au Laos". In *Rercherches Nouvelles sur le Laos/New Research on Laos*, edited by Yves Goudineau and Michel Lorrillard, 113–81. Vientiane-Paris: École française d'Extreme-Orient.

——. 2010–2011. "Par-delà Vat Phu: Données nouvelles sur l'expansion des espaces khmer et môn anciens au Laos". *Bulletin de l'École française d'Extrême-Orient* 97/98: 205–70.

——. 2014. "La plaine de Vientiane au tournant du second millénaire. Données nouvelles sur l'expansion des espaces khmer et môn anciens au Laos (II)". *Bulletin de l'École française d'Extrême-Orient* 100: 38–107.

Luce, Gordon H. 1969. *Old Burma–Early Pagan*. New York: J.J. Augustin, Locust Valley.

Matics, K.I. 1992. *Introduction to the Thai Temple*. Bangkok: White Lotus Press.

McDaniel, Justin. 2015. *The Lovelorn Ghost and the Magical Monk: Practicing Buddhism in Modern Thailand*. New York: Columbia University Press.

Moore, Elizabeth. 1988. *Moated Sites in Early North East Thailand*. British Archaeological Reports (BAR) International Series 400. Oxford: British Archaeological Reports.

——. 2007. *Early Landscapes of Myanmar*. Bangkok: River Books.

Murphy, Stephen A. 2010. *The Buddhist Boundary Markers of Northeast Thailand and Central Laos, 7th–12th Centuries CE: Towards an Understanding of the Archaeological, Religious, and Artistic Landscapes of the Khorat Plateau.* Unpublished PhD dissertation. School of Oriental and African Studies, University of London.

——. 2013. "Buddhism and Its Relationship to Dvāravatī Period Settlement Patterns and Material Culture in Northeast Thailand and Central Laos ca. 6th–11th centuries CE: A Historical Ecology Approach to the Landscape of the Khorat Plateau". *Asian Perspectives* 52, no. 2: 300–26.

——. 2014. "*Sīmā* Stones in Lower Myanmar and Northeast Thailand: A Comparison". In *Before Siam: Essays in Art and Archaeology*, edited by Nicolas Revire and Stephen A. Murphy, 352–71. Bangkok: River Books & The Siam Society.

——. 2015. "How Many Monks? Quantitative and Demographic Archaeological Approaches to Buddhism in Northeast Thailand and Central Laos, 6th–11th centuries CE". In *Buddhist Dynamics in Premodern Southeast Asia*, edited by Christian Lammerts, 80–119. Singapore: ISEAS Publications.

——. 2016. "The Case for Proto-Dvāravatī: A Review of the Art Historical and Archaeological Evidence". *Journal of Southeast Asian Studies* 47, no. 3: 366–93.

——. 2019. "Cultural Connections and Shared Origins between Campā and Dvāravatī: A Comparison of Common Artistic and Architectural Motifs, ca. 7th–10th centuries CE". In *Champa: Territories and Networks of a Southeast Asian Kingdom*, edited by Arlo Griffiths, Andrew Hardy, and Geoff Wade, 303–21. Paris: Études thématiques 31, École française d'Extrême-Orient.

Murphy, Stephen A. and Pimchanok Pongkasetkan. 2010. "Fifty Years of Archaeological Research at Dong Mae Nang Muang: An Ancient Gateway to the Upper Chao Phraya Basin". *Journal of the Siam Society* 98: 49–74.

Nagasena, Bhikkhu and Kate Crosby. 2022. "Sīmā Basics from Buddha to Burma". In *Sīmās: Foundations of Buddhist Religion*, edited by Jason A. Carbine and Erik W. Davis, 18–41. Hawaii: University of Hawaii Press.

Newhall, Thomas. 2022. "The Development of Ordination Platforms (jietan 戒壇) in China: The Translation and Development of Sīmā in East Asia from the 3rd to 7th Centuries". In *Sīmās: Foundations of Buddhist Religion*, edited by Jason A. Carbine and Erik W. Davis, 66–109. Hawaii: University of Hawaii Press.

O'Reilly, Dougald J.W. and Glen Scott. 2015. "Moated Sites of the Iron Age in the Mun River Valley, Thailand: New Discoveries Using Google Earth". *Archaeological Research in Asia* 3: 9–18.

O'Reilly, Dougald and Louise Shewan. 2016. "Phum Lovea: A Moated Precursor to the Pura of Cambodia? Sociopolitical Transformation from Iron Age Settlements to Early State Society". *Journal of Southeast Asian Studies* 47, no. 3: 468–83.

Paknam, No Na. 1981. *The Buddhist Boundary Markers of Thailand*. Bangkok: Muang Boran Publishing House (in Thai and English).

——. 1986. "Phrasatphanomrungkupphuangkhan [Prasat Phanom Rung and Phu Angkhan]". *Muang Boran* 12, no. 2: 63–70 (in Thai and English).

——. 1997. *Simakatahsamotkhongwatsuthatdhepvararam* [Manuscript of *Sīmā* at Wat Suthat Dhepvararam]. Bangkok: Muang Boran Publishing House.

Parmentier, Henri. 1954. *L'art du Laos*. Paris: Imprimerie Nationale.

Pelliot, Paul. 1904. "Deux itineraries de Chine en Inde à la fin du VIIIe siècle". *Bulletin de l'École française d'Extrême-Orient* 4: 131–413.

Pendleton, Robert L. 1962. *Thailand, An American Geographic Society Handbook*. Connecticut: Greenwood Press.

Phanomvan, Phacharaphorn. 2021. "Plai Bat: Reclaiming Heritage, Social Media, and Modern Nationalism". In *Returning Southeast Asia's Past: Objects, Museums, and Restitution*, edited by Louise Tythacott and Panggah Ardiyansyah, 235–63. SAAAP Art and Archaeology of Southeast Asia: Hindu-Buddhist Traditions Series. Singapore: NUS Press.

Phiromanukun, Rungrot. 2009. "Les bornes rituelles du nord-est de Thaïlande". In *Dvāravatī: aux sources du bouddhisme en Thaïlande*, edited by Pierre Baptiste and Thierry Zéphir, 21–5. Paris: Réunion des musées nationaux.

Phonpha and Suthilak. 1974. "Baisematimueangfadaetsongyang [*Sīmā* Stones at Muang Fa Daed]". *Borankadi* 5, no. 3: 379–99 (in Thai).

Pongkasetkan, Pimchanok and Stephen A. Murphy. 2012. "Phitifangsopsāmaikonpra watisatdonplaithawararawadilaktanmaichakdongmaenangmueung [Burial Rites from Late Prehistory to the Dvāravatī Period: New Evidence from Dong Mae Nang Muang]". *Muang Boran* 37, no. 4: 148–59 (in Thai).

Pruess, James. 1976. *The That Phanom Chronicle, A Shrine History and Its Interpretation*. Ithaca, New York: Cornell University.

Renfrew, Colin. 1986. "Introduction: Peer Polity Interaction and Socio–political Change". In *Peer Polity and Socio-Political Change*, edited by Colin Renfrew and John F. Cherry, 1–18. Cambridge: Cambridge University Press.

Renfrew, Colin and John F. Cherry (eds). 1986. *Peer Polity and Socio-Political Change*. Cambridge: Cambridge University Press.

Revire, Nicolas. 2009. "À propos d'une « tête » de khakkhara conservée au Musée national de Bangkok". *Aséanie* 24: 111–34.

——. 2011. "Some Reconsiderations On Pendant-Legged Buddha Images in the Dvāravatī Artistic Tradition". *Bulletin of the Indo-Pacific Prehistory Association*

31: 37–49.

——. 2014. "Glimpses of Buddhist Practices and Rituals in Dvāravatī and Its Neighbouring Cultures". In *Before Siam: Essays in Art and Archaeology*, edited by Nicolas Revire and Stephen A. Murphy, 240–71. Bangkok: River Books & The Siam Society.

——. 2016 "Dvāravatī and Zhenla in the Seventh to Eighth Centuries: A Transregional Ritual Complex". *Journal of Southeast Asian Studies* 47, no 3: 393–417.

Santoni, Marielle. 2008. "La mission archéologique française et la Vat Phu: Recherches sur un site historique exceptionnel du Laos". In *Rercherches Nouvelles sur le Laos/New Research on Laos*, edited by Yves Goudineau and Michel Lorrilard, 81–111.Vientiane–Paris: École française d'Extreme-Orient.

Sathaphon, Khwanyan. 1980. "Kankhuttaengboransathantiamphoenadunchangwatmahasarakham [Archaeological Excavations at Na Dun District, Maha Sarakham Province]". *Silpakorn* 24, no. 2: 71–91.

Schopen, Gregory. 1997. *Bones, Stones and Buddhist Monks: Collected Papers on the Archaeology, Epigraphy, and Texts of Monastic Buddhism in India*. Hawaii: University of Hawaii Press.

Seidenfaden, E. 1954. "Kanok Nakhon, an Ancient Mon Settlement in Northeast Siam (Thailand) and Its Treasures of Art". *Bulletin de l'École française d'Extrême-Orient* 44: 643–8.

Sharrock, Peter D. and Emma C. Bunker. 2016. "Seeds of Vajrabodhi: Buddhist Ritual Bronzes from Java and Khorat". In *Esoteric Buddhism in Mediaeval Maritime Asia: Networks of Masters, Texts, Icons*, edited by Andrea Acri, 237–52. Singapore: ISEAS-Yusof Ishak Institute.

Shorto, Harry. 1971. "The Stūpa as Buddha Icon". In *Mahayanist Art After AD 900: Colloquies on Art and Archaeology in Asia No. 2*, edited by William Watson, 75–81. London: University of London, Percival David Association of Chinese Art.

Siribhadra, Smitthi. 2009. "Introduction". In *Dvāravatī: aux sources du bouddhisme en Thaïlande*, edited by Pierre Baptiste and Thierry Zéphir, 21–25. Paris: Réunion des musées nationaux.

Siribhadra, Smitthi and Elizabeth Moore. 1992. *Palaces of the Gods, Khmer Art and Architecture in Thailand*. Bangkok: River Books.

Skilling, Peter. 2005. "'Buddhist Sealings': Reflections on Terminology, Motivation, Donors' Status, School-Affiliation, and Print-Technology". In *South Asian Archaeology 2001. Vol. II, Historical Archaeology and Art History*, edited by Catherine Jarrige and Vincent Lefèvre, 677–85. Paris: Éditions Recherches sur les Civilisations.

——. (ed.). 2008a. *Past Lives of the Buddha: Wat Si Chum – Art, Architecture and Inscriptions*. Bangkok: River Books.

——. 2008b. "Buddhist Sealings and the Ye Dharmā Stanza". In *Archaeology of Early Historic South Asia*, edited by Gautam Sengupta and Sharmi Chakraborty, 503–25. New Delhi/Kolkata: Pragati Publications (Centre for Archaeological Studies and Training, Eastern India).

——. 2009. "Des images moulées au service de l'idéologie du merit". In *Dvāravatī: aux sources du bouddhisme en Thaïlande*, edited by Pierre Baptiste and Thierry

Zéphir, 107–17. Paris: Réunion des musées nationaux.

——. 2012. "Introduction". In *How Theravāda Is Theravāda? Exploring Buddhist Identities*, edited by Peter Skilling, Jason A. Carbine, Claudio Cicuzza, and Santi Pakdeekham, xiii–xxx. Chiang Mai: Silkworm Books.

——. 2020. "Dvāravatī in Inscriptions and Manuscripts". In *Defining Dvāravatī: Essays from the U Thong International Workshop 2017,* edited by Anna Bennett and Hunter Watson, 64–81. Chiang Mai: Silkworm Books.

Smith, Michael E. 2007. "Form and Meaning in the Earliest Cities: A New Approach to Ancient Urban Planning". *Journal of Planning History* 6, no. 1: 3–47.

Snodgrass, Adrian. 1985. *The Symbolism of the Stūpa.* Cornell: Cornell Southeast Asia Program.

Solheim, Wilhelm G. and Chester Gorman. 1966. "Archaeological Salvage Program; Northeast Thailand, First Season". *Journal of the Siam Society* 54, no. 2: 111–210.

Stadtner, Donald M. 2011. *Sacred Sites of Burma: Myth and Folklore in an Evolving Spiritual Realm.* Bangkok: River Books.

Suksavasti, Suriyvudh. 1991. "Baisemasalakrueangramayana: kanplianplaengkhitlaerupbaebchaksilpathawarawa–disusilpabaebkhmennaiphaktawonokchiangnuea" [*Sīmā* with a Scene from Ramayana: Change of Tradition and Style in 12th-Century Northeast Thailand]. *Muang Boran* 17, no. 1: 105–11.

Supanjanya, T. and P. Vanasin. 1983. *The Inventory of Ancient Settlements in Thailand.* Bangkok: Toyota Foundation.

Swearer, Donald. 1995. *The Buddhist World of Southeast Asia.* Albany: State University of New York Press.

Tambiah, Stanley J. 1976. *World Conqueror and World Renouncer: A Study of Buddhism and Polity in Thailand against a Historical Background.* Cambridge: Cambridge University Press.

Thamrungrueng, Rungrot. 2009. "L'Image du Buddha sur Phanasbodi". In *Dvāravatī: aux sources du bouddhisme en Thaïlande*, edited by Pierre Baptiste and Thierry Zéphir, 83–7. Paris: Réunion des musées nationaux.

Thompson, Ashley. 2011. "In the Absence of the Buddha: 'Aniconism' and the Contentions of Buddhist Art History". In *A Companion to Asian Art and Architecture*, edited by Rebecca M. Brown and Deborah S. Hutton, 398–420. Malden, MA: John Wiley & Sons.

Tian, Haoyu, Guo-An Yu, Ling Tong, He Qing Huang, Akira Bridhikitti and Thayukorn Prabamroong. 2019. "Water Quality of the Mun River in Thailand—Spatiotemporal Variations and Potential Causes". *International Journal of Environmental Research and Public Health* 16, no. 20: 3906.

Tilley, Christopher. 1994. *A Phenomenology of Landscape, Places, Paths and Monuments.* Oxford/Providence USA: Berg.

Vallibhotama, Srisakra. 1975. "Semaisan [*Sīmā* Stones in Isan]". *Muang Boran* 1, no. 2: 89–116 (in Thai).

Vickery, Michael. 1994. "What and Where was Chenla?" In *Recherches Nouvelles sur le Cambodge,* edited by F. Bizot, 197–212. Paris: École française d'Extrême-Orient, Études thématiques 1.

Wade, Geoff. 2014. "Beyond the Southern Borders: Southeast Asia in Chinese Texts to the Ninth Century". In *Lost Kingdoms: Hindu-Buddhist Sculpture of Early Southeast Asia*, edited by John Guy, 25–31. New York: Metropolitan Museum of Art; New Haven: Yale University Press.

Wales, H.G. Quaritch. 1969. *Dvāravatī: The Earliest Kingdom of Siam (6th to 11th century A.D.).* London: Bernard Quaritch Ltd.

——. 1980. "Recent Dvāravatī Discoveries, and Some Khmer Comparisons". *Journal of the Siam Society* 68: 43–54.

Walker Vadillo, Veronica. 2019. "A Historiography of Angkor's River Network: Shifting the Research Paradigm to Westerdahl's Maritime Cultural Landscape". *SPAFA Journal* 3: 1–30.

Wangsuk, Khemica. 2000. *Phattanakanthangwathanthumnailummaenummun: Kann isueksalaengborankadimueangsemaamphoesongnenchangwatnakhonratchasima* [The Cultural Development in the Mun River Basin: A Case Study of the Archaeological Site at Muang Sema, Sung Noen District, Nakhon Ratchasima Province]. Unpublished MA thesis. Department of Archaeology, Silpakorn University (in Thai).

Watson, Hunter. 2013. *Kansueksarupkampasamonboranchakcharuektipopnaiprathetth airawangphutthasattwatti 12-17* [A Study of Old Mon Word Forms from Inscriptions Found in Thailand Dating between the 12th and 17th Centuries B.E]. Unpublished MA thesis. Department of Oriental Language, Silpakorn University (in Thai).

——. 2018. "A Group of Clay Artefacts from Tap Chumphon Inscribed in Pāli and Old Mon". In *Advancing Southeast Asian Archaeology 2016: Select Papers from the Second SEAMEO SPAFA International Conference on Southeast Asian Archaeology, Bangkok, Thailand 2016,* edited by Noel Hidalgo Tan, 119–28. Bangkok: SEAMEO SPAFA Regional Centre for Archaeology and Fine Arts.

——. 2020. "Old Mon Inscriptions and the Extent of Dvāravatī". In *Defining Dvāravatī: Essays from the U Thong International Workshop 2017,* edited by Anna Bennett and Hunter Watson, 82–93. Chiang Mai: Silkworm Books.

Wattanatumphathtanakanthangprawatisateklaksanalaephumipanyachangwat Roi Et [The Historical Development of Culture, Identity, and Wisdom of Roi Et Province]. 2000 Anakrumkanfaipramuanekasanlaechotmaihetunaikhanakrum-kanamnuaikanchotnganchelimphrakiatphrapatsomdetphrachaoyuhua. Bangkok: Rongphimkurusaphalaphrao (in Thai).

White, Joyce C. 1995. "Incorporating Heterarchy into Theory on Socio-political Development: The Case from Southeast Asia". In *Heterarchy and the Analysis of Complex Societies,* edited by R.M. Ehrenreich, C.L. Crumley, and J.E. Levy, 103–23. Archaeological Papers of the American Anthropological Association, No. 6. Arlington, VA, American Anthropological Association.

Winichakul, Thongchai. 2004. *Siam Mapped: A History of the Geo-Body of a Nation.* Chiang Mai: Silkworm Books (orig. publ. Silkworm Books 1994).

Wiraprajak, Kongkaew. 2007. "Charuekbaisemabanpanna [*Sīmā* Inscription at Ban Panna]". *Silpakorn* 50, no. 2: 53–7 (in Thai).

Wolters, Oliver W. 1999. *History, Culture, and Region in Southeast Asian Perspectives.* Ithaca, New York: Cornell Southeast Asia Program Publications.

Wongnoi, Phuyang. 2009. "Les sites du basin de la rivière Phetburi". In *Dvāravatī: aux sources du bouddhisme en Thaïlande,* edited by Pierre Baptiste and Thierry Zéphir, 187–93. Paris: Réunion des musées nationaux.

Wood, Christopher S. 2016/17. "Under the Influence". *Res: Anthropology and Aesthetics* 67/68: 290–8.

Woodward, Hiram. 1997. *The Sacred Sculpture of Thailand.* Bangkok: River Books.

——. 2005. *The Art and Architecture of Thailand, From Prehistoric Times through the*

Thirteenth Century. Leiden, Boston: Brill (orig. publ. Brill, 2003).

——. 2010. "Dvāravatī, Si Thep, And Wendan". *Bulletin of the Indo-Pacific Prehistory Association* 30: 87–97.

APPENDIX: TABLES 1–11

Table 1: Sites in the Chi River system

Site Number	Site Name	Evidence
1.1	Muang Fa Daed	Over 250 *sīmā*, architectural remains (*stūpa*, monastic building), votive tablets.
1.2	Ban Nong Hang	23 *sīmā*
1.3	Ban Na Ngam	5 *sīmā*
1.4	Kunchinarai Town	30 *sīmā*
1.5	Ban Muang Phrai	37 *sīmā*
1.6	Ban Sangkhom Phathana	4 *sīmā*
1.7	Roi Et Town	40 *sīmā*, architectural remains (*stūpa*)
1.8	Maha Sarakham Town	38 *sīmā*
1.9	Kantharawichai	6 *sīmā*, possible Buddha images, architectural remains (monastic building)
1.10	Ban Non Sala	6 *sīmā*
1.11	Wat Phu Kao Putthanimit	6 *sīmā*, one rock carving (image of a monk or Buddha)
1.12	Phu Bor	Rock carving (Buddha in *Mahāparinibbāṇa*)
1.13	Na Dun	5 *sīmā*, large cache of votive tablets
2.1	Ban Kut Ngong	27 *sīmā*
2.2	Ban Khon Sawan	46 *sīmā*, three Buddha images
2.3	Ban Pho Chai	39 *sīmā*, 1 *dharmacakra stambha*
2.4	Ban Fai	5 *sīmā*
2.5	Ban Nong Kai Nun	15 *sīmā*
2.6	Ban Nong Hin Tang	8 *sīmā*
2.7	Ban Muang Kao	6 *sīmā*
3.1	Ban Non Muang	19 *sīmā*
3.2	Ban Phai Hin	9 *sīmā*
3.3	Ban Non Chat	14 *sīmā*

3.4	Ban Bua Simama	14 *sīmā*
3.5	Ban Nong Hin Tang	6 *sīmā*
3.6	Ban Hua Kua	3 *sīmā*
3.7	Ban Pao	2 *sīmā*
3.8	Ban Phan Lam	21 *sīmā*
3.19	Ban Kaeng	10 *sīmā*
3.10	Phu Wiang	Rock carving (Buddha in *Mahāparinibbāṇa*)
4.1	Ban Tat Tong	26 *sīmā*
4.2	Ban Khum Ngoen	19 *sīmā*
4.3	Wat Si Thammaram Temple/ Yasothon Town	13 *sīmā*
4.4	Ban Pueai Huadong	48 *sīmā*
4.5	Muang Ngio	9 *sīmā*
4.6	Ban Song Bueai	3 *sīmā*
4.7	Ban Hua Muang	10 *sīmā*
4.8	Ban Bueng Kae	6 *sīmā*
4.9	Ban Ku Chan	1 *sīmā*
4.10	Ban Nam Kham Yai	1 *sīmā*
4.11	Phanom Phrai Town	4 *sīmā*
4.12	Ban Namoma	16 *sīmā*
4.13	Muang Samsip Town	23 *sīmā*
4.14	Ban Phon Muang	10 *sīmā*
4.15	Ban Phai	*Sīmā* have been reported at this site
4.16	Ban Si Bua	15 *sīmā*
4.17	Ban Thung Yai	Undocumented number of *sīmā* have been reported at this site

Table 2: Sites in the Mun River system.

Site Number	Site Name	Evidence
5.1	Muang Sema	17 *sīmā*, architectural remains (*stūpa*, monastic buildings), *dharmacakra*, 11-metre Buddha image in *Mahāparinibbāṇa*
5.2	Ban Tanot	16 *sīmā*, large bronze bodhisattva image
5.3	Non Ban Jak	Small terracotta Buddha
5.4	Ban Non Wat	Awaiting post-excavation analysis
5.5	Wat Chanthuek	Four large stone Buddha images
5.6	Ban Muang Fai	1 *sīmā*, three stone Buddha images, two bronze bodhisattvas and one bronze Buddha image
5.7	Phu Phra Angkhan	15 *sīmā*
5.8	Ban Pa Khiap	46 *sīmā*
5.9	Ban Prakham	3 *sīmā*
5.10	Ban Lupmok	4 *sīmā*
5.11	Ku Kaeo Sithi	Undocumented number of *sīmā* have been reported at this site, architectural remains (possibly a *stūpa*)
5.12	Prasat Yai Ngao	Undocumented number of *sīmā* have been reported at this site (approximately 8–10)
5.13	Ban Truem	8 *sīmā*
5.14	Plai Bat II	Cache of bronze sculptures, exact number unknown
5.15	Phnom Kulen	2 sets of *sīmā*, approximately 30 in total.
5.16	Ban Slaeng Thon	15 *sīmā*
5.17	Ban Muang Tao	Undocumented number of *sīmā* have been reported at this site
5.18	Phimai	Khmer temple

Table 3: Sites in the Middle Mekong

Site Number	Site Name	Evidence
6.1	Ban Thalat	9 *sīmā*, 1 stone Buddha image, 1 inscribed stele
6.2	Ban Thin Keao	A number of possible Buddha images and *sīmā*
6.3	Ban Muang Kao	Undocumented number of *sīmā* have been reported at this site
6.4	Ban Vieng Kham	Large number of *sīmā* excavated at this site
6.5	Ban Nong Khon	9 *sīmā*
6.6	Ban Na Sone	9 *sīmā*
6.7	Ban Ilai	9 *sīmā*
6.8	Ban Nong Kan Khu	2 *sīmā*, 1 stone Buddha head
6.9	Dan Sung	Rock carvings, *sīmā*, Buddhist sculpture
6.10	Ban Phon Pa Nao	1 *sīmā*
6.11	Ban Dong Phosy	1 *sīmā*
6.12	Ban Saphang Mo	1 *sīmā*
6.13	Ban Nam Pot	1 *sīmā*
6.14	Ban Simano	4 *sīmā*
6.15	Ban Thoun Loua	4 *sīmā*
6.16	Ban Sa Feu	4 *sīmā*
6.17	Ban Somsanouk	4 *sīmā*
6.18	Muang Sanakham	1 *sīmā*
6.19	Vang Sang	Rock carvings of Buddha images
6.20	Phu Phra Bat	*Sīmā*, rock carvings of Buddha images
6.21	Ban Nong Khluem	22 *sīmā*
6.22	Ban Phailom	33 *sīmā*
6.23	Wang Sapung	35 *sīmā*
6.24	Ban Hin Tang	12 *sīmā*
6.25	Ban Phottak	10 *sīmā*
6.26	Wiang Khut	1 *sīmā*

6.27	Ban Daeng	Undocumented number of *sīmā* have been reported at this site
6.28	Ban Khok Khon	Undocumented number of *sīmā* have been reported at this site
6.29	Ban Peng Chan	Undocumented number of *sīmā* have been reported at this site
7.1	Ban Don Kaeo	10 *sīmā*
7.2	Ban Chiang	5 *sīmā*
7.3	Ban Ma	16 *sīmā*
7.4	Ban Ta Wat Dai	15 *sīmā*
7.5	Ban Panna	2 *sīmā*
8.1	That Phanom	9 *sīmā*
8.2	Ban Lak Sila	Undocumented number of *sīmā* have been reported at this site
8.3	Ban Fang Daeng	Undocumented number of *sīmā* have been reported at this site
8.4	Ban Saphang Thong	Undocumented number of *sīmā* have been reported at this site
8.5	Ban Na Ngam	Undocumented number of *sīmā* have been reported at this site
8.6	Ban Sikhai	7 *sīmā*
8.7	Ban Kang	9 *sīmā*
8.8	Ban Na Mouang	8 *sīmā*
8.9	Nong Hua Thong	2 *sīmā*, large amount of excavated Hindu material
8.10	Ban Pha Kha Niai	Approximately 2 or 3 *sīmā*
8.11	Ban Sompoy Noi	Approximately 2 or 3 *sīmā*
8.12	Phra That Phon	Approximately 6 or 7 *sīmā*
8.13	Ban Tak Daet	Approximately 6 or 7 *sīmā*
8.14	Ban Phumma Chedi Tai Nua	Approximately 8 or 9 *sīmā*
8.15	Muang Phin	8 *sīmā*
8.16	Ban Na Pha Bang,	5 *sīmā*
8.17	Wat Phu	Architectural remains (possibly 2 *stūpa*), 2 fragmentary Buddha images, 3 Buddha heads

Table 4: Cluster 1 sites

Site Number	Site Name
1.1	Muang Fa Daed
1.2	Ban Nong Hang
1.3	Ban Na Ngam
1.4	Kunchinarai Town
1.5	Ban Muang Phrai
1.6	Ban Sangkhom Phathana
1.7	Roi Et Town
1.8	Maha Sarakham Town
1.9	Kantharawichai
1.10	Ban Non Sala
1.11	Wat Phu Kao Putthanimit
1.12	Phu Bor
1.13	Na Dun

Table 5: Cluster 2 sites

Site Number	Site Name
2.1	Ban Kut Ngong
2.2	Ban Khon Sawan
2.3	Ban Pho Chai
2.4	Ban Fai
2.5	Ban Nong Kai Nun
2.6	Ban Nong Hin Tang
2.7	Ban Muang Kao

Table 6: Cluster 3 sites

Site Number	Site Name
3.1	Ban Non Muang
3.2	Ban Phai Hin
3.3	Ban Non Chat
3.4	Ban Bua Simama
3.5	Ban Nong Hin Tang
3.6	Ban Hua Kua
3.7	Ban Pao
3.8	Ban Phan Lam
3.9	Ban Kaeng
3.10	Phu Wiang

Table 7: Cluster 4 sites

Site Number	Site Name
4.1	Ban Tat Tong
4.2	Ban Khum Ngoen
4.3	Wat Si Thammaram temple/ Yasothon Town
4.4	Ban Pueai Huadong
4.5	Muang Ngio
4.6	Ban Song Bueai
4.7	Ban Hua Muang
4.8	Ban Bueng Kae
4.9	Ban Ku Chan
4.10	Ban Nam Kham Yai
4.11	Phanom Phrai Town
4.12	Ban Namoma
4.13	Muang Samsip Town
4.14	Ban Phon Muang
4.15	Ban Phai
4.16	Ban Si Bua
4.17	Ban Thung Yai

Table 8: Cluster 5 sites

Site Number	Site Name
5.1	Muang Sema
5.2	Ban Tanot
5.3	Non Ban Jak
5.4	Ban Non Wat
5.5	Wat Chanthuek
5.6	Ban Muang Fai
5.7	Phu Phra Angkhan
5.8	Ban Pa Khiap
5.9	Ban Prakham
5.10	Ban Lupmok
5.11	Ku Kaeo Sithi
5.12	Prasat Yai Ngao
5.13	Ban Truem
5.14	Plai Bat II
5.15	Phnom Kulen
5.16	Ban Slaeng Thon
5.17	Ban Muang Tao
5.18	Phimai

Table 9: Cluster 6 sites

Site Number	Site Name
6.1	Ban Thalat
6.2	Ban Thin Keao
6.3	Ban Muang Kao
6.4	Ban Vieng Kham
6.5	Ban Nong Khon
6.6	Ban Na Sone
6.7	Ban Ilai
6.8	Ban Nong Kan Khu
6.9	Dan Sung
6.10	Ban Phon Pa Nao
6.11	Ban Dong Phosy
6.12	Ban Saphang Mo
6.13	Ban Nam Pot
6.14	Ban Simano
6.15	Ban Thoun Loua
6.16	Ban Sa Feu
6.17	Ban Somsanouk
6.18	Muang Sanakham
6.19	Vang Sang
6.20	Phu Phra Bat
6.21	Ban Nong Khluem
6.22	Ban Phailom
6.23	Wang Sapung
6.24	Ban Hin Tang
6.25	Ban Phottak
6.26	Wiang Khut
6.27	Ban Daeng
6.28	Ban Khok Khon
6.29	Ban Peng Chan

Table 10: Cluster 7 sites

Site Number	Site Name
7.1	Ban Don Kaeo
7.2	Ban Chiang
7.3	Ban Ma
7.4	Ban Ta Wat Dai
7.5	Ban Panna

Table 11: Cluster 8 sites

Site Number	Site Name
8.1	That Phanom
8.2	Ban Lak Sila
8.3	Ban Fang Daeng
8.4	Ban Saphang Thong
8.5	Ban Na Ngam
8.6	Ban Sikhai
8.7	Ban Kang
8.8	Ban Na Mouang
8.9	Nong Hua Thong
8.10	Ban Pha Kha Niai
8.11	Ban Sompoy Noi
8.12	Phra That Phon
8.13	Ban Tak Daet
8.14	Ban Phumma Chedi Tai Nua
8.15	Muang Phin
8.16	Ban Na Pha Bang,
8.17	Wat Phu

INDEX

abhiṣeka tablets, from Phetchaburi, 72
aesthetics and motifs, of Khorat Plateau, 6, 19, 153, 204
agāra, 25
Airavata, Indra mounted on, 52, 72–3
Ālambāyana brahmin, 54
    wrestling with the *nāga*, 80, 93
Amsadeva, 131
Ananda Temple, 71, 118
    arrangement of the *jātaka* plaques at, 118
Aṅgati, King, 55–6
Angkor civilisation, 1, 202
Angkor-period stoneware, 46
Aṅgulimāla bandit
    Aṅgulimāla Sutta, 82
    converting to monk, 82
    as intelligent and keen student in Sāvatthī, 82
    Majjhima Nikāya, 82
    necklace of human fingers, 83
    threat to Buddha, 82–3
aniconic worship, of *stūpa* images, 117
añjalimudrā (both hands pressed together in prayer), 175
Apara-mahavinaseliya sect, 117, 205
Archaeological Salvage Expedition, 189
Arthur, Chris, 6
Arts of Asia, 148
Asian Art Museum, San Francisco, 154
Avalokiteśvara, 81, 134, 145, 156, 185–6, 198
    bronze statue from Ban Tanot, 156
    four-armed Bodhisattva, 151
Ayutthaya, 3, 30, 47
    military campaigns, 131

Ball, Helen, 134
Ban Ilai, village of, 23, 171, 179
Ban Khon Sawan, 26, 90–3, 95–100, 104, 203–4
Ban Na Ngam, site of, 22–3, 75–6
Ban Nong Hang, 42, 62, 73–8, 80, 82–3, 91, 93, 95, 204
Ban Nong Khan Khu, 171
Ban Nong Khon Temple, 169
Ban Non Muang, 110

Ban Tanod bodhisattva, 124, 134–5
Ban Thalat village, 168
Batteur, Charles, 181
Bauer, Christian, 36, 173
bhadrāsana (legs pendant), 67, 108, 198
Bhikkhus, 190
bhūmisparśamudrā (representing the moment of Enlighten-
    ment), 34, 138
Bhūridatta-jātaka, 53–4, 78, 79–81, 92, 93
Bimbisara, King (King Suddhōdana), 30
    Buddha preaching to, 53, 61, 65, 71, 175
bodhisattvas, 4, 54, 56, 59, 65, 69, 94, 96, 106
    from Ban Tanot, 204
    conical hairstyle of, 78
    depicted in ascetic form, 143
    depiction in Khorat Plateau aesthetic, 19
    Dvāravatī facial features of, 56, 81
    four-armed bodhisattva
        Avalokiteśvara, 151
        Maitreya, 151
    head of a bodhisattva image found at Ban Tanot, 132
    images of, 34, 97–9
    jaṭāmukuṭa of, 133
    from the Mun River Valley region, 34
    prevalence of bodhisattva images, 155
    in royal ease posture (*lalitāsana*), 172
    seated in *vīrāsana* on a polygonal throne, 81
    sīmā depicting, 107
    in *tribhaṅga* postur e, 145
    Vajrapāṇi, 186
Bodhi tree, 34, 67, 69, 97, 114, 117, 120
Bo Ika inscription, 130–1, 138
Boisselier, Jean, 133, 148
Boulbet, J., 72, 157
brick building, 159
Bronkhorst, Johannes, 22, 125, 190
Brown, Robert, 15, 29, 71, 83
Buddha, Amitabha, 99, 134
Buddhacarita, 30
Buddha, Gotama, 2

Aṅgulimāla threatening to, 82–3
attaining of Enlightenment, 66–7
depiction of
    bhadrāsana, 67
    dhyānamudrā, 69–70, 84, 99
    tribhaṅga (three bends) posture, 99
    vīrāsana, 52
    vitarkamudrā, 52, 66, 99
Eight-fold noble path, 67
Enlightenment under Bodhi tree, 114, 120
Four Truths, 67
Indra offering fruit to, 65–6
preaching to King Bimbisara, 53, 61, 65, 175
rebirth as
    nāga, 54
    Prince Temiya, 52
reincarnation as Nārada Mahābrahmā, 55
return to Kapilavastu, 66, 67–9, 185
sheltering under the hood of the *nāga* king Mucalinda, 69
sitting under the Bodhi tree to meditate, 67
Sotthiya offering Kusa grass to, 67
stūpa as an aniconic representation of, 120
unidentified life of the Buddha scene, 69
Buddhahood, 52, 78
Buddha images
    from Ban Thalat, Vientiene province, 169
    carved into the rockface at
        Phu Phra Bat, 176
        Vang Sang, 181
    Dvāravatī-style face and hair curls, 129, 154
    with gold leaf paint located under a rock shelter at Dan Sung, 179
    from the Khorat Plateau, 34–5
    mahāparinibbāṇa posture, 110, 126, 128–9, 138
    in *vitarkamudrā*, 162
Buddha Mucalinda, 68, 69–71
buddhapāda (footprint of the Buddha), 175
Buddha preaching
    images depicting, 75
    to king Bimbisara (King Suddhōdana), 53, 61, 65, 71
Buddha Vairocana, 35
Buddhism, 22, 100, 119, 147, 156, 166, 172, 187, 207
    adoption of, 175
    archaeological approach for study of, 5
    dissemination of, 166
    emergence of, 4
    on the Khorat Plateau, 4, 17
    in Magadha in the Middle Ganges basin, 205
    Mahāyāna Buddhism, 144, 205–6

religious practice of, 5
Sanskrit-based form of, 205
Thai Buddhism, 5, 30, 37
theoretical and methodological frameworks for understanding, 4–11
Theravāda Buddhism, 206
types of archaeological and artistic evidence for
    architecture, 33–4
    Buddha images, 34–5
    inscriptions, 36–7
    narrative art, 28–30
    sīmā, 24–8
    stūpa motifs, 30–3
    votive tablets, 35–6
Vajrayāna Buddhism, 35, 155, 162, 205
Buddhist architectural canon, 116
Buddhist architecture, 4, 33–4
    ordination hall (*ubosot*), 33
    stūpa, 33
Buddhist art, 4
    sīmā tradition and, 16
    spread on the Khorat Plateau, 7, 10
    in the upper and lower Chi River system, 89–122
Buddhist centres, development of, 75
Buddhist monasteries, 2, 6, 10, 28, 87, 131, 145
Buddhist monks, 78, 85, 158–9, 176, 182, 198, 206
Buddhist religious practices, 5, 143
Buddhist teachings, 28
Buddhist visual and material culture, recontextualisation of, 203
Bunker, Emma, 148, 150
Buri Ram ceramics, discovery of, 127

cakra, 83, 138, 143
cakrastambha, 158
Canāśapura, princes of, 131
Can Ban, 44, 188
Candakumara, Prince, 64–5
Chaddanta-jātaka, 104
chattravali (architectural term referring to *stūpa* rings), 32, 115, 120
Cherry, Deborah, 38
Chevance, Jean-Baptiste, 158
Chi River system, 100, 175, 182, 186, 188, 202, 206
    archaeological remains for Buddhism in, 42
    Ban Nong Hang site, 42
    Buddhist art in, 89–122
    distribution of sites along, 41
    Muang Fa Daed site, 42–87

Index

sīmā stones, 42
Chutiwongs, Nandana, 176
Citrasena-Mahendravarman, King, 125
Coedès, George, 110, 189–90
Courting of Amarā, 64, 93, 104, 107, 174–5
Crumley, Carole, 7

Dagens, B., 72, 157
Dang Raek Mountain range, 11–12, 123, 156, 197
Dao Ming, 44, 188, 195, 201, 203
Dehejia, Vidya, 116
Denver Post, 149
deva (celestial being), 69
 images, representation of, 145
devarāja ritual, 156
Devedhamma-jātaka, 104
dhāraṇī (a Buddhist chant or mnemonic), 8, 35
Dharma (the Law of the Buddha), 120
dharmacakra (Wheel of the Law), 2, 120, 126, 130–1, 146,
 157, 204
 motif, 32, 109
 on the *sīmā* from
  Ban Phan Lam, 109
  Khorat Plateau, 109
 at Upper Chi River site, 108–9
dharmacakra stambha, 100–1, 108
dhyānamudrā (meditation *mudrā*), 34, 69, 84, 99
Diffloth, Gerard, 16
Diskul, Subhadradis, 15, 18, 67
Dong Mae Nang Muang site, 23, 46
"double-*kumbha*" motif, 115
drapé-en-poche, 18–19, 64, 145, 204
Dvāravatī art and culture, 72, 207
 Buddhist imagery, 162
 in Central Thailand, 15, 17–20
 of Chao Phraya basin, 1, 202
 political structure, 16
Dvāravatī Plateau, 15–19
Dvāravatī technology and style, 134

earthen mounds, 8, 19, 22–3, 33, 100, 113, 171, 196
École française d'Extrême-Orient (EFEO), 195
Enlightenment, under the Bodhi tree, 28, 34, 66–7, 114, 116,
 120–1
ethno-linguistic group, 17

female goblin, 62
Fine Arts Department of Thailand, 128, 149

Gagneux, Pierre-Marie, 168
garuda king, 56
Google Earth satellite imagery, 8
Gorman, Chester, 189
Great Stūpa, at Sanchi, 116
Guillon, Emmanuel, 168
Gupta Vākāṭaka dynasty, 125

Hanwong, Tanongsak, 131, 149
Harihara image, 131, 133
Higham, Charles, 131
Hinduism, 31, 119, 125, 147, 156, 165, 196, 199
"Historical" Buddha. *See* Sākyamuni Buddha
Ho Chi Minh City, 165
Hoshino's hypothesis, 83
Hoshino, Tatsuo, 44–5, 83, 127, 187, 195
Huai Nam Kham River, 14, 193
Huai Soen River, 100, 102
human–environment interactions, study of, 7

Ikṣvāku dynasty, 125
Illustrated London News, 148
Indorf, Pinna, 25
Indra (king of the gods), 56
 as king of Tāvatiṃsa heaven, 72
 mounted on Airavata, 72–3
 offering fruit to the Buddha, 65–6
 reincarnation as Prince Candakumāra, 95
 sitting in *lalitāsana*, 72
 vajra, 72, 172
Indrawooth, Phasook, 45–6, 117, 205
inscriptions, in Southeast Asia, 36–7
 Late Southern Brāhmī inscription, 36
 Old Mon inscriptions, 36–7
Irandatī (*nāga* princess), 59, 81
Iron Age, 20–1, 131, 134
Isan (nation state of Thailand), 11
Īśānavarman I, King, 125, 159

Jacques, Claude, 194
Jālī and Kaṇhā (Vessantara's son and daughter), 81
jātaka tales (past lives of the Buddha), 2, 27
 Bhūridatta-jātaka, 53, 78, 79–81, 92, 93
 categories of, 28
 Chaddanta-jātaka, 104
 Chinese *Fo Benxing Ji Jing*, 29
 depicted at Chula Pathon Chedi, 29
 depicted on *sīmā*, 205
 Devedhamma-jātaka, 104

"Great Section" (*Mahānipāta*), 28
Jātaka-aṭṭhakathā, 29
Jātakamālā of Arya Sura, 28
Khaṇḍahāla-jātaka, 94–5
Kulāvaka-jātaka, 51, 52, 72
Mahājanaka-jātaka, 76–8, 104–5
Mahānāradakassapa-jātaka, 55–6, 93–4
Mahāummagga-jātaka, 59–64, 93, 104, 175
Mahāvastu from the *Vinaya*, 29
Nidāna-Kathā, 29
Pāli *jātaka*, 29
Paṭhamasambodhi, 30
produced by the Mahāyāna schools, 28
renditions of, 28
representations of the life of the Buddha, 71
Sāma-jātaka, 78–9, 183
Sarabhaṅga-jātaka, 51, 52–4, 69
Suvannakakkata-jātaka, 183–4
Temiya-jātaka, 48, 49–52, 96–7, 184–5
Vessantara-jātaka, 64, 79–81, 95
Vidhurapaṇḍita-jātaka, 56–7, 79–81, 95–6, 106, 172
jaṭāmukuṭa, of a bodhisattva, 133, 143, 150, 154
Jayavarman II, King, 124, 156, 159
    palace of, 158
Jayavarman V, King, 133
Jayawickrama, N.A., 29–30
Jia Luo She Fu, 127, 203

Kantharawichai, 32, 44, 45, 83
Karlstrom, Anna, 169
Karpelès, Suzanne, 180–1
Kawaguchi, Keizaburo, 13
Kevaṭṭa (brahmin), 59–60
khakkharaka (a staff carried by Buddhist monks), 77–8, 205
Khaṇḍahāla-jātaka, 64–5, 94–5
Khao Khieo Mountain, 124
Khao Yai National Park, 13
Khmer civilisation, 158
Khmer cultural traits, 46
Khmer Empire, 15, 162
    Dvāravatī art, impact of, 18
    political control of, 18
    presence on the Khorat Plateau, 17
Khmer temples, on the Khorat Plateau, 17
Khon Kaen National Museum, 29, 46, 56, 65, 83, 190
Khorat Plateau, 11–19, 42, 44, 67, 175, 192, 204
    aesthetics and religious culture, 1, 18
    Buddhism, spread of, 4, 17
    Buddhist landscapes of, 201–7

drapé-en-poche, 145
eight clusters on, 7, 9
Khmer presence on, 17
Khmer temples on, 17
motifs of, 1
religious landscape of, 193
rice yield, 12
river systems on, 7
sīmā tradition of, 54
site analysis and settlement patterns in, 19–23
    earthen mounds, 22–3
    moated sites, 20–2
    mountaintop and hillside sites, 23
    undefined sites, 23
Khu Bua, settlement of, 19
Khuddaka-nikāya (Miscellaneous Collection), Pāli *Tipiṭaka*, 28
Kimbell Art Museum, 152, 154
Kingmanee, Arunsak, 72, 104, 114, 183–4
Klokke, Marijke, 184
Krairiksh, Piriya, 29, 44, 59, 76, 81, 190
Kuberu (the guardian god of the north), 191
Kulāvaka-jātaka, 51, 52, 72
kumbha
    motif, 27, 30–2, 83
    pot, 83, 94, 119, 157
    significance of, 119
Kyuma, Kazutake, 13

Lakṣmī, Goddess, 72, 195
lalitāsana ("royal ease posture"), 52, 64, 72, 108, 172
Lalitavistara Sūtra, 30
Lam Nam Yam River, 14
Lam Plai Mat River, 144
Lam Ta Khong River, 126
Land Zhenla, 44
Lang Nam Yang River, 42, 75
Lao rebellion of 1826–1828, 12
La Pa Thao River, 91
Latchford, Douglas, 72, 148–50
late Iron Age (500–600 CE), 131, 134
Life of the Buddha (*jātaka* tales), 2, 27–30, 35, 45, 49, 52, 54, 65, 67, 69, 71, 74, 83, 112, 116, 174, 183, 186, 205
Light Detecting and Ranging (LIDAR) survey, 158
Loei River, 168, 186
Lorrillard, Michel, 168–9, 175, 180–1, 194
Lower Chi River, Buddhist art in, 111–21
    Ban Pueai Huadong and Muang Ngio, 116
    Ban Tat Tong and Ban Khum Ngoen, 113–14

interpreting the *stūpa* motif, 116–21
lower Chi river workshop, 114–15
workshop on, 114–15

mahādhātu, 118
Mahājanaka-jātaka, 76–8, 104–5
Mahājanaka, King
    encounter with his estranged wife Queen Sīvalī, 76–7
    quest to reclaim his father's kingdom of Videha, 76
Mahānāradakassapa-jātaka, 55–6, 93–4, 153
mahāparinibbāna (the Buddha depicted entering nirvana), 19, 34, 85, 86, 110, 126, 160, 204
Maha Sarakham, 13, 32, 35, 42, 74, 83–4, 158, 195, 204
Mahāummagga-jātaka, 59–64, 93–4, 104, 174, 175
    courting of Amarā, 107
Mahāvagga of the *Vinaya Pitaka*, 24
Mahāyāna Buddhism, 145, 205–6
Mahendraparvata, city of, 158–9, 198
Mahendravarman, King, 159
Mahīdharapura Dynasty, 160
Mahosadha, 59, 61–2, 64, 93, 175
Maitreya, 81
    four-armed Bodhisattva, 152
Majjhima Nikāya, 82
Maya, Queen, 72
McDaniel, Justin, 5
Mekong River, 11–15, 124, 165–6, 167, 186, 191, 196, 199, 202–3
Metropolitan Museum of Art, 151, 198
Middle Mekong basin, Buddhist art from, 14, 165–6
    Ban Phailom and Ban Nong Khluem cluster, 182–3
    Buddha seated cross-legged in *vajrāsana*, 185–6
    of Buddha's return to Kapilavastu, 185
    Dvāravatī-period habitation, 175
    Phu Phra Bat, Dan Sung, and Vang Sang, 175–82
    pilgrimage and mountaintop retreats, 175–82
    Sāma-jātaka, 183
    stūpa-kumbha motifs, 186
    Suvannakakkata-jātaka, 183–4
    Temiya-jātaka, 184–5
    That Phanon in Nakhon Phanom province, Thailand, 191–8
    Udon Thani and the Sakhon Nakhon basin, 188–91
    Vientiane and its hinterlands, 166–75
moated settlements, 15, 20–2, 126, 134, 155
modern worship and re-use of ancient objects, 37–40
monastic forest community, 178
Mon language, 16, 168, 190
mountaintop and hillside sites, 19, 23

Muang Fa Daed Mandala (Chi River system), 42–87, 193, 203
    archaeological excavations in, 46
    Ban Na Ngam site, 75–6
    Ban Nong Hang site, 75–6
    Bhūridatta-jātaka, 53
    Buddha Mucalinda image, 69–71
    as capital of Wendan, 45
    Dvāravatī period, 74
    establishment of Buddhism at, 46
    Kantharawichai, Na Dun, and Roi Et site, 83–4
    Khaṇḍahāla-jātaka, 64–5
    Kulāvaka-jātaka, 51
    Kunchinarai site, 75–6
    Lakṣmī, Goddess, 72
    as largest moated sites in the Khorat Plateau, 45–9
    life of the Buddha and *jātaka* tales at, 71, 74
    Mahānāradakassapa-jātaka, 55–6
    Mahāummagga-jātaka, 59–64
    Phu Bor site, 42
    Phu Kao Putthanimit site, 42
    Prataduyaku Stūpa, 46–7
    religious structures in, 47
    Sarabhaṅga-jātaka, 51, 52–4
    settlement at, 15–16, 26
    sīmā tradition, 44–6, 49
    stucco, votives, and inscriptions, 74
    Temiya-jātaka, 49–52
    tribute to China, 45
    Vessantara-jātaka, 64
    Vidhurapaṇḍita-jātaka, 56–9, 60
    village temple of Wat Pho Chai Semaram, 46
Muang Sema site, 10, 16, 20, 33–4, 36, 46, 100, 123–38, 147, 155, 162–3, 202–5, 207
Mūlasarvāstivāda sect, 205
Mun River Dvāravatī Earthenware, 134
Mun River system, 41, 109, 162, 203–4
    Bo Ika inscription, 130–1
    bronze bodhisattva images, 205
    Buddhism along the central and eastern reaches of
        Ban Muang Fai, 138–44
        Ban Pa Khiap and Ban Prakham, 145–6
        Phimai, site of, 160–2
        Phnom Kulen, 156–60
        Phu Phra Angkhan, 144–5
        Plai Bat II, 148–56
        Surin, Si Sa Ket, and Ubon Ratchathani provinces, 146–8
    Chi River and, 124
    important findspots of bronze sculpture, 126

Khmer presence in, 125
Muang Sema site, 126–33
    Buddhist monastery located at, 131
    Mahāparinibbāṇa Buddha images, 128–9
    satellite sites at, 133–8
    sculptural tradition in, 124
    sīmā tradition in, 124–5
    spread of Buddhism in, 125
Musée Guimet, 18, 198

nāga, 18, 54, 69
    brahmin Ālambāyana wrestling with, 80, 93
    dance, 80
    king, 56, 69, 71
Nagarjunakonda, 117
Nam Ngum River, 15, 167, 168–75, 203
Nam Phom River, 100, 102
Nārada Mahābrahmā, reincarnation of Buddha as, 55
narrative art, 2, 5, 28–30, 75–6, 83, 89–92, 97, 99–100, 104,
    112, 121, 126, 145, 165, 172–3, 191, 199, 203–6
National Museum of Cambodia, 119, 128, 138
New Tang Annals (*Xin Tang Shu*), 44, 127, 187, 203
Nidāna-kathā, 29–30, 69, 205
nimitta (boundary marks), 25, 206
No Na Paknam, 72, 104, 145

Pallava Dynasty, in Southwest India, 36
parāmitā, 71
parinibbāna, 116
Parmentier, Henri, 194
Paṭhamasambodhi, 30
pāṭimokkha ceremonies, 25, 33–4
Petchabun Mountain range, 102
Phimai National Museum, 104, 107, 130, 135, 137, 138
Phu Laen Kha Mountain range, 90, 102
Phu Phan Mountain range, 12, 14, 42, 178
Phu Phra Angkhan, 144–5
Phu Wiang National Park, 109
Piliyakkha, King, 78–9, 183
Plai Bat II Temple, 19, 34, 56, 94, 124, 126, 134, 143, 148–9,
    151–2, 154–6, 163, 204–5
pottery, Dvāravatī-style, 134
Prakhon Chai hoard, 19, 124
Prasat Phumphon, 17, 146
Prataduyaku Stūpa, 46–7, 54
pratyāliḍha (a type of dance pose), 161
Puṇṇaka (*yakkha* General from the *Vidhurapaṇḍitajātaka*),
    59, 81, 106
puṇyakṣetra (place of pilgrimage), 110

pūrṇaghaṭa (full pot/vase of plenty), 31
    motif, 27, 30

Quantum Geographic Information System (QGIS), 8

rājabhikṣu, 37
Rājendravarman II (Khmer king), 17
Rama I, King, 12
Ramayana, 190
Ratchathani, Ubon, 12
regional identity, sense of, 12
religious practice, of Buddhism, 5
Renfrew, Colin, 16, 99
Revire, Nicloas, 131
rice cultivation, 12, 14
ritual sacrifice, 65
river systems, on the Khorat Plateau
    Chi River system, 7, 13, 17, 21
    Mun River system, 7, 13–14, 21
rockfaces, 204
rock formations, presence of naturally occurring, 178
rock shelter
    Buddha images with modern gold leaf paint located
        under, 179
    at Dan Sung, 179
    at Phu Phra Bat, 177
    Usa's Tower, 177–8
routes of communication, 159

Sākyamuni Buddha, 2
Sāma-jātaka, 78–9, 183
Sam-Nuk Sam-Roi Ong/Reminiscing the 300 Buddhas, 149
saṅgha (community of monks), 4, 75, 100
Sanskrit *avadāna*, of the Sarvāstivāda school, 29
Sarabhaṅga-jātaka, 51, 52–4, 69
Schopen, Gregory, 5
Se Bang Fai River, 165, 193–4, 199
Setthathirath, King, 193
shipwrecks, 104
Shorto, Harry, 118
sīmā stones
    analysis of, 5, 7–8
    depiction of
        bodhisattva, 107
        Gaja Lakṣmī, 157
    of Dvāravatī-period, 84
    found at Chi River system, 41
    Life of the Buddha and *jātaka* depicted on, 205
    Mon inscriptions, 104

Index

proliferation of, 203
re-uses for, 37–40
at Wat Non Sila Temple, 103
at Wat Si Thammaram Temple, 120
sīmā tradition (stone boundary markers), 1–2, 15, 19, 39,
75–6, 78, 81
and Buddhist art, 16
carvings of Ban Nong Khluem and Ban Phailom, 18
categories of, 28
in the Chi River system, 18
khandasīmā, 25, 39
of the Khorat Plateau, 54
mahāsīmā, 25
at Muang Fa Daed mandala, 44, 49
in Mun River system, 124–5
types of, 26–7
use as archaeological and artistic evidence for Buddhism,
24–8
Siribhadra, Smitthi, 160
Śiva (destroyer and creator of universes)
cult of, 195
image of, 119
Śiva-liṅga, 119, 133
Sīvalī, Queen, 76
Śiva's *jaṭā* (chignon), in Khmer art, 19
Skilling, Peter, 4, 35, 71, 99, 131, 135, 190
Smith, Michael, 43
Snodgrass, Adrian, 117, 119–20
Solheim, William G., 189
Song Dynasty, 127
South China Sea, 165
Śrī Canāśa, kingdom of, 10, 124, 162, 203
golden *liṅga*, 131
location of, 131, 138
marriage alliance with Dvāravatī in Central Thailand, 135
Muang Sema and its related sites, 126–33
rulers of, 133
śrī dharmarājā, 172, 188, 203
stucco decoration, 74
stūpa, 2, 7–8, 19, 26, 33, 143
as an aniconic representation of the Buddha, 120
as *anda* (egg), 119
Buddha-*stūpa-dharmacakra*, 32
concept of Buddha as, 118
as *garbha* (womb or container), 119
motifs, 30–3
in Northeast Thailand and Laos, 192
rising from the *kumbha*, 119
signification of, 119

Snodgrass's seminal work on, 119
votive *stūpa*, 35
stūpa-kumbha, 73, 83, 157
iconography from Ban Tat Tong and Ban Khum Ngoen,
114
motifs, 75, 89, 98–9, 103, 112, 119, 120, 145, 158, 168,
171, 186, 199, 204
Suvaṇṇabhūmi, 76, 104
Suvannakakkata-jātaka, 183–4

Tabachnik, Sam, 149
Ta Muen inscription, 17
Tatsuo Hoshino, 44, 127
Temiya-jātaka, 48, 49–52, 96–7, 184–5
Thagya Paya Stūpa, 62
Thai Buddhism, 5, 30, 37
Thai *thao muang*, 188
Tham Fa Tho Cave, 19
Theravāda Buddhism, 25, 205, 206
Thompson, Ashley, 32, 119
Tibetan Plateau, 14, 165
Trailokyavijaya, 161
tribhaṅga (three bends) posture, 99, 143, 145

Ubolratana Dam, 102
ubosot, 25–6, 33, 39, 114
Udon Thani province, 15, 30, 165, 166, 175–8, 182, 184,
188–9, 199
undefined sites, classification of, 23
uposathagara, 25–6
Upper Chi River
Buddhist art in, 89–100
Ban Khon Sawan site, 90, 91–2
Ban Kut Ngong site, 90, 91–2
Bhūridatta-jātaka, 93
Buddha and Bodhisattva images, 97–9
Dvāravatī Buddha image, 92
historical analysis of, 92, 99–100
Khaṇḍahāla-jātaka, 94–5
landscape archaeology, 99–100
Mahānāradakassapa-jātaka, 93–4
Mahāummagga-jātaka, 93
Temiya-jātaka, 96–7
Vessantara-jātaka, 95
Vidhurapaṇḍita-jātaka, 95–6
tributaries of, 100–10
art historical analysis at, 104–8
dharmacakra and *stūpa* motifs at, 108–9
Huai Soen River, 100

inscriptional evidence at, 103–4
  jātaka and Buddha images, 104–8
  Mahājanaka-jātaka, 104–5
  Nam Phom River, 100
urban settlements, 23, 43
  demographic definition of, 44
Usa's Tower, 177–8
uṣṇīṣa (Dvāravatī-style hair curls), 56, 75, 78, 86, 99, 168, 174

Vadillo, Veronica Walker, 10
vajra (thunderbolt – the attribute of Indra), 52, 65–6, 72, 172
vajrahumkaramudrā, 161
Vajrapāṇi, 186
vajrāsana (the throne of the Buddha), 118, 173, 185
Vajrasattva, 161–2
Vajrayāna Buddhism, 35, 155, 156, 160, 162, 205
Vedeha, King, 59
Veluvana, bamboo grove of, 65
Vessantara-jātaka, 60, 64, 79–81, 95, 96
Vessantara, Prince, 64
  donation of his wife Maddī to Indra, 64
Vickery, Michael, 125
Vidhura, 59, 81, 95
Vidhurapaṇḍita-jātaka, 56–7, 56–9, 79–81, 95–6, 106, 172
Vientiane mandala, 203
vihāra (assembly halls), 2, 34
Vihāra III, in Gautamiputra Cave, 117
Vimayapura, town of, 161
vīrāsana (cross-legged posture), 52, 59, 65, 69, 97, 99
Viṣṇu
  avatars of, 133
  image, 131
vitarkamudrā (the teaching *mudrā*), 18, 34, 52, 56, 59, 65–6, 69, 75, 140, 154, 174, 181
votive tablets, 24, 27, 30, 32, 35, 36–8, 40, 46, 74, 83–4, 133, 204

Wales, H.G. Quaritch, 18
Wangsuk, Khemica, 128
Wanna, Lord, 168
Wat Chanthuek Temple, 135
water management technologies, 12
Wat Ho Phra Keo Temple, 168, 173
Wat Kut Nong Temple, 91
Wat Non Sila Temple, 103, 182, 184
Wat Pho Seng Arun Temple, 168
Wat Phu complex, in Champassak, 15, 197
Wat Si Chum Temple, 71
Wat Si Thammaram Temple, 113–14, 120

Wat Si That Temple, 189
Watson, Hunter, 17, 36, 94
Wat Sribunruang Temple, 60, 64
Wat Suthat Dhepvararam temple, 24
Wendan hypothesis, 45
Winichakul, Thongchai, 11
Wiraprajak, Kongkaew, 190
Woodward, Hiram, 44–5, 110, 131

yakkha (nature spirit) general, 56–9
Yaśodharā (Buddha's estranged wife), 67, 69, 185

Zhenla civilisation, 1, 202